PENGUIN BOOKS

THE YEAR OF HENRY JAMES

David Lodge was born in London in 1935. He taught in the English Department of the University of Birmingham from 1960 until 1987, when he retired to become a full-time writer. He is Emeritus Professor of English Literature at Birmingham and lives in that city. He is a Fellow of the Royal Society of Literature, was awarded a CBE for services to literature and is also a Chevalier de l'Ordre des Arts et des Lettres.

David Lodge's novels include *The Picturegoers* (1960); *The British Museum is Falling Down* (1965); *Out of the Shelter* (1970); *Changing Places* (1975), for which he was awarded both the Hawthornden Prize and the *Yorkshire Post* Fiction Prize; *How Far Can You Go?*, which was Whitbread Book of the Year in 1980; *Small World*, which was shortlisted for the Booker Prize in 1984, *Nice Work*, which won the 1988 *Sunday Express* Book of the Year Award and was also shortlisted for the Booker Prize; *Paradise News* (1991); *Therapy*, regional winner and finalist for the 1996 Commonwealth Writers' Prize; the novella *Home Truths* (1999); *Thinks* (2001); and most recently *Author, Author* (2004).

David Lodge wrote his own adaptation of *Nice Work*, which won the Royal Television Society's Award for the best drama serial of 1989, and adapted Dickens' *Martin Chuzzlewit* for the BBC in 1994. He has also written two stage plays, *The Writing Game*, which he adapted for Channel 4 TV, and *Home Truths*. He is the author of numerous works of literary criticism, including *The Art of Fiction* (1992), *The Practice of Writing* (1996) and *Consciousness and the Novel* (2002).

David Lodge

The Year of Henry James

The Story of a Novel

PENGUIN BOOKS

PENGUIN BOOKS

Published by the Penguin Group
Penguin Books Ltd, 80 Strand, London WC2R ORL, England
Penguin Group (USA) Inc., 375 Hudson Street, New York, New York 10014, USA
Penguin Group (Canada), 90 Eglinton Avenue East, Suite 700, Toronto, Ontario, Canada M4P 2Y3
(a division of Pearson Penguin Canada Inc.)
Penguin Ireland, 25 St Stephen's Green, Dublin 2, Ireland (a division of Penguin Books Ltd)
Penguin Group (Australia), 250 Camberwell Road, Camberwell, Victoria 3124, Australia
(a division of Pearson Australia Group Pty Ltd)
Penguin Books India Pvt Ltd, 11 Community Centre, Panchsheel Park, New Delhi – 110 017, India
Penguin Group (NZ), 67 Apollo Drive, Rosedale, North Shore 0632, New Zealand
(a division of Pearson New Zealand Ltd)
Penguin Books (South Africa) (Pty) Ltd, 24 Sturdee Avenue, Rosebank, Johannesburg 2196, South Africa

Penguin Books Ltd, Registered Offices: 80 Strand, London WC2R ORL, England

www.penguin.com

First published by Harvill Secker 2006
Published in Penguin Books 2007

2

Set in Monotype Dante
Typeset by Palimpsest Book Production Limited, Grangemouth, Stirlingshire
Printed in England by Clays Ltd, St Ives plc

ISBN: 978-0-141-02680-0

To Tom Rosenthal

contents

The genesis, composition and reception of a novel may be loosely likened to three stages in the life of a human being (very loosely, because literary genesis is usually parthenogenetic). There is a moment of conception, when one of the myriad thoughts that continually stream through the consciousness of a writer penetrates his or her imagination and fertilises it.* This is usually described as 'getting an idea for a novel'. Many such ideas quickly die, or miscarry, and are forgotten. Even if they survive to full term, the writer may be unable to recall the precise moment of conception, but sometimes – as with several novels discussed in this book –

---

* Henceforward in this preface, and throughout the book, for the sake of stylistic economy and smoothness I use the masculine pronoun alone to refer to 'the writer', 'the author', 'the novelist', 'the biographer', and 'the reader', but all such generalisations are meant to apply equally to male and female writers and readers unless otherwise indicated or implied.

we have reliable accounts of when and how it happened. The initial idea, however, always has a pre-history in the writer's life, in his experience and in his reading, which it is interesting to try and trace. That is also part of the work's genesis, as is the process by which the idea is developed, brooded on and modified, in the writer's mind or notebook, before the actual writing begins.

In this analogy, the composition of a novel corresponds to parents' nurturing and education of their offspring from birth until the time when the child 'leaves home' and becomes independent of parental control. Much of this compositional work also goes on in the writer's head, or in memos to himself in a notebook, as well as in the actual production of the text in a growing pile of numbered pages. One tries to make one's novel as strong, as satisfying, as immune to criticism as one can, a task that usually involves a great deal of rereading and rewriting; but when the novel is published and passes into the hands of other readers it has an independent life which the writer can never fully anticipate or control (though he may of course seek to influence it by commenting publicly on the work or taking issue with his critics). In some, rather rare cases – Henry James's *Daisy Miller* being an example – a writer may significantly revise and reissue a work of fiction after its first publication, but in that case he has written another work, which will then have its own reception, distinct from the reception of the original.

'Reception' is a term that covers several different phenomena. It can mean the process by which an individual reader negotiates a text, from sentence to sentence, paragraph to paragraph, chapter to chapter, 'making sense' of it, or 'producing' it, as a fashionable academic jargon says. All descriptive and analytical criticism is this kind of reception in action, and there is a good deal of it in the essays in this volume. Such criticism also, by implication, throws light on the process of composition, since it describes effects of which the author is the conscious or unconscious cause. But 'reception' can also have a more institutional meaning, i.e., the evaluative response of the literary community, the media, and the reading public to a particular book, as measured by reviews, sales, prizes and other evidence. Reception in that sense is a recurrent topic in this book.

The person best qualified to give an account of a novel's genesis and composition is the author. He or she is also the person most affected by its reception. In the first part of this book I describe in some detail all three stages in the life of one of my own novels, *Author, Author*. Such an undertaking obviously risks seeming narcissistic or presumptuous – all the more because the novel is about Henry James, whose Prefaces to the New York Edition of his novels and tales probably constitute the most impressive feat of authorial self-examination in the English language. It seemed to me, however, a story worth telling because it had several curious and unusual features, notably the nearly simultaneous publication of several other novels about or inspired by Henry James, a phenomenon which stirred up considerable interest and speculation in the literary world, and had for me personally some painfully ironic consequences. I have called this piece 'the story of a novel', but it is also the story of a novelist, over a few years of his professional life, and much of it is written in an anecdotal autobiographical mode. I hope that 'The Year of Henry James' may have some general interest and value for the light it throws on the psychology, sociology and economics of authorship in the early twenty-first century, as well as on the creative process itself.

The essays collected in Part Two are more conventional literary criticism. They were written for different occasions (although three of them are published here for the first time), as introductions to reprints, as reviews, and in one case as a lecture, and they do not apply a common or systematic method to the texts they examine. The degree of emphasis on genesis, composition and reception, respectively, varies from one essay to another, though most of them deal with all three aspects of a single novel. Two essays discuss a wider range of texts. The one on Graham Greene focuses on the sources of a writer's work in his reading, and also on the way he may use his criticism of other writers to try and influence the reception of his own. 'The Best of Young American Novelists, 1996' examines a very recent development in the reception of literary fiction, the public listing of meritorious books or authors, usually attached to the award of a prize, which in this case began as a marketing wheeze and then acquired institutional status.

In arranging the order of the contents, it seemed appropriate to follow 'The Year of Henry James' with an essay about one of James's own tales, and that with an essay on Wells's *Kipps*, the reception of which included a notable appreciation by James. After backtracking in time to take in George Eliot, the essays are ordered historically, according to topic. 'Henry James: *Daisy Miller*' is closely based on the introduction to my forthcoming edition of the novella for Penguin Classics. 'H. G. Wells: *Kipps*' is substantially the same as my introduction to the Penguin Classics edition of that novel, edited by Simon J. James, published in 2005. 'The Making of "George Eliot": *Scenes of Clerical Life*' is a substantially revised version

of the introduction to my edition of the three tales for Penguin Classics, originally published in 1973. 'Graham Greene and the Anxiety of Influence' is the text of a lecture delivered at the Graham Greene Festival at Berkhamstead, October 2004. 'Vladimir Nabokov: *Pnin*' was written as an introduction to the Everyman Library edition, published in 2004. 'Umberto Eco: *The Name of the Rose*' will be the introduction to the Everyman Library edition of that novel to be published in 2006. 'The Best of Young American Novelists, 1996' was originally published in *The New York Review of Books*, 8 August 1996, and 'J. M. Coetzee: *Elizabeth Costello*' in the same journal, 20 November 2003. I am grateful to the editors and publishers concerned for the original stimulus to write these pieces, and to Colm Tóibín for permission to quote passages from his book *The Sign of the Cross* (1994), and from his article 'The Haunting', published in the *Daily Telegraph*, 13 March 2004. I am indebted to Professor Michael Caesar of the University of Birmingham for advice and information regarding *The Name of the Rose*. Bernard Bergonzi, Tony Lacey, Geoff Mulligan, Jonathan Pegg, Tom Rosenthal, Mike Shaw and my wife Mary read various parts of this book when it was in preparation and made useful comments, for which I am very grateful.

D.L.

PART
ONE

THE YEAR OF
HENRY JAMES

or, Timing Is All:
the Story of a Novel

I

*If anyone deserves to win this year's Man Booker Prize, it's Henry
James. During 2004, he has been the originator of no fewer than
three outstanding novels.*

Thus began Peter Kemp's review of my novel, *Author, Author*,
in the *Sunday Times* of 29 August 2004, a few days before its
official publication date. The other two novels to which he
referred were Colm Tóibín's *The Master*, published in March
of that year, and Alan Hollinghurst's *The Line of Beauty*,
published in April. Henry James is the central character of
both *The Master* and *Author, Author*. The central character of
The Line of Beauty, which is set in the 1980s, is a young man
who is writing a postgraduate thesis on Henry James, and
Hollinghurst's novel was seen by several critics as a stylistic
hommage to him. In due course *The Line of Beauty* won the
Booker Prize, and *The Master* was shortlisted for it.

Peter Kemp did not mention another novel about Henry James which had been published in November 2002 and was reissued as a paperback in the spring of 2004, Emma Tennant's *Felony*, which spliced together an account of James's relationship with the American novelist Constance Fenimore Woolson and a speculative retelling of the source story of his novella, *The Aspern Papers*. Nor did Kemp mention – probably he was not aware of its existence – yet another novel about James, by the South African writer Michiel Heyns, which was being offered to London publishers in 2004. Entitled *The Typewriter's Tale*, and narrated from the point of view of James's secretary, it concerned James's involvement, in the years 1907–10, in a love affair between two of his closest friends, the novelist Edith Wharton and Morton Fullerton, bisexual journalist and man of letters. We know all this about a book which is still unpublished because Michiel Heyns wrote an eloquent and poignant article in the magazine *Prospect* in September 2004 about coming last in the procession of James-inspired novelists. These were its opening words:

> My agent forwards to me another polite letter of rejection: 'I am so sorry but timing is all – and there has been a spate of fiction based on the life of Henry James published here. I don't know how such coincidences happen . . . something in the atmosphere? So regretfully I must say no.'

Henry James was unkindly portrayed, thinly disguised as 'Jervase Marion', by Vernon Lee in her story 'Lady Tal' in 1893, and there may have been other fictionalised portraits in his lifetime, or after his death in 1916, but as far as I am aware he never appeared as a character in a novel under his own name prior to Emma Tennant's novel in 2002. Yet within two years of the appearance of *Felony* two more novels about him were published and a third was looking for a publisher.* It can be inferred from the available evidence that the preparation and composition of all these books overlapped chronologically and that none of the authors was aware of the projects of the others until their own was under way or actually completed. On the face of it, this convergence of novelistic attention is a remarkable phenomenon, and the anonymous publisher who regretfully declined Michiel Heyns's novel is not the only person to have wondered what could explain it. Something in the atmosphere – or, to use a more philosophical term, the *Zeitgeist*? Needless to say I have given the question some thought myself, and have come to the conclusion that it was a coincidence waiting to happen.

Although Henry James's reputation suffered a certain eclipse in the decades immediately following his death, he has been firmly established as a major modern writer for at least the last sixty years, required reading for any serious student of the English and American novel, and the subject of a steady stream of scholarly books and articles. He has always been a writer's writer because of his technical skill and dedication to his art, a critic's writer because of the challenge his work presents to interpretation, and a biographer's writer because of the intriguing enigmas of his character and personal relationships. The facts of his private and professional life have been available in rich detail since the completion of Leon Edel's

---

* There might have been a fourth. I was reliably informed in the spring of 2004 that the publishers of the American novelist David Leavitt were expecting his new novel to be about Henry James, but when it was delivered it turned out not to be. Perhaps he discovered that Colm Tóibín was working on the same subject and dropped it. I presume Leavitt's novel was *The Body of Jonah Boyd*, published in the USA in May 2004.

massive five-volume biography, published between 1953 and 1972. So what's new that would explain the appearance of a clutch of novels about him in quick succession between 2002 and 2004?

There have been two fairly recent developments in the academic study of literature which have some bearing on this question: feminism and so-called Queer Theory. Probably no male novelist of the period created so many memorable women characters as Henry James, from Daisy Miller and Isabel Archer at the beginning of his career to Milly Theale and Maggie Verver in his late, 'major phase'. Feminist critics, or critics influenced by feminism, have taken a keen interest in this aspect of his work, and they have also been intrigued by his intimate personal relationships with women, notably his cousin Minny Temple, who died young of consumption in 1870, his sister Alice, who died of cancer in 1892 after years of neurasthenic illness, and Constance Fenimore Woolson, who took her own life in 1894. Although James was attracted to Minny, and enjoyed close companionship with Fenimore (as he called her), he never committed himself emotionally to either of them, and there is evidence that he felt some guilt on this account after their deaths (he had less with which to reproach himself in his treatment of Alice). The most thorough and persuasive investigation of this aspect of James's life and character is Lyndall Gordon's *A Private Life of Henry James*, published in 1998, which may have inspired Emma Tennant to write *Felony*. She states that she is 'deeply indebted' to it in a prefatory note to her novel. I too am deeply indebted to this remarkable book, but I read it fairly late in my preparatory research for *Author, Author*. It convinced me that I would have to find room in my novel for extensive treatment of James's relationship with Fenimore, but it was not one of the original stimuli of my project.

James's ambivalence towards women is inevitably associated with the belief of most of his biographers, including Edel, that he was a repressed homosexual who probably never admitted this orientation explicitly to himself or acted it out in a physical relationship. Not surprisingly James has been the object of intense interest from exponents of Queer Theory, which asserts the centrality to literature and the human condition of forms of sexuality traditionally regarded as deviant or transgressive. They have combed his work for rhetorical clues to suppressed homoeroticism (Eve Kosofsky Sedgwick's claim to have discovered imagery of anal fisting in the Prefaces to the New York Edition of James's *Novels and Tales* being a notable example),[1] and are sympathetic to the view that he may not have suppressed it after all. In his biography, *Henry James: the Young Master* (2000), Sheldon M. Novick argued that James was initiated into sexual love in the spring of 1865 by the jurist Oliver Wendell Holmes Jr.[2] Both Colm Tóibín and Alan Hollinghurst are identified as gay writers and are interested in this aspect of James's life and work. Tóibín has a scene in which the young James is affected by sharing a bed with Holmes, both being naked (though nothing happens between them), and deals with James's much later and better documented attraction to the sculptor Hendrick Andersen (an episode in his life which falls just outside the chronological scope of my own novel). But comments and asides of both novelists in articles and reviews suggest a certain scepticism about the efforts of Queer theorists to co-opt James into their cultural mission, and Tóibín has stated that for him the initial stimulus to write a novel about James came from reading Edel's biography, which he picked up at a writers' colony where he was working on a quite different subject.[3]

In short, although these currents in the stream of critical and biographical commentary on Henry James may have contributed something to the almost simultaneous composition of several novels about him, they do not wholly explain the phenomenon. Each of the novelists had their own 'take' on the subject, and their own starting point. A more important factor, in my view, is that the biographical novel – the novel which takes a real person and their real history as the subject matter for imaginative exploration, using the novel's techniques for representing subjectivity rather than the objective, evidence-based discourse of biography – has become a very fashionable form of literary fiction in the last decade or so, especially as applied to the lives of writers. It is not of course a totally new phenomenon. Anthony Burgess wrote a novel about Shakespeare, *Nothing Like The Sun*, in 1964, and later published *Abba, Abba* (1977) and *A Dead Man in Deptford* (1995) about Keats and Marlowe, respectively; Peter Ackroyd's second novel was *The Last Testament of Oscar Wilde* (1986) and he subsequently produced *Chatterton* (1987), *Milton in America* (1996) and *The Lambs of London* (2004), a novel about Charles and Mary Lamb. But both these novelists are, among their contemporaries, distinguished by a consistent interest in historical and biographical subjects of all kinds as sources for fiction. What is notable about the last decade or so is the number of novelists who have taken up the biographical novel at a relatively late stage of their careers, and their focus on *writers* as subjects. Emma Tennant published such a novel about Sylvia Plath and Ted Hughes, *The Ballad of Sylvia and Ted* (2001), before she turned her attention to James and Constance Fenimore Woolson. Other examples which come

to mind include J. M. Coetzee's *Master of Petersburg* (1994),
Penelope Fitzgerald's *The Blue Flower* (1996), Michael
Cunningham's *The Hours* (1999), Malcolm Bradbury's *To the
Hermitage* (2000), Beryl Bainbridge's *According to Queeney*
(2001), Edmund White's *Fanny: a fiction* (2003), Kate Moses's,
Wintering (2003), Alberto Manguel's *Stevenson under the Palm
Trees* (2004), C. K. Stead's *Mansfield* (2004), Andrew Motion's
The Invention of Doctor Cake (2004) and Julian Barnes's *Arthur
and George* (2005), novels about Dostoevsky, Novalis, Virginia
Woolf, Diderot, Dr Johnson, Mrs Frances Trollope, Sylvia
Plath, Robert Louis Stevenson, Katherine Mansfield, Keats,
and Sir Arthur Conan Doyle, respectively. It is important to
distinguish the biographical novel from the romantic biography, a once popular but now somewhat discredited genre
which purports to be history but insinuates a good deal of
authorial invention and speculation into the narrative. The
biographical novel makes no attempt to disguise its hybrid
nature, though each writer sets himself or herself different
rules about the relationship of fact to fiction. Some keep very
closely to the historical record, as I did in *Author, Author*, and
others invent freely, sometimes to the point of travesty – for
example, Lynn Truss's amusing *Tennyson's Gift* (1996), which
brings together on the Isle of Wight in July 1884 the poet
laureate and his wife, Charles Dodgson (Lewis Carroll), the
painter G. F. Watts and his sixteen-year-old wife, Ellen (née
Terry), and the pioneering photographer, Julia Margaret
Cameron, with farcical consequences that are entirely
fictitious.

Why the biographical novel should have recently attracted
so many writers as a literary form is an interesting question,
to which there are several possible answers. It could be taken
as a symptom of a declining faith or loss of confidence in the

power of purely fictional narrative, in a culture where we are
bombarded from every direction with factual narrative in the
form of 'news'. It could be regarded as a characteristic move
of postmodernism – incorporating the art of the past in its
own processes through reinterpretation and stylistic pastiche.
It could be seen as a sign of decadence and exhaustion in
contemporary writing, or as a positive and ingenious way of
coping with the 'anxiety of influence'. The same trend is
observable in contemporary drama – for example: Tom
Stoppard's *Travesties* (1975), about James Joyce, Lenin and
Tristan Tzara, and *The Invention of Love* (1997), about A. E.
Housman and contemporaries; Michael Hastings's *Tom and Viv*
(1985), about T. S. Eliot and his first wife, Vivien, and *Calico*
(2004), about James and Nora Joyce, Samuel Beckett and Joyce's
daughter, Lucia; Alan Bennett's *Kafka's Dick* (1987), and April
de Angelis's *A Laughing Matter* (2002), about David Garrick, Dr
Johnson and Oliver Goldsmith.

In short, the biographical-novel-about-a-writer has
recently acquired a new status and prominence as a subgenre
of literary fiction, and it was only a matter of time before
this kind of attention was turned on Henry James. That is
what I meant by saying that the decision of several novelists,
independently but at approximately the same time, to write
novels about James was a coincidence waiting to happen.*
Speaking for myself, I would certainly not have thought of
writing a book like *Author, Author* twenty years ago; not
because I was uninterested in James – I have been reading,
teaching and writing criticism about him since I was an under-

---

* I might have realised this earlier, in January 2003, when I was deep into my own
novel, and my friend, fellow novelist and Birmingham resident, Jim Crace, guessed
its subject with astonishing ease and the minimum of clues ('Historical? Late 19th
century, early 20th? A writer? Henry James.'). But I did not.

graduate – but simply because my concept of what consti-
tuted a novel, especially my own kind of novel, did not then
include the possibility of writing one about a real historical
person. The fact that for much of my life I pursued a dual
career, split between writing fiction and literary scholarship,
publishing books of each kind in alternation, may have
delayed my perception of the possibility of combining both
kinds of interest and expertise in a biographical novel. For
the same reason I perhaps overlooked the professional pitfalls
of such a project.

There is a sense in which all literary novels published in the
same year or season compete with each other – for readers,
for sales (not quite the same thing, though the two are of
course connected), for critical approval, and (a fairly new
phenomenon, this) for prizes. The proliferation in the last
few decades of literary prizes like the Booker, with their
published shortlists and (more recently) longlists, has inten-
sified and institutionalised the element of competition in the
writing and publishing of fiction – a development which may
have been good for the Novel, inasmuch as it has increased
public interest in literary fiction, but not for the equanimity
of novelists, publishers and agents. Normally, however, novels
compete in all these ways as independent works of art, not
as different treatments of the same subject matter. If it
happens that two new novels have a theme in common, or
the same historical background, they are likely to be
compared and contrasted more directly. Writers are always
uncomfortable when they find themselves in this situation,
because it threatens to detract from the originality of their
work – originality being a highly valued quality in modern

literary culture.* But in such cases there is bound to be a significant difference between the two narratives. It is impossible to imagine (outside the pages of Jorge Luis Borges) two novelists independently inventing the same fictional story enacted by identical characters, except at the very deep structural level where narratologists work, reducing all possible plots to a few basic archetypes. When two novelists take the life of the same historical person or persons as their subject, however, the possibility of duplication is much more real, the element of competition between the two novels becomes more specific and overt, and the stakes are higher. Biographers are familiar with this danger, and live in dread of finding that someone else is working on the same subject as themselves. Such a coincidence is invariably bad news for one, if not both, of the writers involved. There have been men and women whose lives were so interesting and important that there is always a receptive readership for a new biography of them – but seldom for two or more in the same year. If they are published simultaneously, the potential audience is split; if separated by an interval, the earlier book is likely to arouse more interest than the later. The same conditions apply to the biographical novel.

Of the recent spate of novels about Henry James, the two that were most directly in competition with each other in 2004 were *The Master* and *Author, Author. The Line of Beauty* merely alluded, occasionally and glancingly, to the life and character of Henry James. Heyns's novel was unpublished. *Felony* had been first published over a year before; only about half of its brisk 190 pages were about James, and that part was narrowly focused on his relationship with Constance Fenimore Woolson,

* For further discussion of this topic see 'Graham Greene and the Anxiety of Influence', below, pp. 202–23.

treated in a manner highly prejudicial to James. Colm Tóibín's novel and mine had much more in common than either had with any of the others. (For reasons to be explained, I have not read *The Master*, but I have assimilated some information about it indirectly, and have had the facts checked by others.) Both are long, extensively researched books, sympathetic to James, which attempt to represent known facts of his life from inside his consciousness, using a novelist's licence to imagine thoughts, feelings and spoken words which can never be reliably documented by a biographer. It is true that the structure of each book is different, and that they deal in part with different aspects and episodes of James's life. The backbone of my novel is Henry James's friendship with George Du Maurier, who does not figure in Tóibín's book at all; he deals extensively with James's relationship with Lady Louisa Wolsey, who is not mentioned in mine. Both of us have invented some incidents – Tóibín perhaps more boldly than I (at least, I have received that impression) and I feel safe in assuming that these additions to the record are quite different in each book. The main story of my novel is framed by an account of Henry James's last illness and death, which is not covered by Tóibín. But there is nevertheless a significant amount of overlap between the narrative content of the two novels. The calamitous first night of James's play *Guy Domville* in January 1895 is central to both. Tóibín begins with this traumatic experience, and traces James's gradual recovery from it and rededication to the art of prose fiction, following his life, with occasional retrospective digressions, up until and just beyond his acquisition of Lamb House in Rye in 1897. The first half of my main story leads up to the first night of *Guy Domville*, and the second half corresponds almost exactly to the chronological span of *The Master*.

It never occurred to me when I was researching my novel that another writer might have had a very similar idea. Much later, when I was already well into the composition of the book, I experienced a qualm of uneasiness on reading a piece by Colm Tóibín in the *London Review of Books* which showed a remarkable familiarity with some fairly obscure details of the life and work of James, who was not the ostensible subject of the book under review. But there were many possible reasons for this interest – a work of non-fiction in progress, for instance. Tóibín's most recent book at the time was a biographical study of Lady Gregory, *Lady Gregory's Toothbrush* (2002). If any fears that he might be engaged on a novel about James flitted through my mind, I quickly suppressed them, and forgot all about the review until later events reminded me of it.

I first learned about the existence of *The Master* at the end of September 2003, a few weeks after delivering the typescript of *Author, Author* to my publishers, as I recorded in the last paragraph of the 'Acknowledgements, etc.', appended to the novel. At a literary party some six months later, the writer and television presenter Joan Bakewell told me she was much moved by this note, and asked me if I burst into tears on hearing the news. I did not, but I appreciated her understanding of the emotional impact of such a discovery on a writer who had just brought three years' work to a satisfactory completion. I was at first incredulous, then divided between dismay (that a novel by a highly respected writer on much the same subject was due to be published before mine) and relief (that I had not known about it sooner). It would have been deeply disturbing if I had made this discovery while I was actually writing my book, and had I made it very much earlier I might have abandoned or never started what turned out to be one of the most satisfying creative projects I have ever undertaken. But I immediately recognised the damaging effects that the prior appearance of *The Master* was likely to have on the way my novel would be read and received, and in due course all my fears were realised. I can truthfully say of *Author, Author* that I have never enjoyed writing a book more, and publishing one less.

I am usually secretive about my work-in-progress. I am afraid of being excessively influenced, and perhaps discouraged, by the reactions of others to what would be, if I were more open, an account of something in a fluid and incomplete state. I want to know what effect the novel will have on readers in its fully finished form, and that depends to some extent on their not knowing in advance what to expect, so I keep the subject to myself, even though it is in a way what I would most like to talk about, since it is what I am thinking about most of the time, whether or not I am at my desk. Perhaps I am afraid that some other writer might 'steal my idea' if I were to broadcast it widely; or perhaps there is a more devious and largely unconscious motivation at work: a denial of the possibility that anyone else might have had the same idea, illogically combined with a wish not to know about it if they have, because that might entail giving up the cherished project. However, there are inevitably a few people – family, friends, agent, publishers – in whom I confide sooner or later, and as the book approaches completion, and its form and content are pretty well established, I become more relaxed about mentioning it in casual conversation. There are writers – my friend Malcolm Bradbury was one – who take the opposite route: they announce the subject of their next novel in advance and read at public events from the work-in-progress. This may be a way of warning other writers off the subject, or a way of making themselves finish the promised novel. In Malcolm's case I think he genuinely wanted to try out his ideas and his texts on others, and found the feedback of audiences useful.

I do not know in which category of writers Colm Tóibín would place himself, but I suspect it is the same secretive clan to which I belong. Even so, it was surprising that I had no inkling (a word which has a punning appositeness in this context) of the existence of *The Master* until several months after he delivered it to his publishers and a few weeks after I delivered mine. Once his novel was received by his publishers, in the spring of 2003, I might have picked up news of it on the literary grapevine. But, long before that, our common involvement in researching the same subject, consulting some of the same sources and visiting some of the same places, might well have alerted either of us to the other's project. Michiel Heyns tells the story of an encounter with Colm Tóibín at Lamb House in Rye (Henry James's principal residence from 1898 until his death in 1916) which might as easily have happened to me as to himself:

> On a summer afternoon, shortly before the completion of my novel, my agent and I made a pilgrimage to Lamb House, now a National Trust property. There we met Colm Tóibín, whose presence was the first ominous inkling either of us had of his intentions. The custodian of the house kindly allowed us upstairs, normally closed to the public. Both of us made surreptitious notes, Tóibín's, it seems, enabling him to write the passage in his book in which Henry James, in his bedroom, can hear his young guest and the object of his adulation, Hendrick Andersen, undress in the adjoining guest room.[4]

Colm Toíbín told the same story, with more amusing details, in an article in the *Daily Telegraph* in March 2004, when *The Master* was published. He described going to visit Lamb House, 'on a bright Saturday afternoon two years ago, when I was close to completing a draft of my novel about Henry James', and being moved on discovering a piece of needlework by Constance Fenimore Woolson over the mantelpiece of the front parlour. Then:

> Suddenly, that day, as I stood staring at this object, a voice called my name. It was a London literary agent whom I knew. She was with one of her clients. She asked me what I was doing in Lamb House. I said that I was writing a book about Henry James.
>
> 'So is my client,' she said. She introduced me to her client, who was standing beside her.
>
> 'Are you writing about this house?' the agent asked.
>
> I told her I was. As I spoke, I noticed a neatly dressed man whom I presumed was American listening to us carefully, moving closer.
>
> 'Did you both say you are writing books on James?' he asked. 'Because so am I.' He shook our hands cheerfully.
>
> By this time a small crowd had gathered, marvelling at three writers pursuing the same goal. We were very careful with each other, no one wishing to say exactly how close to finishing we were. We were also very polite to each other. Then the man who rents the house from the National Trust and has the upstairs rooms as his private quarters, having heard all this, invited us to view James' old drawing room on the first floor, as a special privilege.[5]

Tóibín does not identify the American writer, but one may safely assume from his cheerful demeanour that he was a scholar rather than a rival novelist. For me there are other intriguing features of the episode, and the two reports of it. If we put Tóibín's 'two years ago' and Heyns's 'a summer afternoon' together, it took place in the summer of 2002. I also visited Lamb House with my notebook and pencil that summer – on 1 August, to be precise – privately, by appointment. Tony Davis, the tenant/curator of Lamb House mentioned by Tóibín, is sure that my visit preceded that of the other writers, which he thinks took place in October, or September at the earliest. This sequence of events put him in a unique and sensitive position: he was the only person in the world who knew that both Colm Tóibín and I were working on novels about Henry James, because I had told him and his partner Sue confidentially of the reason for my interest in Lamb House when I arranged my visit. He was subsequently very helpful to me in supplying information and documents relating to Henry James's servants, but he did not tell me about Colm Tóibín's interest in James, nor Tóibín about mine, which was entirely the right and proper thing to do, and for which I am grateful, since the information would only have disturbed me. There was never any chance of my overtaking Colm Tóibín in the Henry James stakes even had I known there was the possibility of a race, since he was near to completing a draft of *The Master* when he went to Lamb House, whereas my visit was the last piece of research I did before actually starting to write *Author, Author*. But I had been in Lamb House – and indeed slept in Henry James's bedroom – three years earlier, when *Author, Author* was just a gleam in my eye, so to speak.

I first made a note about the relationship between Henry James and George Du Maurier as a subject for imaginative treatment in November 1995. I had just finished reading Du Maurier's novel *Trilby* for the first time. An independent television company had approached me about adapting this work as a drama serial, so I obtained the Penguin Classics edition, edited by Daniel Pick, and read it. I thought the early chapters had a certain period charm, but as a narrative it was poorly constructed, melodramatic and sentimental. Pick records that Sir Frank Kermode told him it was the worst novel he had ever read. This seemed to me a rather harsh judgement, but I told the company, via my agent, that I could see no way of making the story credible or interesting to a modern television audience, and as far as I know the project was never realised.[6] But two facts in Daniel Pick's introduction made a strong impression on me. The first was that Henry James had been closely involved in the genesis of *Trilby*. The two men were good friends and often took walks together, on Hampstead Heath and in London. On one of these walks, in March 1889, Du Maurier summarised the story of Trilby and Svengali (both as yet nameless), which he had dreamed up as a young man, when he was toying with the idea of trying his hand at fiction, but never completed, and offered it to James, who had been complaining of a dearth of ideas for plots. According to Du Maurier's later account of this episode, James said that he lacked the requisite musical knowledge to write the story, and suggested that his friend should write it himself. Du Maurier, whose sight was failing and threatening to curtail his career as an artist and illustrator, was prompted by this conversation to start writing a novel – but on another subject. This was *Peter Ibbetson*, published in 1891. Its modest success encouraged him to try again, this time with *Trilby*, which appeared in 1894. The second fact in Pick's introduction that struck me – indeed, astounded me – was that *Trilby* is thought to have been the bestselling novel of the nineteenth century. I had known it was popular, but not *that* popular.

This was the starting point for *Author, Author* – the moment of conception, if you like. The basic facts were in Edel's biography, but I had not read that enormous work from cover to cover at that stage. I had only dipped into the parts that concerned my critical and editorial work on James, just as I had only dipped into *The Notebooks of Henry James* edited by Matthiessen and Murdock, which contains James's own, slightly different account of his seminal conversation with Du Maurier, and reveals that he himself was genuinely intrigued by the possibilities of the Trilby story. It was reading *Trilby* and Pick's introduction that prompted that first entry in my own notebook, which concludes:

> I am much taken with the idea of a play (or even musical?) of the story of (behind) *Trilby*, in which H. James and Du M. would be the main characters, framing extracts from the more dramatic scenes of *Trilby*. It would turn on the irony of the great master of modern fiction turning down an idea that made his friend a bestseller, something J. hankered after and never achieved.

In retrospect it seems clear to me that I thought first of a dramatic rather than a novelistic treatment of the subject partly because, as mentioned above, it had never previously occurred to me to write a novel about a real, historical person. Also, in the late 1980s and the 1990s I had begun to combine novel-writing with writing scripts for film, television and the stage. I had written one play (*The Writing Game*) first produced in 1990, and had been working intermittently on another one (which became *Home Truths*, produced in 1998). As I noted earlier, there were lots of contemporary models for theatre pieces about writers and artists. I think I had particularly in mind Tom Stoppard's *Travesties* and Stephen Sondheim's *Sunday in the Park with George*. As I turned the idea over in my mind, however, I soon began to think of it as a novel. Only the discourse of prose fiction would allow me to render the effect of the success of *Trilby* on James's supersensitive consciousness, and even a cursory reading around the subject revealed a richness of detail and ramification of effects that would require the expansiveness of the novel form to encompass them. I observed that Du Maurier's success with *Trilby*, first as a novel, and then as a play (adapted by other hands), in the years 1894–5, coincided with the catastrophic climax of Henry James's long campaign to achieve fame and fortune as a playwright, when he was booed onstage at the first night of his play *Guy Domville* on 5 January 1895. I had been fascinated by the story of that first night, and the people, some famous, others to become famous, who were present at it, ever since I encountered it in Edel's biography some ten years earlier. I was then editing the Penguin Classics edition of *The Spoils of Poynton*, the first work of fiction James started after the debacle of *Guy Domville*, and had acquired from researching the background to that novel a vivid sense of the pain of James's humiliation and the effort it required to lift himself out of the consequent depression and resume his career as a novelist. The thought of exploring and exploiting this rich material in a novel was exciting, all the more so because I was aware of the element of risk involved: first, in writing a novel completely different in form and content from anything I had attempted before; and secondly in taking on a formidably difficult subject, a writer about whom a great deal was known, and on whose life and work there were many expert and proprietorial authorities.

I obtained and read Leonée Ormond's excellent biography of George Du Maurier which confirmed my hunch that he was an interesting figure in his own right whose relationship with HJ would be worth exploring in some detail. But I did not begin serious work on the project for several years. If I had done so at once, I might have been the first instead of the third novelist to publish a novel about Henry James. When I made that initial note in November 1995, however, I was well into the preparatory research for another novel, which had priority. This was *Thinks...* , a novel about two contrasting and conflicting views of consciousness: the scientific and the literary (the latter being informed by both humanistic and religious ideas). These views are represented respectively by the hero, Ralph Messenger, a cognitive scientist specialising in Artificial Intelligence, and the heroine, Helen Reed, a novelist seeking distraction from the recent death of her husband by teaching creative writing for a semester at Ralph's university. It was a long time before I felt I had acquired a sufficient grasp of the key issues and the vocabulary of consciousness studies to begin writing the novel, and then it progressed very slowly. I was always glad to have an excuse to put it aside for a while, to work on something else – film scripts of my novels *Paradise News* and *Therapy*, which were 'in development' during this period (and never emerged from it), and *Home Truths*, which finally reached the stage in January 1998, and which I turned into a novella early in 1999. But to begin work on another entirely new novel would have been effectively to abandon *Thinks...* .

Although the labour of researching and writing this book

postponed systematic work on the Henry James–George Du Maurier project, that idea was always simmering quietly on the back burner of my own consciousness, and in consequence there are several allusions to and quotations from Henry James in *Thinks...* . He was probably the first novelist in the English language to have a theoretical as well as an intuitive under-standing of the importance of 'point of view' in fiction – i.e., the perspective(s) from which a story, involving several char-acters through any or all of whom it could be focalised, is told; and he was a virtuoso in the art of telling a story through a limited or unreliable 'centre of consciousness' (to use his own term). It seemed useful and plausible therefore to make my heroine an admirer of Henry James, very familiar with his work from having once begun (but not completed) a DPhil thesis on it at Oxford. Early on in the novel there is a con-versation in which Messenger explains that the problem for cognitive scientists is that consciousness is a first-person phenomenon but science is a third-person discourse. Helen quotes from memory the opening paragraph of *The Wings of the Dove* to demonstrate how novelistic discourse can overcome the first person / third person dichotomy through the device of 'free indirect style', in which the inner voice of the point-of-view character is fused with the voice of a covert narrator:

> She waited, Kate Croy, for her father to come in, but he kept her unconscionably, and there were moments at which she showed herself, in the glass over the mantel, a face positively pale with the irritation that had brought her to the point of going away without sight of him.

The subjectivity of consciousness – the fact that we can never know for certain what anyone else is thinking – makes it easy for human beings to deceive each other, and this was a theme that Henry James often explored, though with the greatest reticence and decorum, in stories of infidelity. In a crucial episode of *Thinks...* , when Helen unexpectedly encounters Ralph's wife Carrie engaged in a romantic assignation with one of his colleagues (generally supposed to be a celibate homosexual), she is conscious of re-enacting a celebrated scene in Henry James's novel, *The Ambassadors*, where the hero Lambert Strether, on a solitary walk in the French countryside near Paris, sees and is seen by Chad Newsome and Madame de Vionnet in a rowing boat on the river and realises the true nature of a relationship he had been led to believe was entirely innocent. It is Helen's interest in James (and at a second remove my own) that brings her to the town of Ledbury where she makes this discovery.

In the summer of 1999, by which time I was well into the writing of *Thinks...* , Philip Horne published *Henry James: A Life in Letters*, which told the story of the novelist's life through a generous selection of his letters, many of them not previously published, with linking passages of editorial commentary and comprehensive notes. It was just the book I needed to refresh my knowledge of James's life as the prospect of actually starting work on the James–Du Maurier novel appeared on the horizon. Among the early letters I was particularly struck by one from James to a friend in America (Charles Eliot Norton) describing a long walk he made in the spring of 1870 from Malvern, in Worcestershire, where he was seeking a cure for his chronic constipation, to Ledbury, where he saw 'a noble old church (with detached campanile) and a churchyard so full of ancient sweetness, so happy in situation and characteristic detail, that it seemed to me . . . one of the memorable sights of my European experience'.[7]

I decided that Helen should come across this letter in a book (though in fact she couldn't have done, because Horne published it for the first time and the action of *Thinks...* takes place in 1997) and decide to make a literary pilgrimage to Ledbury, where she would encounter Carrie Messenger and her lover. Ledbury is no great distance from Cheltenham, Gloucester and environs, where I had set the action of my novel, inventing the greenfield University of Gloucester for this purpose (having checked on the Internet that no such institution existed, but overlooking the fact that there was a Cheltenham & Gloucester College of Higher Education which was seeking university status, and would acquire it within a year of the publication of my novel). In October '99 I was in Cheltenham myself to take part in the literary festival, and I took the opportunity to drive the following day to Ledbury, where I lunched at the Feathers, a fine old black-and-white inn, the perfect setting for my projected scene, and noted other details of local colour which would be useful.

The festival event that had brought me to Cheltenham was a panel discussion with Andrew Davies and Adrian Mitchell about the adaptation of novels for TV, film and stage. It was a subject in which I had a personal interest, having adapted my own *Nice Work* and Dickens's *Martin Chuzzlewit* as serial TV dramas for the BBC. But the main example I used in my brief presentation at Cheltenham was the juxtaposition of a passage from James's *The Portrait of a Lady* with the corresponding scene in Laura Jones's published screenplay for Jane Campion's 1996 feature film of that novel. I had been thinking a lot lately about the adaptation of James's fiction for the screen.

At the beginning of that same year, 1999, I had received an invitation to give the annual Henry James lecture at the

Rye Festival in September. It came from Hilary Brooke, the organiser of the festival. She and her husband Gordon were then the custodians of Lamb House. She mentioned that they would be glad to offer me hospitality at Lamb House if I accepted. I had been in Rye on two or three occasions in the past, and looked at Lamb House from the outside, but these visits never coincided with the limited hours when the interior and the garden were open to the public. The prospect of actually being able to stay there overnight as a guest was irresistible. I agreed to give the lecture, and proposed as my topic the feature film adaptations of James's novels, of which there had been several in recent years, notably *The Bostonians*, *The Portrait of a Lady*, *The Wings of the Dove*, and *Washington Square*, while a film of *The Golden Bowl* was about to go into production. There had also been many adaptations of James's novels and tales for television, especially by the BBC, going back to the 1960s and '70s, and several successful stage adaptations including *The Heiress* (*Washington Square*), *The Aspern Papers*, and several versions of *The Turn of the Screw*, as well as Benjamin Britten's celebrated opera. These did not come within the scope of my lecture, but they reinforced the irony that Henry James, who always bemoaned the limited circulation and appreciation of his fiction and failed disastrously as a playwright, who was heard to exclaim late in life, 'I should so much have loved to be popular!',[8] achieved a huge global audience posthumously through the adaptation of his work in dramatic form by other hands. This would in due course become a minor theme of *Author, Author*.

I went to Rye early in September, with my wife, Mary, who had been included in the Brookes' invitation, and gave my lecture, illustrated with video clips, in the Methodist Hall. I shall say no more here about the lecture, which was published

later in a much expanded form,[9] nor expatiate on the charms
of Lamb House and its walled garden, which are amply
described in the pages of *Author, Author*, but the occasion still
glows in my memory with a kind of halo of happiness. It
took place on a very warm evening, of a kind rare in England,
when the heat of the day lasts long into the night and it is
comfortable to be outdoors in shirt-sleeves or summer frocks
as darkness falls. There was a drinks party at Lamb House
after the lecture and guests sipped their white wine on the
lawn and under the boughs of the mulberry tree which
replaced the one blown down in the great storm of 1915. One
of the pleasures of the occasion was a reunion with Graham
Watson, who had been my literary agent at Curtis Brown
until his retirement in 1979. He and his wife Dorothy had
themselves been the curator-tenants of Lamb House at that
time, though I was then unaware of it, and had subsequently
moved to a pretty cottage on Church Square. Later in the
evening there was a convivial supper kindly provided by our
hosts in the modern extension discreetly attached to the back
of the house. And so to bed – in Henry James's bedroom!
Not in his actual bed, which was disposed of along with most
of his other furniture long ago, but in the panelled bedroom
on the first floor at the front of the house, known as the King's
Room since George I slept there in 1726, having been shipwrecked in a storm on nearby Camber Sands, and where the
Master slept during his occupancy of Lamb House. I had no
idea that a few years later I would write a scene in which
Henry James, waking early in this room, and lying content-
edly in bed, as the rising sun peeps between the gap in his
curtains, thinks back over his recent acquisition of the house,
and looks forward to the work he hopes to accomplish there.
My plans to write a novel about him were at that point

extremely vague and fluid. I knew that the James–Du Maurier relationship, and the contrasting fortunes of *Guy Domville* and *Trilby*, would be at the heart of it, but the structure and scope of the whole novel remained to be decided, or rather discovered, first in the process of reading and research, then in the process of writing. In September 1999 I was still preoccupied with the task of finishing *Thinks...* .

It was in fact not until April of the following year that I delivered the completed manuscript of *Thinks...* to my publishers, and was free to begin serious preparation for the Henry James novel. I started by reading Edel's *Life* carefully from cover to cover, and rereading Leonée Ormond's biography of George Du Maurier, and worked outwards from those basic sources in all directions. I compiled a calendar of noteworthy events in the lives of the two men, and noticed some interesting convergences in the process. I began to get a much clearer idea of the shape of each man's life. But that did not give me the shape of my novel – 'life being all inclusion and confusion, and art being all discrimination and selection', as Henry James himself observed, in the Preface to *The Spoils of Poynton* in the New York Edition. No one wrote or spoke more eloquently about the connections and discontinuities between life and art, but of his many remarks on the subject the one that seemed most relevant to my task is in his Preface to *Roderick Hudson*:

> Really, universally, relations stop nowhere, and the exquisite problem of the artist is eternally but to draw, by a geometry of his own, the circle within which they shall happily *appear* to do so.

Relations stop nowhere because the existence of each human being, and every action and every thought of each human being, are determined by pre-existing circumstances which themselves were subject to the same kind of determinations, and to trace the chains of cause and effect which extend outwards in space and time from even the most trivial event, in a complex web of connections, is a task which if, *per impossibile*, it were pursued exhaustively would eventually encompass the history of the universe. Laurence Sterne's Tristram Shandy discovers this to his cost when he sets out to give a faithful and comprehensive account of his 'Life and Opinions', starting with his own conception. He is led into so many explanatory digressions and retrospective sub-narratives that by the fourth volume he has progressed no further than the first day of his life, which has taken him a whole year to narrate, and it dawns on him that the longer he lives, accumulating more experience which demands the same exhaustive treatment, the less likely he is to complete his work:

> – was every day of my life to be as busy as this – and why not? – and the transactions and opinions of it to take up as much description – and for what reason should they be cut short? As at this rate I should just live 364 times faster than I should write – it must follow, an' please your worships, that the more I write, the more I shall have to write – and consequently, the more your worships will have to read.
>
> Will this be good for your worships' eyes?[10]

The ninth volume was the last, because Sterne himself died shortly after publishing it, but however long he had lived the novel would never have been finished in the usual sense of the word. *Tristram Shandy* is the ultimate metafiction, which achieved an unprecedented truthfulness to life by continually exposing the irreducible gap between the world and the book. Tristram's failure is Sterne's triumph. But if all novels were like *Tristram Shandy* we should soon become bored with them. The human mind demands pattern, order, cohesion and a certain degree of closure in narrative discourse, and can only occasionally be teased into accepting a radical departure from these conventions.

Readers bring such expectations to non-fictional as well as fictional narratives, but the method of the writer in each kind is quite different. The historian or biographer describes a circle which contains the facts he considers necessary for a proper understanding of his subject, and excludes an infinity of other connected facts. Skilful writers in these genres are able to give their narratives a satisfying form, with elements of suspense, enigma and irony such as are found in novels, but their liberty to shape their narratives in this way is limited by a duty to historical truth-telling and the availability of evidence. The solution to the enigmas may be irrecoverable; the great climactic moments in the subjects' lives may never have been recorded. The writer of fiction is quite differently situated. He must draw a circle and then fill it with invented facts which connect interestingly, plausibly and meaningfully with each other to make a narrative which had no previous existence. Because his story is not in the ordinary sense 'true', it requires a much greater degree of patterning to satisfy the reader. In historical writing every discrete, documented fact about the subject has a certain value, but in fiction 'facts' are redundant if they do not have a literary function (metonymic, symbolic, thematic, didactic, etc.). In historical writing some facts *must* be included, whereas in fiction this is completely a matter for the writer to decide. It is hard to imagine a biography which did not, for instance, include an account of the subject's parentage. But many novels make no mention of their principal characters' parents (or, to put it another way, the novelist did not bother to invent these characters) simply because such information would have been irrelevant to the work's narrative content and design. (Philip Swallow and Morris Zapp, for example, characters who figure prominently in three of my own novels, are parentless.)

The biographical novel, being a hybrid form, brings both kinds of selection and exclusion into play. As the writer of such a book you are constrained by the known facts of your historical characters, but free to invent and imagine in the interstices between these facts. How free is a matter of individual choice. When I first conceived my book I assumed I would invent some minor characters, but the more research I did the more convinced I became that the historical persons in whose lives James's life was embedded were so interesting that there was no need to invent any more, and that it would immensely enhance the effect of authenticity I aimed at if all my named characters were real people.* Writing, and preparing to write, *Author, Author* was an entirely new compositional experience for me: instead of creating a fictional world which wasn't there until I imagined it, I was

---

* This had an amusing and ironic consequence. Long before I started writing *Author, Author* I took part in a so-called 'Immortality Auction', organised by the charity Medical Foundation for Victims of Torture, at which people bid to have their name used for a character in the next novel by a participating writer of their choice. Dr John Plater bid successfully for that privilege in my next novel, and later generously doubled his donation to the charity. As I got deeper and deeper into writing *Author, Author,* and became more and more committed to using only historical personages in the story, I was increasingly concerned about honouring my contract. For a while I thought of calling George Alexander's business manager at the St James's Theatre, *continued overleaf*

trying to find in the multitudinous facts of Henry James's life a novel-shaped story.

The connection between HJ and Du Maurier which had first prompted the idea of the book was its key structural component, because it gave me a criterion of relevance for the inclusion and exclusion of material uncovered in reading and research. I decided that my story should begin around 1880, when the two men first became friends, which meant that all James's previous life could either be excluded or alluded to briefly and retrospectively. The climax of the story was always to be the failure of *Guy Domville* and the contemporaneous triumph of Du Maurier's *Trilby*. The closing sequence would interweave Du Maurier's rapid physical decline and death following the success of *Trilby* with HJ's gradual recovery from his humiliation, his rededication to the art of fiction and his acquisition of Lamb House. I foresaw a potential difficulty in keeping the two strands of the narrative intertwined until the very end, because Du Maurier died in 1896 while HJ did not sign the lease for Lamb House until a year later, and did not actually move in until another year had passed. However, the posthumous publication of George Du Maurier's disappointing third novel, *The Martian*, in 1897, and James's long postponement of writing a memorial essay about his friend, happily (to adopt his own word) allowed me to

---

John Plater, but then discovered that this person's real name, Robert Shone, appeared on the theatre's playbills, and I must therefore use it. I seriously contemplated repaying Dr Plater his donation, but a friend who had read the MS pointed out that the man who taught Henry James how to ride a bicycle in Torquay had no name, nor was it likely that his real name could ever be discovered. So I gave the name of my patron to a character so minor that he never actually appears, but is only quoted. I wrote to John Plater explaining all this, and expressing the hope that the unique status of this character in the book would compensate for his obscurity, and he accepted the solution good-humouredly.

keep Du Maurier in the foreground of James's thoughts and within the circle of the main narrative. But around this circle I planned to draw a second one – or, to change the metaphor, to enclose it in the story of Henry James's last illness and death, divided into two parts which act as bookends to the main story.

There were several reasons for wanting to include this material in my novel. First and foremost, it was an irresistible and well-documented human story, involving several interesting people with different and sometimes conflicting attitudes to the dying and periodically demented novelist: members of the James family, his last secretary-assistant Theodora Bosanquet (who kept a diary of the events of this period on which Leon Edel drew extensively), and the servants who cared for him. Among the latter I was particularly interested in the character of Burgess Noakes, whom James, shortly after moving into Lamb House, had hired as a house boy when he was only twelve or thirteen, and subsequently trained to become his valet. With James's approval Noakes had volunteered for service in the British army at the beginning of the war in 1914, served in France as one of the 'Old Contemptibles', was wounded and partially deafened by a mortar shell in the spring of 1915, hospitalised in England, and given indefinite medical leave to care for his dying master, which he did with great tenderness and devotion.

Another reason for having this frame story was that it would enable me to put James's literary career into a deeper and truer perspective than would be possible if my book ended in the late 1890s, with James happily ensconced in Lamb House, and looking forward confidently to writing the masterpieces of his later career. One of the things I discovered (or rediscovered, with a keener apprehension of the pain involved) from my reading in the biographies and letters of James was that for the novelist himself his 'Major Phase', as critics would later term it, was a bitter disappointment as regards public recognition, culminating in the critical and commercial failure of the great New York Edition of his novels and tales, which triggered a nervous breakdown in 1910 even more severe than the depression he suffered and successfully overcame after the collapse of his theatrical ambitions. This second crippling experience of failure could be referred to in the frame story, and I also hoped somehow to work into this part of the book a reference to his posthumous success.

There was great poignancy as well as drama in the story of James getting the Order of Merit in the New Year's Honours list of 1916, just two months before his death. When Edmund Gosse brought him the news in his bedroom he seemed barely conscious, but after his old friend had left James told his maidservant Minnie Kidd to blow out the candle to 'spare my blushes'. He was, I believe, ironically exaggerating his gratification. The honour, though no doubt welcome, was too little and too late to make up for all the unfulfilled ambitions of his literary career. Edel mentions that among the many messages of congratulation which James received was a telegram from Sir George Alexander, the actor-manager who had mounted the doomed production of *Guy Domville*, and the man who at the end of the play had, either mischievously or foolishly, invited James on to the stage to take a bow, whereupon he was loudly booed by the gallery. I imagined James, his customary decorum undermined by his dementia, responding to Alexander's message (which actually referred to the play, and claimed still to take pride in his association with it) with an angry expletive. I decided to invent another telegram (though it is not impossible that there was a real one) from Gerald Du Maurier, George's younger son and by this time a famous actor, which I thought would provide a convenient opportunity to suspend the frame story and begin the main story. And if I ended the main story with HJ hiring the young Burgess Noakes that would provide a fitting, and hopefully moving, link to the second half of the frame story.

This description of the structure of *Author, Author* gives a very misleading impression of how I arrived at it, as if in a smooth series of logical steps. In fact it evolved slowly and hesitantly while I was researching the novel, the subject of frequent speculative memos to myself in my notebook. This 'notebook' was actually a very capacious lever arch file in which I kept my research notes, correspondence and other documents, as well as ongoing thoughts about the projected novel. Most of the notes were also filed on the hard disk of my computer. Although it was my customary practice to make notes on reading and other research in handwritten form, I realised fairly early in working on this fact-based novel the advantage of having them instantly accessible by using the computer's Search facility. Partly for that reason, *Author, Author* was the first novel I wrote entirely on my computer. (Previously my practice had been to write a rough draft by hand, a few pages at a time, transferring it to the computer for revision and expansion.)

I did more 'field work' than usual for this novel, visiting several sites that were important to my story, beginning with De Vere Gardens, Kensington, where Henry James occupied a fourth-floor flat for most of the duration of the main action, and whence he would often walk up to Hampstead Heath on

a Sunday in the 1880s, to visit the Du Mauriers. What astonishing distances the Victorians covered on foot! I did not walk
up, but I did walk down the long steep incline of Fitzjohn's
Avenue to Swiss Cottage, after I had located and photographed
George Du Maurier's house in Hampstead, visited the parish
church in whose churchyard he is buried, and walked over the
heath, approximately retracing the steps of the two men on
their Sunday strolls. I was unable to find the bench on which
they liked to sit and talk, and which long after Du Maurier's
death was photographed on James's instructions for the
frontispiece to the volume dedicated to tales of literary life
in the New York Edition, but no doubt it was removed or
replaced long ago. I viewed the outside of Carlyle Mansions,
Cheyne Walk, Chelsea, where James acquired a flat in 1913,
and took photographs of this stretch of the Thames which
he never tired of looking at from his front room windows
until he died there at the end of February 1916.

I took opportunities that arose to view places with Jamesian
connections further afield. After spending a weekend with
friends in Leeds we drove to Whitby, a place with many other
literary associations (Caedmon, Mrs Gaskell, Bram Stoker)
where he often joined Du Maurier and James Russell Lowell
when they were holidaying there, and then to the little fishing port of Staithes a few miles further up the north Yorkshire
coast, a favourite walking destination of Du Maurier's. On
another occasion I escaped from a family holiday in the Center
Parcs holiday village at Longleat to stay overnight at the
Osborne hotel, part of a striking white Regency crescent overlooking the sea just outside Torquay, where James spent a re-
cuperative summer in 1895, the year of *Guy Domville*. Apart
from the open-air swimming pool embedded in the front lawn,
its appearance and situation have changed very little since

James described it in his letters. I had never visited these places before, and doing so suggested scenes for my novel that I would not otherwise have thought of. Venice I *had* visited before, but I went back there after attending a literary festival in Mantua and, like James himself, hung around the environs of the Casa Biondetti on the south side of the Grand Canal, peering up at the second-floor window from which poor Constance Fenimore Woolson had fallen to her death in January 1894.

Researching a novel had never been so enjoyable. But there is no limit to the amount of facts you can discover about a relatively recent historical personage like James. At some point you have to decide that you have accumulated enough raw data to work with, and begin writing. In the summer of 2002 I decided I had reached that point. The last piece of fieldwork I did was to revisit Rye, spending three days there at the end of July and beginning of August, staying at the Mermaid, the medieval inn where Henry James used to dine when his cook and butler had a day off. My previous hosts at Lamb House, Hilary & Gordon Brooke, were no longer its tenants, but they gave me generous assistance. Through them I was able to visit the cottage at Point Hill, Playden, just outside and above the town, which Henry James rented in the summer of 1896 from the architect Reginald Blomfield who built it, and to appreciate from its garden the view of Rye and the Romney marshes stretching towards the sea which caused James to fall in love with the place. The Brookes also introduced me to James Davidson, custodian of the Rye Museum which occupies the ancient Ypres Tower on the town ramparts, whose wife was a great-niece of Burgess Noakes. When I asked him if Burgess Noakes ever married, he replied in the negative, and said that some members of the family suspected he was gay. When I subsequently spoke to Mrs Davidson, by phone, however, she told me that he did marry, some time after the death of Henry James (in fact, as I later discovered, in 1930, after returning from America where he worked for many years as butler to James's nephew Billy and his wife), a woman called Ethel, whom nobody in the family liked and whom they suspected of marrying Burgess for his money. There were no offspring from the marriage, which Burgess was heard to describe as the worst thing he ever did. From this and other evidence I formed the opinion that Burgess Noakes was, like his master, a man without a clearly defined sexual identity or an active sexual life – which would explain the bond between them. Mrs Davidson was very helpful later, sending me further useful information and documents relating to Burgess Noakes. I knew she was in poor health, but I was very sorry to learn from her husband, when I sent her an inscribed copy of my novel, with its acknowledgement of her assistance, that she died not long before its publication.

During that visit to Rye I drove around the delightful surrounding country, visiting the places James used to walk or cycle to – the neighbouring Cinque Port of Winchelsea, the villages of Lydd, New Romney, Newchurch and Brookland, with their ancient churches – and went as far as Folkestone, where James visited the Du Mauriers, who were on holiday there in September 1895, when the success of Trilby was at its height. I planned a conversation between Henry and George as they walked up and down the clifftop promenade known as the Leas. And, as previously mentioned, I went back to Lamb House, to refresh my memory of its interior and garden, just a month or two before Colm Tóibín and Michiel Heyns encountered each other there.

In the article in *Prospect* from which I quoted earlier, Michiel Heyns reminded his readers of Henry James's extreme and uncompromising hostility to literary biography, and his almost obsessive desire to preserve his private life from public scrutiny even beyond the grave, recalling that the novelist confided to a correspondent in 1914: 'My sole wish is to frustrate as utterly as possible the postmortem exploiter . . . I have long thought of launching, by provision in my will, a curse not less explicit than Shakespeare's own on any such as try to move my bones.' It is a fair assumption that James would have anathematised novels about himself even more vehemently than biographies. Heyns concludes his article by saying, 'I am starting to suspect, as yet another letter of rejection arrives, that James's curse is taking effect – at least on one writer.' His suspicion was understandable in the circumstances, and if I were of a superstitious nature I might experience some uneasiness myself on this score, since I certainly feel that *Author, Author* has been an unlucky book. But if the outraged spirit of HJ *were* responsible, it is not obvious why Heyns should have suffered much worse luck than I, or why Colm Tóibín has enjoyed a seemingly trouble-free and favourable reception for *The Master* (unless being shortlisted for the Booker Prize but not winning it counts as a misfortune).

No, I do not feel that I have been cursed, but rather that by daring to write imaginatively about Henry James I entered a zone of narrative irony such as he himself loved to create, especially in his wonderful stories (which are among my favourite works of fiction) about writers and the literary profession: 'The Lesson of the Master', 'The Death of the Lion', 'The Figure in the Carpet', 'The Middle Years', 'The Next Time', and several others. I became – we all became, Colm Tóibín, Michiel Heyns and I – characters in a Jamesian plot. Consider, for example, that comical convergence in the sanctum of Lamb House of three writers all secreting works-in-progress about its distinguished former owner. Could anything be more Jamesian? It was, to use a phrase of Lambert Strether's in *The Ambassadors*, when he encounters Chad Newsome and Madame de Vionnet at the riverside inn, 'as queer as fiction, as farce . . .'. Or consider the delicate situation of Tony Davis when he was taken into the confidence of two novelists unknowingly competing with each other to write novels about the writer of whose home he was custodian. Or consider the ironies and symmetries that have characterised my own slender acquaintance with Colm Tóibín, which I will now relate.

We first met not, as writers usually do these days, at a book launch or literary festival, but on top of a small mountain in Galicia, in north-west Spain, in the summer of 1992. I was making a television documentary for the BBC about the pilgrimage to Santiago de Compostella, and we had reached the little village of Cebrero, about 150 kilometres from Santiago, which has a special place in the history of the pilgrimage because of a miracle said to have taken place there in the Middle Ages. It has a *refugio* (one of the hostels free to genuine pilgrims that are dotted along the Camino) with a more than usually commodious canteen attached, where I was having lunch with the team (director, production assistant, cameraman, sound technician) during a break in filming, when a dark-haired young man came in and sat down, since there were no other places free, at the end of our refectory table. Colm Tóibín was also following the pilgrimage trail, gathering material for a book entitled *The Sign of the Cross: Travels in Catholic Europe*, which was published two years later, and which I reviewed, not knowing in advance that I would find in it his description of our encounter:

> As I looked at the menu I realised that the other people at the table were of the English persuasion and did not look like pilgrims. Nor did they look like a family on holiday; most of them were in their thirties and it was hard to work out the relationship between them. I looked at one of them and was sure I knew him from somewhere; he was careful to look away. I asked them a question about the pilgrimage and found out quickly that they were a television crew making a film about the route to Santiago. I told them I was writing a book about it, and wondered out loud if everyone else in the dining room was engaged in similar activities. They were all jolly and friendly in a very English way, and it was a great relief from the gruff Galicians I had been dealing with.
>
> I looked at the man who had looked away earlier: he had glasses and straight hair, he was in his late forties. Suddenly I realised who he was.
>
> 'What did Chad's family make their fortune from in Henry James's "The Ambassadors"?' I asked him.
>
> 'No one knows,' he replied. He did not seem surprised by the question.
>
> 'But there's a solution in your first novel,' I said.
>
> 'In my second novel,' he corrected me.
>
> 'You're David Lodge,' I said, and he agreed that he was.
> He was the presenter of the BBC film.[11]

Note that the very first utterance Colm Tóibín addressed to me was an abstruse question about Henry James. To use a currently fashionable formula: how weird is that? (The 'solution' is in *The British Museum is Falling Down*, actually my third novel, published in 1965, in which a postgraduate friend of the hero called Camel, who is writing a doctoral thesis on 'Sanitation in Victorian Fiction', argues half-seriously that the unnamed, 'small, trivial, rather ridiculous object of the commonest use', on the manufacture of which the Newsome family fortune in *The Ambassadors* is based, is a chamber pot.) Note too that Colm Tóibín, discovering that I was making a film about the pilgrimage to Santiago, revealed that he was writing a book on the same subject (not quite true – it was only one chapter of his book) and immediately wondered aloud if everyone else in the canteen were similarly engaged, anticipating the moment ten years later when he found himself at Lamb House in the company of two men also writing books on Henry James.

The passage continues:

> We had lunch then. The crew was full of jokes and nicknames for each other, completely bonded as a group. They even called David Lodge 'Lodgie'. He seemed disturbed that I had not got an official book of the route which should be stamped regularly. I knew he was trying to be helpful but brief exchanges between Irish people and English people can be difficult, and I thought for a moment that he felt he was hectoring me, and he soon stopped and smiled and I smiled back.
>
> He and his crew had a minibus. I really wanted to go with them and abandon my own solitary manoeuvrings. I sat for ages over my coffee talking to them, but I knew it could not last and I stood up to go.

It is always disconcerting to encounter a description of yourself unexpectedly in someone else's book – like catching sight of yourself on a CCTV monitor. Tóibín captured very well the bantering camaraderie of the production team and the slightly awkward tone of our own conversation, between two writers meeting each other in untypical circumstances and slightly fraudulent roles. For, as his book revealed, Colm was hardly more of an authentic pilgrim than Lodgie. At times we had both walked for a while in the wrong direction – I because the cameraman said the light was better that way, and he because he was lost. I drove most of the route, while he hopped on to trains and buses. I wasn't of course really disturbed by his lack of a pilgrimage 'passport' – one of the devices that the Catholic Church and the Spanish Tourist Board have dreamed up to promote the Camino – but merely trying to help him in his reportorial task. Also I was more disconcerted than I showed by the knight's move by which he identified me, and a little embarrassed by the fact that I knew little about his own work while he seemed to know mine rather well. *The Sign of the Cross* was in fact the first book by him that I read. I enjoyed it, and reviewed it favourably. In 1999 he and Carmen Callil did me the honour of including *Changing Places* in a book they co-authored called *The Modern Library: 200 Best Novels Published Since 1950*. We had no correspondence about these publications.

Up until the time I published *Author, Author* I thought that the encounter in Cebrero was our only meeting, and said so to several enquirers, including some journalists. But in mid-September 2004 I met Colm Tóibín again, in Rye, where we were both speaking about our respective novels at the festival, and he reminded me that we had met on another occasion, only two years before, which to my great embarrassment I had to admit I had completely forgotten. I had forgotten the meeting because I had scarcely been aware of it, for reasons which are worth recalling for their comic and ironic aspects. It happened at the Harbourfront literary festival in Toronto at the end of October 2002. This is one of the major international festivals, on a par with Edinburgh, Hay-on-Wye and Adelaide, and is very much the brain-child of Greg Gatenby, a peppy, extrovert, bearded bibliophile who has run it very successfully for many years. He had invited me on a couple of previous occasions when I had been unable or disinclined to go, but in 2002 I agreed to take part in the festival, partly because writers I knew spoke well of it (Malcolm Bradbury was particularly enthusiastic and had been more than once), and partly because Greg had invited me to talk about my book of essays, *Consciousness and the Novel*, which had just been published in America and was about to appear in England. Books of literary criticism are not usually showcased at literary festivals. I would also be able to read from the recently issued paperback edition of *Thinks...* . Writers are invited to Harbourfront for several days, fed at a different restaurant every evening, and do one onstage interview and one reading during their stay. There was an optional excursion to the Niagara Falls, which I had visited only once, many years before, on the American side of the border and in mist so thick that I could only hear them. And I have relatives in Toronto. So there were several reasons to say yes, and in the spring of 2002 I did so. By the time I packed my bag for Toronto I was about three months and some 20,000 words into the writing of *Author, Author*, but I was not averse to putting it aside for a week – an enforced break of that kind allows you to reread your over-familiar text with a fresh eye when you return home. I saw from the festival programme that the British writers who would be in Toronto at the same time as myself included Michael Holroyd, Rachel Billington and Simon Gray, all of whom I knew. I noticed that Colm Tóibín would be appearing after I had departed (the festival lasts for two weeks).

My trip began dramatically. I arrived at Heathrow's Terminal Four to find the Departure Hall in turmoil. *CANCELLED, CANCELLED, CANCELLED, CANCELLED*: the word ran down the right-hand columns of the monitor screens as if announcing some apocalyptic catastrophe. It transpired that all that day's flights had been cancelled because of high winds. Was it possible that the awesome power of modern aviation could be brought to a halt by mere wind? Apparently so. There was nothing to do but go back to London, spend the day and night in my London pad, and return to Heathrow next day. The awkward consequence of this delay was that, instead of having a day to rest and recover from jet-lag, I had to do my onstage interview within a few hours of arriving in Toronto, at what was two o'clock in the morning by my body-clock. Simon Gray had a similar experience, arriving on the same day on a later plane to perform in the same evening, and wrote very amusingly about it in the next instalment of his delectable journals, *The Smoking Diaries* (2004).

Fired up by the challenge of the circumstances I believe I acquitted myself pretty well in my onstage interview, which was deftly conducted by the Canadian novelist Wayne Johnston; but perhaps for that reason the rest of my visit, though pleasant enough, seemed slightly anticlimactic. To be honest, I found the venue something of a disappointment. Though I had been to Toronto before, and should have known better, the name 'Harbourfront' had summoned up in my mind the image of something like Fisherman's Wharf in San Francisco, a busy picturesque quayside crammed with yachts and fishing boats and lined with bars and restaurants. Toronto's Harbourfront is a somewhat soulless development of big hotels and apartment blocks spread out along the lake shore, where a bitter wind already blew off the water in late October, and the festival itself took place in a modern building lacking in charm. It did, however, have a bar, and there one evening near the end of my stay, after attending some event, I had a drink with a friendly Canadian who was connected with the festival in some way. I cannot remember his name. There was a crowd of people around the bar and a roar of talk.

At this point I must inform the reader that in recent years I have become quite deaf, and am obliged to wear a hearing aid in both ears. Though it is a state-of-the-art digital device with a programme to damp down background noise, it cannot always cope with extreme conditions such as obtained in that bar. Names are always especially difficult to hear when nothing in the context gives you any clue as to what they might be. My Canadian friend greeted a man whose name I did not catch and whom I did not recognise, though he smiled warmly as if he knew who I was. He spoke animatedly for some time, but I heard and understood almost nothing of what he said, and responded with phatic murmurs and complaints about the circumambient noise level, until his attention was drawn by some other person. As we moved away from the bar I said to my companion, 'Who *was* that man?' 'Colm Tóibín,' he replied. 'Good God,' I said, 'was it really? I didn't recognise him.'

If this seems improbable, bear in mind that I had only seen Colm Tóibín in the flesh for about an hour, ten years previously, and in the meantime his physical appearance had altered. It is not surprising that he recognised me: I am famous among my acquaintance for not changing much in appearance, and looking younger than my years. (It is just the luck of the genetic draw.) At the time of our first meeting, when Colm Tóibín described me in his book as being in my late forties, I was in fact fifty-seven. The passage of time since then had left its mark more deeply on him than on me. The young man who walked into the canteen at Cebrero had a head of dark curly hair. The man in the Harbourfront bar was bald, and his features triggered no memory. (I am sorry to be so personal, but it is the only way I can explain what happened. I would gladly trade my hair for his ears.) I was embarrassed that I had not recognised him and hoped that it had not been too obvious, but the episode did not bother me for long, and I soon forgot it completely. There is no mention of it in the brief notes I made of my time in Toronto. I wonder now what Colm Tóibín said in the conversation that I was unable to hear or meaningfully contribute to. Did he perhaps drop some hint of working on a novel about Henry James? If so, I didn't pick it up, and returned to England blissfully ignorant of this threat to the originality of my own project, only to encounter immediately another from a different source.

I arrived in London early on Saturday morning, 2 November, and bought the *Guardian* to read on the train to Birmingham. Although a copy was waiting for me at home, I was eager to read the lead article in the Review section, which was an edited extract from the title essay of *Consciousness and the Novel*. I read it through with the quiet complacency that seeing one's work prominently in print usually generates, and then idly turned the pages of the magazine. My eye was caught by the opening sentence of a review by Toby Litt of a novel by Emma Tennant called *Felony*:

I don't know what Henry James ever did to Emma Tennant, but it must have been something pretty awful. Enough to have her take revenge upon him by making him the villain of her latest novel.

BAD NEWS BAD NEWS BAD NEWS . . . The message raced through the synapses of my brain and sent the adrenalin pumping through my arteries and veins. Seated in a crowded railway carriage, I could not express my shock or relieve my feelings by an exclamation or expletive. Another writer had scooped me by publishing a novel about Henry James! I hardly dared to read on to discover how similar it might be to the one I had recently started. I let my eye skim the surface of the newsprint, picking up the gist of the review; then I read it from beginning to end. I was relieved to discover that *Felony* was only partly about Henry James, and dealt with only a fairly small segment of his life, in a style evidently very different from my novel. I also observed from the header that it was very short. Nevertheless its publication was a blow. It would take some of the bloom of originality off my own novel, and if I had not already made a substantial start on *Author, Author*, the effect would have been far more demoralising. As soon as I got home I reread what I had already written (the first half of the frame story, and the first chapter-and-a-bit of the main story), and was reassured. It worked, I thought, and I knew how I meant to go on with it. To avoid any more interference in the creative process from *Felony*, I resolved not to read that novel, and to avert my eyes from any more reviews of it that might come my way. An additional ironical twist, of a kind with which I would become familiar, was that it was published by Cape, a Random House imprint like my own publishers, Secker & Warburg. I had not yet told my publisher, Geoff Mulligan, the subject of my novel-in-progress, except to say that it was a period piece. I now put him in the picture. He was sympathetic and supportive, and said there was no need to speak to anyone else in Random House at present about the clash with *Felony*. So I went on with my novel in a calmer state of mind, and in the months that followed the existence of Emma Tennant's bothered me less and less. Subconsciously I must have assumed that, having survived this unwelcome surprise, I would not experience another of the same kind. Little, as the old novelists used to say, did I know.

Writing a novel could be accurately described as a process of continual problem-solving or decision-making. Most of these decisions are made at the level of the scene or paragraph or sentence: this action or thought rather than that, this word or phrase rather than that. But there are macro-decisions which govern the whole narrative, and there are limits to one's freedom to revise or modify them once the work is well under way. I have already touched on one of these matters, the handling of time. Another, perhaps the most important, is the question of the point of view from which the story is to be presented, which concerns not only the perspective from which events are perceived, but also the style or voice in which they are narrated. The possibilities are numerous: you can have one point of view or several; you can let the point-of-view character or characters narrate their story/stories in their own voice(s), in literary or colloquial styles, or you can narrate it in an authorial voice which may be intrusive or impersonal, and may merge to a variable degree with the inner voices of the characters through the device of free indirect style. You can narrate the novel entirely in the form of documents: letters, emails, depositions – even, as in Nabokov's *Pale Fire*, in the form of a poem and editorial apparatus. But always, at any given point in the narrative, there is a point of view which focuses and controls our interest as readers in the unfolding story.

While I was researching *Author, Author*, I gave much thought to this aspect of the projected novel, as my notebook shows, e.g.:

> *9 Dec 2000. I still have a very open mind as to how the story should be told. Not first person – would be too like the notebooks and the essays. Probably not focalised through HJ throughout. Perhaps multiple viewpoints . . . [Undated] A question to be considered is whether the main story should proceed chronologically within the frame of James's last illness and death, or in a series of jumbled flashbacks in the mind of the dying James . . . 10 July 02. Still turning over the options re. pov. I am coming to the conclusion that HJ must be the only char whose consciousness is represented mimetically, through free indirect speech etc . . . To 'do' GDM in the same dense detail and interiority as HJ would be inconsistent with HJ being the main character of the frame story, and would probably extend the book inordinately.*

A persistent theme in many of the notes, widely separated in time, is an anxiety that the novel should not read like a biography, and the hope that I could avoid this effect by foregrounding the machinery of narration itself, through abrupt time-shifts, switches of point of view and 'postmodernist' authorial interpolations. In late July 2002, I wrote:

I think of beginning the novel something like this:

December 1915. In the master bedroom (never was the estate agent's epithet more appropriate) of Flat xx [check], 21 Carlyle Mansions, Cheyne Walk, Chelsea, the novelist was dying – slowly, but inexorably. In Flanders, a mere 150 miles away [check] men were dying more quickly, more painfully, more pitifully, blown to bits by shells, perforated by machine gun bullets, disembowelled by bayonets, drowned in mud-filled craters, poisoned by infection – young men, most of them, with their lives still before them, lives never to be lived. The novelist was 72 [check] he had lived a full life, travelled widely, moved in society (one winter he dined out 172 times [check]), enjoyed the arts, owned a charming old house in Rye as well as leasing his spacious London flat with its view of the Thames. He had never experienced sexual intercourse, but that was by his own choice, unlike the many young men in Flanders who died virgins either for lack of opportunity or because they believed in chastity outside marriage. The novelist was propped up in bed among starched sheets and plump pillows, attended by three servants and two professional nurses working in rotation, while the young men were dying in No Man's Land, caught on barbed wire, or in trenches amid mud and excrement and rats, or on jolting stretchers, or on camp beds in field hospitals filled with the moans and screams of their wounded comrades. So, why should one expend much retrospective sympathy on the old man when so many young ones were suffering much crueller fates? Because there is no quantifying the significance of a death. The end of every human life has inexhaustible pathos, poignancy, irony, if we know the person well enough. But we cannot know everybody. The half million [check] who died in the Battle of the Somme – I wonder at the immensity of loss as I wonder at the number of years it takes for the light of the nearest star to reach Earth – but I cannot imagine those deaths. Whereas the last illness and death of a novelist, one whose work I am reasonably familiar with, whose life is recorded and recoverable in some detail, is a subject that stirs my sympathies, invites my speculations, no doubt in part because I am a novelist myself, not so far away from the age of Henry James when he died.

The next note reads:

On reflection I think it would be a mistake to draw attention to myself as the 'real' author in this way. I couldn't then 'invent' freely. The authorial narrator must have authority.

What this first attempt revealed to me was that I really wanted to write a novel in which the joins between documented facts and imaginative speculation would be seamless and invisible, and that drawing attention to myself as narrator would entail coming clean about the extent to which I was selecting from and embellishing the historical record – thus forfeiting the great advantage of writing a novel about a real person, namely, the reader's trusting involvement in the story. I also felt that there was too much rhetorical emphasis on the horror of war in this opening paragraph. There was a value to be obtained from the circumstance that James died at a dark moment in the history of European civilisation, and in the way the big public tragedy impinged on the small private one, but it needed to be handled more subtly. Eventually, after much tinkering, the published novel began thus:

LONDON, December 1915. In the master bedroom (never was the estate agent's epithet more appropriate) of Flat 21, Carlyle Mansions, Cheyne Walk, Chelsea, the distinguished author is dying – slowly, but surely. In Flanders, less than two hundred miles away, other men are dying more quickly, more painfully, more pitifully – young men, mostly, with their lives still before them, blank pages that will never be filled. The author is 72. He has had an interesting and varied life, written many books, travelled widely, enjoyed the arts, moved in society (one winter he dined out 107 times), and owns a charming old house in Rye as well as the lease of this spacious London flat with its fine view of the Thames. He has had deeply rewarding friendships with both men and women. If he has never experienced sexual intercourse, that was by his own choice, unlike the many young men in Flanders who have died virgins either for lack of opportunity or because they hoped to marry and were keeping themselves chaste on principle.

The narration is still authorial, and continues to be throughout the frame story, controlling the frequent shifts from one point of view to another among the people grouped around the dying James, and providing necessary contextual information; but it is an impersonal narrative voice, stripped of autobiographical references and personal reflections. Between the two versions I had decided to use the present tense as the basic tense for the frame story (though there are retrospective passages within it written in the past tense) to heighten the contrast between it and the main story, and this also increases the effect of impersonality, inasmuch as the conventional narrative preterite is a grammatical sign of a narrator's existence.

When I came to write the main story I adopted a more traditional method: a past-tense, third-person narrative focalised through the consciousness of my main character. I aimed at a style which would be compatible with James's own without being an exact imitation of it, for two reasons: first that the latter would risk seeming like parody, and secondly that people, even professional writers, do not think in the same consciously rhetorical style that they employ in writing. (I was bolder in trying to imitate James's style of speech, from what we know of it.) I also kept to a basically chronological sequence of events in the main story. It seemed the best way to get my readers, most of whom would not be familiar with Henry James's life and work, and perhaps not enthralled by what they did know, to understand and sympathise with his private and professional crises. In particular I felt that they would better apprehend the pain he suffered at the disastrous first night of *Guy Domville* if I took them through the whole history of his five-year campaign to establish himself as a playwright. This was a part of James's story with which I found it very easy to identify, having myself in mid-life and mid-career as a novelist tried my hand at writing for performance, and acquired considerable personal experience of the frustrations and disappointments, as well as the occasional moments of euphoria and hope, involved in writing plays and screenplays. One of the challenges of writing a novel about a novelist is that novel-writing is essentially a private, solitary and largely mental activity, whereas writing and producing plays is essentially collaborative and interactive – the stuff of fiction.

Accordingly I treated James's first play to be professionally produced, an adaptation of his own novel, *The American*, in considerable detail, and gave briefer accounts of his subsequent, abortive attempts to write and find producers for new plays, before coming to the inception and composition of *Guy Domville*, interweaving this theatrical history with the other more personal strands of the novel involving Du Maurier, Fenimore and Alice James. As I approached the crucial years of 1894 and 1895, however, I was conscious that to treat their events in the same fashion – at the same deliberate pace, in chronological order – would diminish the pivotal importance of the disastrous first night. A radical change of tempo and narrative method was called for. I decided to divide the main story into two parts, ending the first of them (Part Two of the whole novel, Part One being the first half of the frame story) with James, just after Christmas 1893, having been bitterly disappointed by the last-minute cancellation of his play *Mrs Jasper*, deciding to give his theatrical ambitions 'one more year'. The first chapter of Part Three takes place just over one year later, on the day of the premiere of *Guy Domville*. It begins with Henry James lying restlessly awake in the small hours, anxiously contemplating the coming make-or-break trial of his dramatic ambitions, and thinking back over the traumatic suicide of Fenimore, the astonishing success of *Trilby* and the agonisingly slow progress of *Guy Domville* towards production, topics which continue to occupy his thoughts throughout the day as he kills time with humdrum activities.

I was pleased with the way this chapter came out, and it provided a model for the last chapter of Part Three, which again begins with Henry James lying awake in bed, this time in a happier mood, thinking back over the acquisition of Lamb House, which he now occupies, and looking forward confidently to the work he hopes to accomplish there. But it was not a viable template for the second chapter, which had to describe the first night of *Guy Domville*, for the simple reason that the anxious James was not present for most of the performance at the St James's Theatre, having gone to see Oscar Wilde's *An Ideal Husband* at the Theatre Royal Haymarket, in an ill-judged attempt to distract himself. He turned up in the wings of the St James's only just in time to be drawn on to the stage by Alexander. He would, of course, subsequently have acquired some knowledge of the circumstances that caused him to be booed, but this would not be enough to support a prolonged retrospective stream of consciousness about what happened. In short, there were many aspects to that evening's events, of rich human and historical interest, that could not be accommodated while at the same time preserving the integrity of the main story's chosen point of view – something James himself insisted on as a theorist and practitioner of the novel. The solution I arrived at was to hypothesise that over the many years that followed he did in fact acquire from various sources, oral and written, directly and indirectly, most of the facts that we now know about that notorious first night, and became belatedly aware that while 'his story, with its drastically limited point of view, was proceeding, other connected stories were in progress, other points of view were in play, at the same time, in parallel, in brackets, as it were'. Those stories are then told, literally inside brackets, in the rest of the chapter, in passages that alternate with passages narrated from James's point of view. It was a kind of cheating, but it turned out to be most readers' favourite chapter.

There is another decision that has to be made about every novel, and that is what to call it. Some writers keep an open mind about this until the very last moment before the book goes to press, but for me deciding on the title is an important part of the creative process. It is a way of defining for oneself, and for one's potential readers, what the novel is essentially

about. Usually in the early stages of working on a novel I entertain several possible titles, hesitating between them and thinking up new ones as the book takes shape. Initially I thought
of calling this novel *HJ*, but that seemed to suggest too narrow
a focus. When I started writing, my working title was *The
Madness of Art*, a phrase in a passage from one of James's stories
which I intended to use (and did use) as an epigraph, the words
of a dying novelist: 'We work in the dark – we do what we
can – we give what we have. Our doubt is our passion and
our passion is our task. The rest is the madness of art.' Out
of its original context, however, 'the madness of art' would
not, I decided, make a particularly appealing or appropriate
title.* On 3 October 2002 I made an entry in my notebook:

> Last night in the bathroom while getting ready to go to bed
> I had an idea for my title which is the one I think I shall stay
> with (though undecided about punctuation):
> *Author, Author*
> *Author Author*
> *Author! Author!*

I was pleased with this title, and never considered any other
afterwards. The primary reference is obviously to the climax
of the novel, when James is lured on to the stage by cries of
'Author! Author!' at the first night of *Guy Domville*. The whole
novel is a kind of tribute to James, as the curtain comes down
on his life, reversing that humiliation (and I already had a
vague idea of inviting him to take a bow at the end). But the

---

* Jim Crace, who had already guessed the subject of my novel early in 2003, aston-
ished me even more by writing in an email in August, 'I'm really looking forward
to your Henry James novel (Title? "The Rest is Madness"?)'. I had told nobody about
my working title. He said it was just a lucky guess.

title also indicates that there is more than one author in the story, and that the career of George Du Maurier is symmetrically paired and compared with James's. In a more abstract sense the novel is about authorship as a profession and vocation, and the repetition of the word (I felt there was a Blakean rhythm to it, 'Author, author, burning bright . . .') expresses the obsessive and all-consuming commitment of writers like James to their art. To incorporate all these suggestions I decided to omit the exclamation marks that belonged to the main, literal meaning of the title, but to have no punctuation at all would have struck too modern a note. So *Author, Author* it was, and remained.*

II

I am rather unusual among contemporary British novelists in being published by different publishers in hardback and paperback (Secker & Warburg and Penguin, respectively). When I began writing fiction it was common practice for hardback publishing houses to sell the paperback rights in a novel to a specialist paperback publisher, but from the 1980s onwards, as bigger and bigger conglomerates were formed, and these set up their own paperback imprints, it became customary to publish novels 'vertically' in hardback and paperback editions produced by the same group. I was reluctant, however, to change an arrangement which suited me very well, and managed to resist pressure to do so. Eventually it was agreed that Secker (who were acquired by Random House in the late '80s) and Penguin would make a joint offer for both hardback

---

* Exclamation marks were, however, used for the French edition of the novel, *L'Auteur! L'Auteur!*, because there is no tradition of calling for the playwright to take a bow in the French theatre, and this level of meaning in the title could not therefore be merely allusive.

and paperback rights of any new novel on which they had an option. It has never been my practice to sign a contract and accept an advance for a novel which was unwritten or partially written. I submit my new novels in a finished form with which I am satisfied (though always open to editorial suggestions) and wait for an offer.

I explain all this because it had some bearing on the timing of the publication of *Author, Author*, and consequently on its reception. In the late spring and early summer of 2003, as I drew near to the end of Part Three of the novel, I began to consider when I was likely to be able to deliver the finished work. The publishing of literary fiction in Britain, as of most trade books (as they are called) sold through bookshops, is divided into two seasons, or six-month periods, spring/ summer (actually January to June) and autumn/winter (July to December). Information about forthcoming books is circulated to the book trade, the media, and other interested parties (such as the organisers of literary festivals) in two corresponding catalogues which are compiled long before the books are published. For this reason, among others, most books are published between nine months and a year after they are accepted. I much prefer to bring out a new novel in the January–June period, when the publication of leading fiction titles is well spread out. The Booker Prize, for which submissions must be published before the end of September in any given year, has made that a very crowded month for literary fiction, to such an extent that important novels are now published in July and August, traditionally considered a bad time to bring out new hardback fiction because so many people are away on holiday.

I had hoped therefore to publish *Author, Author* in the spring of 2004. By the end of May 2003 I had nearly finished Part

Three and had only the second 'bookend', Part Four, to write. But Mary and I had arranged (now rather to my regret) to take a two-week holiday in France in mid-June, and it wasn't feasible to think of delivering the finished novel until late July. The Random House catalogue for the next spring/summer season would go to press early in August. Taking into account the number of people at Random House and Penguin who would have to read the novel and consult each other, and their various planned absences on holiday, it was obvious that there simply wouldn't be time to do a deal and get copy into the Spring/Summer '04 catalogue. Of course I could have submitted the 90 per cent of the novel I had already written by the end of May, and invited an offer on that basis; but having worked so long and hard on the book, and having what I thought of as the makings of a very strong concluding section in my head, I couldn't bear to have it judged in an incomplete form, like an arch with the keystone missing. So I resigned myself to publishing the novel in the autumn of 2004. Had I taken the other course of action *Author, Author* would almost certainly have appeared at the same time as *The Master*, for it is a fair assumption that the two publishers, having discovered by one means or another the coincidence of subject matter between the two books, would have brought them out as early as possible in 2004, and perhaps agreed on simultaneous publication (as had happened the previous year with two competing biographies of Primo Levi). What the consequences of that would have been is impossible to assess with certainty, though I was later to attempt such an exercise; but it would have made a significant difference, I believe, to the reception of both books.

At the time, still ignorant of the existence of *The Master* (which Colm Tóibín later told me he had delivered to his publishers in March of 2003) I felt only a mild disappointment, more than balanced by a comfortable feeling that I could finish my novel without any pressure, and would have plenty of time to show it to a few people in whose opinion I was particularly interested and to give it a final polish before I submitted it to the publishers. There was no point in delivering it any earlier than the beginning of September, when all the publishing folk would be back at work after their summer holidays.

I enjoyed writing Part Four. I nearly always do enjoy writing the concluding sequence of a novel. It seems to come with a kind of ease and inevitability, so very different from the effort and hesitancy with which one begins, doubtless because one is no longer held up by a multiplicity of choices and decisions about the development of the story. There are very few pieces of the jigsaw left lying on the table, and it suddenly seems very obvious where they must go, and how they fit together, with a satisfying click-click-click, to complete the picture. I found a way of including the theme of James's posthumous success in acquiring a large, global audience for his work, by putting another frame around the frame story itself. A brief, italicised 'Author's Note' was already in place before the opening paragraph of the novel. It reads, in part:

> Nearly everything that happens in this story is based on factual sources . . . all the named characters were real people. Quotations from their books, plays, articles, letters, journals, etc., are their own words. But I have used a novelist's licence in representing what they thought, felt, and said to each other; and I have imagined some events and personal details which history omitted to record.

It seemed to me that my readers would appreciate some kind of guidance on the relation of fact to fiction in the novel, and by guaranteeing the authenticity of the written documents quoted I would give them a kind of 'reality check' on the events described: they could be certain that anything referred to in such sources was 'true'. This note would also, I decided later, provide a formal basis for an italicised authorial intervention in the last pages of the novel, where I fantasise being transported to the dying James's bedside to try and deliver the consoling news of his future fame. It was a risky conceit, but I liked it. I wrote the last line of the book with a great sense of satisfaction: 'Henry, wherever you are, take a bow.'

Mary is normally the first person to read my books. To save time, and because she happened to be exceedingly busy herself, I gave her Parts One–Three to read while I finished off Part Four. She was surprised by how different it was in style from my other novels, but favourably impressed. Her main criticism was that there was an excessive amount of factual detail in the first half of the main story. I took this criticism seriously and went over Part Two, trimming it as much as I felt able to, before passing the completed MS to other readers for their comments and corrections. I was particularly eager to know what our friends and neighbours Joel Kaplan and Sheila Stowell would think of it. Joel had recently retired as head of the Drama Department at Birmingham University, where his wife Sheila had also been a senior Research Fellow. I was aware they had a special interest in Oscar Wilde and nineteenth-century British drama, but not until I was well into writing Author, Author did I discover that they probably knew more about George Alexander and the St James's Theatre than any other two people in the world, and that they possessed, framed and hanging on the walls of their early Victorian house, posters, publicity photos and programmes for many of Alexander's productions, including the first one of *The Importance of Being Earnest*, which he mounted hastily after the failure of *Guy Domville*, using several of the same actors who had performed in James's play. It was an extraordinary and (I thought) auspicious coincidence to find this invaluable research resource at the corner of our street. Where else could I have discovered, for instance, that the first name of the actress known professionally as Mrs Edward Saker (a form designed to confer respectability on actresses in those days) was 'Rose'?

From the Kaplans, and from Bernard Bergonzi, Emeritus Professor of English at Warwick University, a very old friend who also knows his Henry James extremely well, I got encouraging overall reactions to the novel and valuable comments and corrections. The other readers of the MS at this stage were Mike Shaw, my agent at Curtis Brown since 1979, who had recently retired and was celebrating by sailing round the British Isles with his son Daniel in their oyster-dredger, the *Susan J*, and his former assistant Jonny Pegg, who had taken over my account. To assist the handover, and contrary to my usual practice, I had already shown both of them the first half of the novel in draft, and taken some notes from them at that time. I was pleased to get their positive responses to the completed novel. I did a final revision of the text, and sent it off at the very end of August to Curtis Brown for copying and forwarding to Secker, Penguin, and my American publisher, Viking. The novel had taken me almost exactly a year to write, during which time I did very little other work.

Waiting for a publisher's verdict on a new book is always a somewhat tense experience, and in this instance the suspense was heightened by my awareness that *Author, Author* was a quite different kind of novel from anything I had written before, and that it might not immediately appeal to a large number of my regular readers. It was my first 'period' novel, and my first about a real person; its predominant mood was elegiac, its comedy muted, and its hero was celibate from start to finish. I did not doubt that Secker and Penguin would want to publish it, but I was not sure with what degree of enthusiasm or commitment. That would be indicated by the kind of advance they offered, which in turn would be based on their assessment of how many copies they would sell. Or, to put it another way: the more they paid for the novel, the more copies they were likely to sell, because the more effort they would put into promoting and marketing the book in order to recoup their investment. In the early part of my career I never expected or aspired to be a novelist whose books appear in bestseller lists, but in the 1980s, through a combination of factors (including Booker Prize shortlist nominations and TV serialisations of two successive novels, *Small World* and *Nice Work*) I acquired quite a large readership; and preserving it, without compromising my literary aims, is important to me. I don't think I am alone in that respect among contemporary novelists who have had the same good fortune. In short, the offer that would be made for *Author, Author* was of more than merely financial interest to me.

Geoff Mulligan called me in the first week of September, having just read the novel, to say, with obvious sincerity, that he liked it very much, but that he needed to show it to other people in Random House before Secker could make an offer. This was exactly what I had expected, but when the second week of September went by without any further news, I began to get uneasy, suspecting some resistance higher up in the Random House hierarchy. It so happened that I had accepted invitations to two literary launch parties in London on the Monday and Tuesday of the following week. I went to these events, with Mary, in a state of concealed excitement and uncertainty about my own book, not guessing how many people I would meet who were or would be involved in its fortunes. The first party was for Antonia Byatt, marking the paperback publication of the last of her Frederica Potter novels by Vintage, and the issue of the completed quartet in a boxed set. It was held in the House of Barnabas, a handsome eighteenth-century building at the top of Greek Street, off Soho Square. The windows of the high-ceilinged reception room on the first floor were wide open to the warm evening. One of the first people I saw and spoke to was Dan Franklin, head of Cape, and formerly head of Secker when it belonged to Reed, where he had published my *Paradise News*. He immediately told me that he had started reading *Author, Author* at three that afternoon and was enjoying it enormously. This was a huge relief, because Dan is a senior and influential figure at Random House, even though, with his boyish features, owlish spectacles and short-back-and-sides haircut, he somewhat resembles a studious sixth-former from a 1950s grammar school. I assured him that if he had enjoyed the first hundred pages so much, he was bound to enjoy the rest of the book even more. We talked about Martin Amis's new novel, *Yellow Dog*, which Cape had just published (the occasion of the following night's party), and its largely hostile reception in the press. Dan felt that an injustice had been done, and I agreed with him. I was reading *Yellow Dog* myself, and although I didn't think it was entirely successful it hadn't shaken my conviction that Martin is the most original and inventive prose stylist of his generation of English novelists. On the other side of the room, I spotted the tall, bulky figure of the novelist Tibor Fischer, who had achieved some noto-riety recently by vilifying *Yellow Dog* as 'not-knowing-where-to-look-bad' in an article in the *Daily Telegraph*, well ahead of its publication, something writers don't usually do to their peers, especially when they have a novel coming out them-selves at the same time.

Yellow Dog had, however, been longlisted for the Man Booker Prize (as it was now known, since acquiring a new sponsor), whereas Tibor Fischer's novel, *Voyage to the End of the Room*, had not. The shortlist was due to be decided and announced the following day, and one of the judges, the novel-ist and critic D. J. Taylor, was present at the party. Though we crossed swords on television and in print early in his career we have since got on to amicable terms. 'I'm sick of the Booker Prize,' he said morosely, when I asked him how it was going. As a former chairman of the judges myself, in 1989, I recog-nised the symptoms of a familiar syndrome. Booker judges usually begin their task glowing with a sense of their own importance, and trusting in 'the common pursuit of true judgement'; but sooner or later disillusionment in the objec-tivity of their fellow judges sets in, along with a daunting sense of the enormous pressure of conflicting expectations from friends, acquaintances and colleagues in the literary, publishing and media worlds. They realise that they too are going to be judged, and begin to wish they had never agreed to serve.

The next evening's party was a bigger and more glamorous affair. The venue was the Roof Gardens in South Kensington, a rather wonderful place on top of the old Derry & Toms department store. As well as a large indoor reception area it has surprisingly extensive gardens, with full-grown trees, shrubbery, flower beds and a stream with flamingos and other water birds in it (their wings presumably clipped). The greenery screens out the London rooftops and the noise of traffic, and it is hard to believe that you are a couple of hundred feet above Kensington High Street. On a fine midsummer evening it is a magical place. But this was mid-September, and the party was from '9 till late', so it was already dark by the time the first guests arrived. The weather continued warm, and it was pleasant to be outdoors, but the lighting of the Gardens is patchy. Guests gathered under patio lights in a noisy heaving throng just outside the main reception area, where musicians played to an empty dance floor, or they wandered in ones and twos through the dark, shadowy alleys, peering at the people they met to see if they recognised them. The party never quite gelled – but it wasn't just on account of the lighting. Our hosts were in a sombre mood. The Booker shortlist had been announced that afternoon, and there wasn't a single title on it from any of the Random House imprints, which include Cape, Secker, Hutchinson and Chatto & Windus – not even the much-fancied *The Curious Incident of the Dog in the Night-time*, by Mark Haddon. Random House had accounted for a third of the titles on the longlist, so their hopes had been high, and their disappointment was correspondingly severe. Geoff Mulligan, dressed down to an almost penitential degree in a black crew-neck pullover, described himself as being in shock. He was particularly disappointed at the omission of J. M. Coetzee's *Elizabeth Costello* which Secker had published. (Ample compensation would soon come in the form of the Nobel Prize, but he wasn't to know that.) I had missed the shortlist announcement and asked him for the details, but apparently it was full of surprises and he could only remember that Margaret Atwood was on it, and a completely unknown novelist published by the tiny Tindall Street Press in Birmingham.* It did not seem an auspicious moment to pump him about *Author, Author*, nor did he seem eager to discuss it. I saw Dan Franklin standing lugubriously alone, a glass of red wine in his fist. 'So sad! So sad!' he exclaimed as I approached. He was not referring to the shortlist, but to the chapter in *Author, Author* about the first night of *Guy Domville*, which he had just reached in his reading of my typescript. But he made it clear that this episode in James's life chimed with his own sense of professional defeat.

The failure of *Yellow Dog* to make the shortlist cannot have come as a complete surprise, given its reception in the press, but it was hard on Martin Amis to have his party on this ill-starred evening. He arrived late, and looked as if he would have preferred to be somewhere else, but manfully played the part of guest of honour. I chatted with him briefly about *Yellow Dog*, whose tone of apocalyptic farce had reminded me distantly of Evelyn Waugh's *Vile Bodies*, and he said he had reread *Scoop* to warm up for the journalistic strand in his novel, and how good it was. He was at the noisy epicentre of the party, so I soon moved away, and met Simon Master, a big wheel at Random House, who told me that *Author, Author* had been passed to him but he hadn't yet looked at it. He added that *Thinks...* hadn't sold as well as they had hoped, which made me think he was softening me up for a modest offer for the new novel. Altogether I wasn't enjoying this party much, in spite of the large number of literary friends and acquain-

* This was *Amazing Splashes of Colour* by Clare Morrall. The other shortlisted authors were Monica Ali, Damon Galgut, Zoë Heller and D. B. C. Pierre, who eventually won the prize with his first novel *Vernon God Little*.

tances who were present. By about midnight I was ready to leave, as was Mary.

Before then I had a brief conversation that seemed insignificant at the time, but which turned out to belong to the 'zone of irony' into which I had unwittingly strayed when I embarked on *Author, Author*. This was with Peter Straus, whom I had first met at a champagne reception held some years before, in the grand, gilt-encrusted rooms of Lancaster House, to mark the thirtieth anniversary of the Booker Prize. He was then the head of Picador, a Macmillan imprint with a reputation for publishing interesting literary fiction: a softly spoken, dark-suited man, youngish for his position. He frankly admitted to being 'obsessed' with the Booker Prize, and he certainly seemed to have a *Mastermind*-standard knowledge of its history. When I said I had just met Julian Rathbone, and that he had claimed the melancholy distinction of having written the only shortlisted novel (*Joseph*, 1979) that was never issued as a paperback, Peter Straus instantly informed me that this was also the fate of T. W. Wheeler's *The Conjunction*, shortlisted in 1970. I had never even heard of T. W. Wheeler.

Straus seemed familiar with my work, and hinted that he would be very receptive if I ever contemplated a change of publisher. At long intervals in the years that followed he would drop me a friendly note, perhaps about a book he was publishing, or an enquiry on behalf of a friend of his who collected my work. Picador published Malcolm Bradbury's last novel, *To the Hermitage*, in 2000; and after Malcolm sadly died in that same year Peter Straus asked me if he could reprint an obituary essay of mine at the front of the paperback edition, along with a similar piece by Ian McEwan. I agreed gladly, and also agreed in principle to write the introduction to a selection of Malcolm's unpublished or previously uncollected writings which Picador intended to bring out.* Before that was contracted for, however, I heard that Peter Straus had resigned from Picador, and had become a literary agent. He is not the only publisher to have made such a career move in recent times: it is symptomatic of the tension between cultural mission and corporate business principles in modern publishing.

The party at the Roof Gardens was the first time we had met since he took up his new profession, which he claimed to be enjoying. One of his clients was Adam Thirlwell, who had just published a racy Kundera-esque first novel called *Politics*, which I had read in proof and enjoyed. Probably Peter Straus had sent it to me – I can't remember. We chatted about it for a while. Then he asked me if I was writing a new novel, and I said that I had just delivered one. 'What's it about?' he asked. 'Henry James,' I said, smiling. 'Henry James and George Du Maurier. A new departure.' 'That's interesting,' he said. His expression revealed no more than ordinary curiosity. 'What's it called?' *'Author, Author,'* I said. I don't remember saying much more before we parted.

I went back to Birmingham the following day, Wednesday 17 September. On Friday Jonny Pegg called to say that Random House and Penguin had made an offer: it was exactly the same as they had paid for *Thinks...* , a substantial figure in the usual three instalments (on signature, hardback publication and paperback publication). Geoff Mulligan said they all loved the book, but didn't think they could offer any more because

---

* Published in 2006 as *Liar's Landscape*, edited by Dominic Bradbury, with an Afterword (not an introduction) by D. L.

it was a new departure for me and its prospects were difficult to assess. It was the best outcome I had hoped for, and I didn't hesitate to accept. Geoff called immediately to say he was delighted. In the evening I got an email from Paul Slovak, my editor at Viking in New York, to say that he was finding the book 'very enjoyable and moving' and that they would like to publish it in the fall of 2004 – he promised to get back with an offer soon. So the week ended very satisfactorily.

The following week also began well. On Monday Geoff emailed me to say Secker aimed to publish in September '04. It would be their lead title and 'a massively important book for us'. Tony Lacey, my editor at Penguin, who had felt inhibited from contacting me while Random House was making up its collective mind, called to say how much he loved the book – had been totally gripped by it, read it in two sittings, had no criticisms to make. A day or two later his assistant editor, Zelda Turner, forwarded a letter to me, 'which gives me an excuse to write and say how much I LOVED Author, Author'. Publishers and other media folk often flatter authors, of course, and throw words of praise around rather extravagantly, but in my experience when they say they 'love' something, they usually mean it. I had always had faith in the book myself, but it was gratifying to have this confirmed by others. It was more than gratifying – it was exciting; and I quote these enthusiastic responses to convey some idea of the euphoric mood I was in when it was abruptly shattered by a phone call from Jonny Pegg on the Thursday morning of that same week.

He said he was calling about two things. One was that Viking USA had, like Random House and Penguin, made the same offer as they had for *Thinks...* (a more modest advance than the British one, but very acceptable for the same reasons). The second item was 'not very nice, really'. His voice faltered somewhat as he gave me the bad news. One of Curtis Brown's foreign sub-agents had been sent the MS of *Author, Author*, and had just reported that they had already sold the rights in another forthcoming novel about Henry James, by Colm Tóibín, to my publisher in that country. Jonny read out to me a brief agency synopsis of *The Master* – it began with the first night of *Guy Domville*, traced James's recovery from this setback, ended with the acquisition of Lamb House, etc., etc. It was 200 pages long and due to be published in England in April 2004. I have already described my emotions on receiving this news. Jonny did not need me to spell out my reasons for dismay, or my first thought of how to respond. 'There *is* time to bring forward the publication of *Author, Author*,' he said immediately, before I raised the question.

He meant that it would be feasible to edit and produce the book so as to bring it out at about the same time as Tóibín's. (There was no way it could be published significantly earlier.) That would of course entail by-passing the catalogue for the relevant season, a procedure which has considerable practical disadvantages, but is not unheard of. Our initial feeling was that this was the best way to limit the damage to the prospects of *Author, Author*, and Jonny said he would put it to Geoff when he told him the news. As I brooded on the matter in the course of the day, however, I turned against this idea. The two books would inevitably be paired together in reviews, and compared as if they were rival biographies rather than novels. Colm and I would be doing the publicity circuit of interviews, bookshop signings, festival appearances, etc., at the same time, and the media would enjoy setting up something like a gladiatorial contest between us – a horrible prospect. It seemed to me that September publication, leaving a good stretch of time between the two books, was the lesser of two evils.

Jonny called in the afternoon to say that Geoff had reacted calmly to the news. He had taken counsel with colleagues, and they all agreed that to rush the book out would suggest a lack of confidence in it and that it would be better to avoid a head-to-head competition. Geoff made the point that my readership was bigger than Colm Tóibín's and did not overlap much with his. I said that I had come to the same conclusion on different grounds, which was something of a relief to Jonny. Later Paul Slovak and my agent at Curtis Brown New York, Emilie Jacobson, emphatically concurred. So the publication of *Author, Author* in both countries in the autumn of 2004 was confirmed. I did not know that the information we had been given about the length of *The Master* was incorrect. It was quite a fortunate mistake, because the apparent brevity of *The Master* was the only crumb of comfort I could glean from the situation. It seemed to me that it must be a very different, and perhaps slighter, piece of work than mine. Had I known that it was in fact on the same scale and very nearly as long as *Author, Author* (359 pages compared to 382) I would have been even more anxious and apprehensive than I was in the months that followed.

While I was dealing with this crisis, I had a curious exchange of messages with Peter Straus. In the afternoon of the fateful Thursday I received an email from him, saying that he had been delighted to see me at the Martin Amis launch, and 'it is very exciting about your new novel'. He thanked me for my comments on *Politics*, and said that Adam Thirlwell was reading from it at the London Review of Books Bookshop in November, and another writer was required to partner him. 'I hope I am not being impolite to ask if you would be able or be inclined to read with him at that event – hopefully from AUTHOR, AUTHOR?' This request puzzled me because the main point of such events is to sign and sell books, as Peter Straus knew very well, and he must have realised that if I had only recently finished mine it wouldn't be on sale in November. I pointed this out in politely declining. The next morning he replied:

> Dear David,
> Thank you for this. When will there be proofs of *Author, Author*, or is that a question which is far too early to answer?
> Best, Peter

I replied:

> Dear Peter,
> Yep, too early. I delivered it only three or four weeks ago. Publication is scheduled for next September, so you can probably work it out . . .

Something about his insistent curiosity must have made me suspicious, because I added: 'Any special reason for your eagerness to read it?' before signing off. As soon as I clicked on the Send button, I knew the answer to my own question. I had been in an extremely agitated state over the past two days, and had failed to make some obvious connections, but now the penny dropped. The publisher of Tóibín's forthcoming novel, and of most of his previous books, was Picador. Peter Straus must have been still in charge there when Tóibín was writing *The Master*, possibly under contract, and it was quite likely that he was now Tóibín's agent. I quickly confirmed this last guess with an email to Geoff Mulligan. Soon afterwards Peter Straus answered my question:

> Well I would love to read it and also I am enquiring on behalf
> of my friend, the collector of your work who is trying to
> get everything you wrote!

I didn't reply, and he didn't communicate with me again. He
had got the information he wanted, though he didn't know
that I knew why he wanted it. (As I was saying, Henry James
might have made all this up.) I was annoyed with myself for
giving away the publication date of *Author, Author* so readily,
but I didn't really resent Peter Straus's devious efforts to
discover it. In fact – and this is the reason for telling the story
in such detail – he had unknowingly done me a huge favour.
If he had told me at the Martin Amis party about Colm
Tóibín's novel, I would have been morally bound to apprise
Random House, Penguin and Viking USA of its existence
while negotiations for my novel were still in progress, and it
is unlikely that they would have reacted to my book with such
unqualified enthusiasm or made such generous offers.
Common business sense would have made them more
cautious, and my disappointment and despondency would
have been much more acute. Timing was all.

III

Usually the interval between the satisfactory completion of a
book and the run-up to publication is one of the happiest and
most serene times in a writer's life – certainly in mine. One
has a virtuous sense of having earned a spell of rest and recre-
ation. There is time to catch up on all the reading you put
aside so as not to be distracted from your own task. The anxieties of composition are over and anxieties about the book's
reception have not yet begun. One dreams of success, of
course – all writers do; but it is precisely that, a free flow of

agreeable anticipation unimpeded by the intervention of coarse fact. In the case of *Author, Author*, however, the shadow cast by Colm Tóibín's novel robbed the interlude between completion and publication of all its usual pleasure – indeed made it into an ordeal, which stretched ahead of me for a whole year. It would be five or six months before I could discover how closely *The Master* resembled my novel, and another six before I could know how the reception of *Author, Author* would be affected by it.

I took full advantage of the leisurely production schedule to fine-tune my text. I solicited notes from my three editors, Geoff Mulligan, Tony Lacey and Paul Slovak, and revised the novel in the light of them. I read it aloud to myself to test the cadence of every sentence, seeking to eliminate inelegant repetitions of words and what Henry James called 'abominable assonance'.[12] I had detailed consultations with my publishers about the design of the book and its jacket. But there was a limit to how much tinkering and polishing one could usefully do. At the end of November I sent in my final version of the novel for copy-editing. There would be more queries to deal with after that, and proofs to be corrected in due course, but how would I fill up the rest of the time that yawned ahead? I wasn't ready to start another novel. I had two vague ideas, but one was another historical subject which would require a lot of research merely to discover if it were viable – an effort which I did not feel like making in the circumstances – and the other needed some more ingredients which I would have to wait for inspiration to provide. So instead I worked on various non-fiction commissions – critical essays, introductions to classics, reviews – some of which are included in this book. I was happy enough when absorbed in these projects, but naturally they could not occupy all my waking hours, including some when I should have been asleep. I doubt if a day passed in that twelve-month period when I did not devote some time to cogitation and speculation about the fate of my novel.

When I confided my anxieties to friends I was struck by how clearly they fell into one of two categories: either they immediately grasped the reason for my concern, and empathised with it, or else they thought I was worrying unnecessarily (because Colm Tóibín and I were such different writers, and he was bound to have a quite different take on Henry James, because my readership was different from his, and so on). Ian McEwan, for instance, did his generous best, over a sandwich lunch and in a follow-up email, to persuade me that I had no reason to worry. I asked him if he would not have been worried if some reputable novelist had published a novel about the retreat to Dunkirk a few months before he was due to publish *Atonement*, and he said, 'No.' Well, perhaps if you are Ian McEwan you can shrug off any competition, but I didn't feel such confidence. As a literary form, the novel is well named: it offers, or pretends, to tell a story the reader has not heard before. It seemed to me obvious that if two novels on substantially the same subject and of comparable intrinsic merit were published in the same year, the one that appeared first would cream off much of the interest, curiosity and surprise that such a book might excite in critics and ordinary readers.

I wondered whether reading *The Master* would settle my mind, and resolved to do so as soon as it became available. But after that happened (proof copies began to circulate early in 2004, and it was published in mid-March, a month earlier than previously announced) I found reasons more than once to postpone reading it. First I decided that I would not read it until I had done all the pre-publication media interviews for *Author, Author*; then not until my programme of readings and signings after publication was completed. I did not want to get drawn into making comparisons between the two novels. On the contrary, I wanted to distance my book from Tóibín's as far as possible, and nothing I might say about the latter could appear unbiased. By not reading *The Master* I could avoid all questions about it with a simple and irrefutable excuse.

There was a deeper reason for this decision. Although I averted my eyes from reviews of *The Master* when it was published (all the more scrupulously because I received the proofs of *Author, Author* at exactly the same time) I gathered indirectly that it was being very well received, and I discovered that it was not after all a short novel, but a very substantial one. Reading it in this context could not be anything but a painful experience, and utterly unlike what reading a novel should be – a willing suspension of one's own concerns in order to attend to the product of another's imagination for the sake of intellectual and aesthetic pleasure. I would read *The Master* resisting pleasure and resenting, with a jealous proprietary interest, every overlap with my own book. So I decided I would not read it until the publication of *Author, Author* was well and truly over. But that turned out to be a moveable feast. British publication in September 2004 was followed by the American in October; the American by the French in January 2005, each entailing another round of public interrogation. The ideal conditions for reading *The Master* seemed to recede indefinitely. But I anticipate.

The first mention in the media of the coincidential similarity between these two novels (the first one I saw, anyway) was a paragraph in John Dugdale's 'Diary' column in the book pages of the *Sunday Times*, for 28 March:

At some point in recent weeks, it's fair to surmise, David Lodge read an email, profile or review containing the words 'Colm Tóibín' and spluttered. For Lodge's just-announced autumn offering from Secker centres on Henry James, and specifically in the 1890s 'anxiously awaiting the first night of his make-or-break play Guy Domville'; and that's precisely the subject of Tóibín's *The Master*. With novels by Elsie Burch Donald (recent) and Alan Hollinghurst (imminent) also featuring James, it's all getting rather spooky, possums.

Apart from the allusion to Dame Edna Everage, this was the kind of comment, tinged with *Schadenfreude*, that I had steeled myself to expect, and would encounter again in the coming months. The existence of Elsie Burch Donald's novel was news to me, and I never saw it referred to again in this connection* But I had known for some weeks that Alan Hollinghurst's forthcoming novel contained a Jamesian element. My first reaction to that information had been incredulous hilarity. I even took some transient comfort from the thought that the more such coincidences there were, the merrier, and the less the clash between my novel and Tóibín's would signify; but I soon changed my mind. When I bumped into Dan Franklin

---

* Donald's *A Rope of Sand* describes the romantic intrigues and entanglements of some American college girls in Europe and Egypt in the 1950s, which the first-person narrator self-consciously compares, from time to time, to situations in Henry James's novels and stories. Also published in 2004 was Toby Litt's *Ghost Story*, which one reviewer, Joanna Briscoe, described as 'fiction by another Henry James enthusiast to add to all those suddenly and mysteriously gracing publishing schedules and the Booker shortlist' (*Guardian Review*, 2 October 2004). '*Ghost Story* seemingly pays homage to *The Turn of the Screw*,' said Ms Briscoe. I couldn't see the resemblance myself, though Litt is certainly a declared admirer of Henry James and has written about him. In May 2005 A. N. Wilson published *A Jealous Ghost*, an explicit retelling of the story of *The Turn of the Screw* in a modern setting, presumably written the previous year, when all the other James-inspired books were appearing.

and heard that he had recently been sent the MS of yet *another* novel about Henry James, told from the point of view of his typist, incredulity seemed a barely adequate response and hilarity a quite inappropriate one. The situation was spookier than John Dugdale knew.

One of the most obvious changes over the last few decades in the way literary fiction is marketed and publicised is that writers themselves are now expected to take a leading part in the process, a consequence of increased financial investment in the publishing of literary fiction and increased financial rewards for those who write it. When MacGibbon & Kee published my first novel *The Picturegoers* in 1960 I doubt if they did more by way of publicity than send out the review copies (and they weren't very good at that).* Once I had delivered the revised text of my novel, and corrected and returned the proofs, I was not troubled further by my publishers. But I received an advance of only £75, in three instalments, on signature, delivery and publication, which, even allowing for inflation, was a fairly small risk for the publisher. The average advance for a first novel in 2005 was £5,000.[13] Publishing now operates in a completely different business environment, and success depends crucially on publicity. Although such ideas as the 'impersonality' of art, 'the intentional fallacy' and 'the Death of the Author' have dominated academic theorising about literature since the 1920s, the general reading public remains inveterately curious about the human beings who

---

* I have described in the introduction or afterword to reissued editions of *The British Museum is Falling Down* (1965) how the entire first batch of review copies was mysteriously lost and never reached a single newspaper or magazine, and how, demoralised by the total absence of reviews, I was the first to discover this fact.

create the books they read, and publishers have found that interviews with writers in the press, and on TV and radio, or as a component of readings, signings and similar meet-the-author events in bookshops and at literary festivals, can boost a writer's sales more than reviews. If you have accepted a substantial advance for a book, both self-interest and a sense of obligation make it hard to refuse to participate in such activities, and some writers positively enjoy the opportunity to explain their work, the personal contact with their readers, and the element of performance involved. I quite enjoy these activities myself, in moderation (though not so much since hearing loss set in).

I collaborated very willingly with Tasja Dorkofikis, my experienced and efficient publicist at Random House, in planning a publicity schedule for *Author, Author* because I felt this novel would need all the help I could give it. It probably received more media attention in the run-up to publication than any previous book of mine – not, however, without occasional snags and unwelcome surprises. The main featured interview was to have appeared in the *Daily Telegraph*, which, as is customary, required 'exclusive' rights (i.e. a guarantee that no interview would appear elsewhere beforehand). I independently offered the *Guardian Review*, which had published several pieces of mine in the recent past, an edited extract from the novel, naively supposing that this would not compete with an interview in another newspaper, but when the *Guardian* accepted it, and I informed Tasja, I discovered I was wrong. Each paper wanted to be first, and neither paper would budge (in spite of the fact that almost nobody except journalists reads both). So we passed on the *Telegraph*, and looked for another place for the first press interview. The *Sunday Telegraph* eventually did it in a great rush. The unfortunate

journalist assigned this task had insufficient time to prepare
for the interview, which when it appeared was composed
partly of information and quotations from other, quite old
interviews, including the headline, 'A Bad Review Spoils My
Lunch', which was not the note I wished to strike just before
publication.* It was illustrated by a large photo of a rather
grim and dishevelled-looking author, evidence that the stress
of imminent publication was already beginning to tell. It is
only fair to add that several friends said they enjoyed the article and my elder son said he learned more about me from it
than anything else of the same kind he had read.

Meanwhile, the *Grauniad* (as *Private Eye* immortally dubbed
the chronically misprint-prone newspaper) had published the
extract from *Author, Author* on 14 August. It was an impressive three-page spread and when I first opened my copy of
the *Review* I was delighted. But when I began to read the
extract I was dismayed to discover that my main character,
referred to in the original text as 'Henry', was here called
'James' throughout. I fired off an email to the editor involved:

> You have given me a magnificent spread in today's *Guardian*,
> beautifully illustrated – but why oh why did you change
> 'Henry' to 'James' throughout, and without consulting me?
> It makes the discourse sound like biography, which was just
> the effect I was trying to avoid. The intimacy and familiar-
> ity of 'Henry' is appropriate to the fictional focusing of the
> narrative through HJ's consciousness and point of view.
> That's why it is used throughout the novel.

---

* In the previous interview – I can't remember where or when – I had recalled a
remark of Kingsley Amis's, that 'a bad review spoiled your breakfast, but it
shouldn't spoil lunch', and commented that I thought one such review could spoil
quite a few lunches.

The editor apologised swiftly and abjectly. What had happened was that a junior sub-editor assigned the task of preparing the copy for printing had taken it into her head to apply a rule about proper names in the *Guardian*'s style book, designed primarily for factual reporting, to the extract from my novel, and the editor had failed to spot the changes. Needless to say, I had not been shown the proofs. (One rarely is shown proofs by newspapers in these days of emailed copy and just-in-time editing.) The editor had failed to spot the error, I'm sure, because 'James' is a given name as well as a surname. If my character had been called Henry Winter-bottom the surname would have stuck out like a sore thumb.

The *Guardian* took the matter very seriously. An apology was published at the first opportunity in the paper's 'Corrections and Clarifications' column on the leader page (a daily feature so rich in interest and amusement that it has been anthologised), an emended text was posted on the *Guardian* website, and a week later the paper's ombudsman or 'Readers' Editor', Ian Mayes, devoted the whole of his Saturday column to a description of the affair and a denun-ciation of the over-literal application of the style book. If there is any truth in the adage that there is no such thing as bad publicity I should have been delighted at all this extra atten-tion being focused on my novel – and in the most important pages of the newspaper. But, as Ian Mayes astutely observed, the mistake 'intruded upon and distorted the relationship the author wanted to establish with his subject and with the reader'. It undid with a single unthinking stroke the delicate balance I had striven to attain between fidelity to fact and imaginative empathy in my portrayal of Henry James, and thus drained the prominent serialisation of most of its pleas-ure for me. As far as I was concerned, it was another episode in the history of *Author, Author* to be indexed under: 'Irony, zone of'. Or did I perhaps after all need another entry: 'James, Henry, curse of'?

On Thursday 26 August, a week before publication, the longlist for the Booker Prize was announced, and *Author, Author* was not on it. The shortlist is always something of a lottery, but omission from the longlist feels more like a snub. I would have minded less if *The Master* had not been one of the twenty-two novels selected. Timing again played its part: it was a downer to receive this news on the eve of my first public event to promote *Author, Author*, at the Edinburgh Book Festival.

Then the reviews began to appear. Different writers have different strategies for dealing with reviews. Some read them avidly as they appear, others wait for their publishers to send them; some don't read them at all, and others claim not to but covertly learn what they contain. My own practice is to skim the reviews as they come to me, to get a sense of how a book is being received, and then let them accumulate for a while, to be read later, with closer attention and in a calmer state of mind. When in due course I surveyed the British reviews of *Author, Author* it was clear that the favourable ones greatly outnumbered the unfavourable. But in the first week or two it didn't seem like that: the needle of critical opinion swung abruptly between the admiring and the dismissive, and my spirits with it. The *Sunday Times* was gratifying but *The Times* was sniffy. The *Telegraph* was a rave, but the *Guardian* was lukewarm. The *Scotsman* commended me for following James's injunction to himself to 'dramatise, dramatise', while the *TLS* declared that I 'utterly neglected' it. In the *New*

Statesman George Walden concluded: 'As a novel . . . it doesn't work, and had it not been a novel at all it might have been a better biography', while in the *Spectator* Anita Brookner declared: 'This is a compelling book, which reads seamlessly, organically, as a novel.' Most of the reviews made reference to Colm Tóibín, and several compared the two novels, sometimes in his favour, sometimes in mine. 'It's not that David Lodge has written a weak novel about Henry James. It's just that it suffers in comparison to a brilliant one', said Adam Mars-Jones in the *Observer*. 'Lodge has settled James more comfortably into his own skin than any other biographer, or novelist, to date', said Jonathan Heawood in the same day's *Independent on Sunday*. My ego bounced like a ping-pong ball between these opposing bats.

Anita Brookner's review gave me particular pleasure, especially as it came out on the day of my launch party, where a kindly sales director from Random House slipped the folded cutting into my hand to read afterwards. Geoff and Tasja had early on had the happy idea of holding this event in the splendid library of the Reform Club, Henry James's own club, and the setting of a scene in the novel. I had made a research visit there when doing my final revision of the text, to check some details concerning the lavatory, and obtained the secretary's informal agreement to the party on that occasion, but when Tasja later enquired about available dates she was told by an assistant administrator that we could not use the club for our party because Henry James was no longer a member. This was undeniable; but when we pointed out that Henry James was actually dead, and found a living member who would act as nominal host, as the club rules required, all went smoothly, and the date was fixed for 9 September. The elegantly printed invitations bore as a motto some words from James's letter to his father triumphantly announcing his election to the club in 1878, '*J'y suis, j'y reste* – forever and a day.' The party was particularly enjoyable because the thick carpets, tiers of leather-bound books, and upholstered chairs muffled the usual din of such occasions and made it possible to have real conversations in comfort.

Among the guests was Danny Moynihan, to whom *Author, Author* is dedicated, and his wife, Julia. Dedications are an interesting feature of books, worth an essay in themselves. Originally addressed to patrons, in modern times they are private messages attached to public documents, though they may also send covert signals to readers and reviewers (*I am a model spouse and parent, I have glamorous and powerful friends, I am a pussycat so please treat me gently*) but my simple dedication 'To Danny Moynihan' was innocent of any such intention. Danny is the oldest friend with whom I am still in contact. His mother and mine had been schoolfriends, and his family lived near ours in south-east London in the 1940s until they moved to Hastings, where I used to visit him occasionally. He left school at sixteen and was apprenticed as a cabinet-maker, but round about 1950 he daringly chucked it in and came back to London to live with his grandmother, just up the road from our house, with the aim of becoming an actor. He took a clerical job in the City while attending classes in acting at Morley College, and won a scholarship to the Webber Douglas school of drama. I was then in the sixth form at school (Danny is a couple of years older) and used to attend the end-of-term presentations by the students at Webber Douglas, usually consisting of short extracts from classic plays, from which I got a valuable introduction to world drama. In due course he became an actor on stage and television (best known perhaps as the prosecuting counsel in the long-running series, *Crime of Passion*). We continued to see a good deal of each other in the '50s, and only a professional engagement prevented him from being my best man in 1959. When I moved to Birmingham and he went back to live in Hastings, the intervals between our meetings inevitably grew longer, but we have kept in touch. St Leonards-on-Sea, where he and Julia now live, is not far from Rye, and we had a bar lunch at the Mermaid in the summer of 2003 when I was doing my research there. The formation of my own desire to write is closely entwined in memory with Danny's youthful determination to become an actor, and it seemed to me that *Author, Author*, with its focus on the agonies and ecstasies of literary and theatrical life, might be appropriately dedicated to him. I also co-opted him for my next public presentation of the novel, on the Monday following the party, at the Rye Festival.

The Rye Festival is a fairly modest affair, and I did not expect a huge audience there, but this event mattered to me more than any other in my programme because of the intimate connections between the town and my novel. Hilary Brooke was still organising the literary side of the festival and had put me in the same 'Henry James Lecture' slot as before, though it was understood that I would be doing a reading, with an introductory talk. In mid-July, in the course of email correspondence about the arrangements, she wrote: 'We could, if you would like, provide additional readers to share readings with you, particularly of dialogues. Rye has quite a lot of local talent, as you may imagine. Let me know what you think.' I don't know whether this suggestion was the result of unfortunate experiences with novelists reading from their work, but I was rather taken with it. It occurred to me that I could easily adapt part of the chapter about the first night of *Guy Domville*, with its multiple points of view, as a reading for several voices. I prepared a script and sent a copy to Danny, asking him if he would do the Henry James passages (he agreed readily) and another to Hilary asking if she could find two readers for the characters of Elizabeth Robins and Florence Alexander. I would read the linking narrative passages, and between the four of us we would do the fragments of dialogue from James's play and *An Ideal Husband*. I wasn't aiming at a full dramatisation of the text, but rather a vocalisation of its use of free indirect style in the shifts of point of view.

I had assumed that Hilary was offering me the assistance of some talented amateur actors, and was surprised and delighted when two highly qualified professionals who live near Rye offered their services: Elizabeth Seal, the star of *Irma La Douce* and many other shows, and Sue Schlesinger, semi-retired from a stage career under the name of Sue Robinson, and married to Roger Schlesinger, brother of the late John Schlesinger, the film director. The reading was scheduled at the Methodist church in the evening of Monday 13 September, and it was agreed that we would all meet there for a rehearsal in the afternoon, and adjourn to Lamb House for tea or drinks. I looked forward to the occasion immensely. It was, however, sandwiched between two other engagements, both involving Colm Tóibín, about which I had misgivings.

Hilary had told me months before that Colm and his publishers were keen that he should talk about *The Master* at the Rye Festival, and he was slated to do so in the afternoon of the day following my event. Hilary asked me if I would like to stay on and attend his session. I said it was the last thing in the world I would want to do, and guessed that he would feel similarly about attending mine, but I suggested that we might have lunch together on the Tuesday before I departed. I asked her to convey this to Colm, and to book a quiet restaurant for us if he were agreeable – as, in due course, he was. When I made the proposal it seemed like a good opportunity to meet again, to talk, and perhaps laugh, over the strange circumstances that had brought us into unforeseen rivalry. But timing is all. Our contrasting fortunes in the Booker competition, and the comparisons between our novels being made in the reviews of *Author, Author*, were bound to place a constraint on the meeting, certainly as far as I was concerned, and I did not look forward to it with any eagerness – or to a conversation with Colm on Radio Four's *Today* programme about the current vogue for Henry James, linked to our joint appearance at the festival. Hilary had been approached about this by the BBC, and after some hesitation I agreed for the sake of the publicity that would accrue, not only to *Author, Author*, but to the festival.

Mary accompanied me to Rye. It's a long drive from Birmingham, so we had decided to leave a day early, and break our journey at Tunbridge Wells, partly because we had never visited this legendary spa town before, and partly because a hotel there was recommended in the *Good Hotel Guide*. Our room was indeed spacious and comfortably furnished, but it had an unusual open-plan design which incorporated the bathroom. Only the toilet made a concession to modesty with a frosted glass door. The shower was open-sided and the big bathtub was mounted on a kind of plinth in full view of the double bed. It looked like the stage set for a play called *Sexual*

Perversity in Tunbridge Wells, or perhaps an art installation entitled *The Death of Privacy in the Age of Publicity*.

I was booked to pay my own dues to the Age of Publicity the next morning on the *Today* programme, 'down the line' from the studio of the BBC's local station, Radio Kent, situated quite near the hotel, and I had been asked to present myself there at just before eight. It was pouring with rain when I went out at about seven thirty, but having ascertained that Radio Kent was accommodated in a small shopping mall on a main road with no parking, I decided to walk. When I got to the mall I found entrance barred by a kind of portcullis, and there was no sign of life in the Radio Kent reception office. I discovered a side door on the street which seemed to be for the use of the studio's employees, but there was no bell or entryphone. I banged repeatedly on the steel door, to no effect. I did not have a mobile phone with me, or a relevant number to dial from a call box. The rain dripped from my umbrella. The minutes were ticking away. Surely the BBC in London would have made contact with Radio Kent by now and be urgently concerned about my non-appearance? Surely somebody would think of coming out into the street to look for me? But there was no sign of life in the building. I banged on the door again, and shouted, to no avail. I could think of nothing else to do but return to the hotel and try to contact somebody from there. I had moved some distance in this direction when I saw a hunched figure slanting across the road through the rain, clutching a beaker of takeaway coffee, and making for the steel door. I ran back and managed to get inside just before he slammed it shut again. He seemed mildly surprised at my appearance but escorted me upstairs and into the studio where his colleagues nodded genially and directed me to a microphone. I had about a minute to spare before

John Humphrys's jaunty voice came down the line, followed shortly by Colm's mellifluous brogue. I had prepared a joke to deal with the inevitable opening question ('It's like London buses, you wait years for a novel about Henry James and then three come along at the same time') but after that Colm sounded, not surprisingly, the more fluent and composed speaker. I never did discover how I was supposed to have gained admission to the studio.

That evening I climbed into the pulpit of the Methodist church, and the three actors stood in a row beneath me in front of the sanctuary (if that's what Methodists call it) facing the audience in their pews. It occurred to me that the ecclesiastical setting might have been inhibiting if I had been presenting one of my raunchier comic novels, but it seemed quite appropriate to *Author, Author*. My collaborators did me proud and the audience responded warmly to their performance. Afterwards we adjourned to a nearby pub with them and some of Danny's family, and then Sue and Roger Schlesinger took Mary and me back to their home in the country near Rye for supper and to stay the night. Tony and Sue Davis (recently married) were leaving for Germany early the next morning, and could not entertain us at Lamb House. The wind rose in the night, and was still blowing next morning, gusting to gale force. We had some hours to pass before lunch, so I took Mary on a tour of some of the Romney churches. We headed back to Rye along the coast road that runs below the sea wall at Camber Sands and noticed a crowd of people gathered on the beach above our heads, all gazing at something that was obviously of interest. When we stopped the car and joined them we saw an astonishing sight: a fair-sized cargo ship was stranded high and dry on the beach, listing at an angle of about thirty degrees but apparently undamaged, as if a giant hand had plucked it out of the sea and plonked it down like a child's toy on the pebbles. Obviously it had been blown ashore by wind and tide during the night, and the waters had receded. It was on this very beach that George I had been shipwrecked in 1726, and from which he had been brought to Rye to shelter in Lamb House. The connectedness of things I encountered in the course of my Jamesian project was a constant source of wonder.

I was afraid this diversion would make us late for our rendezvous at the Mermaid with Colm Tóibín but he himself was delayed, having been a victim of one of the endemic cock-ups of the British railway system, and obliged to take a taxi from Hastings. He was dressed in the regulation loose black suit and black shirt of the contemporary writer and carried a soft leather overnight bag that looked as if it contained mostly books. When I referred to our encounter on the road to Santiago as our only meeting, he corrected me, to my considerable embarrassment, as I have already described; but he seemed not to mind that I had not recognised him or caught his name in the Harbourfront bar, and charitably recalled that I had complained of the noise on that occasion. He had come to Rye from the wedding of Zadie Smith and Nick Laird, the most coveted invitation of the year for the younger glitterati, and described himself as both exhausted and exhilarated by the experience.

Hilary had booked a table for us in the Mermaid's restaurant. It was certainly quiet, as I had stipulated – we were the only diners – but the food was pretty dire. (I have always found the bar-food there very good, but the more pretentious restaurant menu should be avoided, unless we were exceptionally unlucky.) It wasn't, however, the kitchen's fault that our meal lacked authentic conviviality. We all performed creditably, but there was a slight sense of strain in the air. Needless to say, the Booker Prize was not mentioned between Colm and myself. We did touch lightly on some of the coincidences and ironies that linked our novels, including our visits to Lamb House. I had not yet read his account of meeting Michiel Heyns there in the *Telegraph*, but I had read the latter's article in *Prospect*, which Colm had not seen. He was genuinely sorry to hear that Heyns had been unable to find a publisher for his book. I learned that Colm had started his novel in 2000, put it aside for a year or so, then resumed work on it and delivered it in March 2003. I had often wondered what his feelings were when he first heard about mine, presumably from Peter Straus, some five months later, but I was not ready for an exchange of confidences at that level. I was glad of Mary's presence to keep the conversation going on other topics. She is of Irish parentage, and I am a quarter Irish, so discussion of recent changes in Irish culture and society occupied quite a lot of the time until Hilary turned up to take Colm off to his three o'clock talk. Before he left he took from his bulging bag a mint copy of *Author, Author* and asked me to sign it, which I found disconcerting. I muttered that I had bought a copy of *The Master*, but hadn't read it yet, though (*hypocrite lecteur!*) I was looking forward to doing so. I picked up the bill, since I had initiated the lunch, and Colm accepted gracefully. We shook hands and parted.

So that was that. I felt a great sense of relief as we drove away from Rye and back to Birmingham. I had met Colm again and shared an amicable if unappetising meal with him: now perhaps I could free myself from unprofitable brooding on the possible damage the prior publication of *The Master* had inflicted on *Author, Author*. But a week later the Booker shortlist was announced, and *The Master* was on it. This was not unexpected, but it revived all my dark, obsessive thoughts. Once again in this narrative, timing was all: the shortlist was in the newspapers on the day I departed for the book fair in Gothenburg. This is the biggest event of its kind in Sweden and is designed for readers and book buyers rather than the trade. Thousands of people make an annual pilgrimage to it from all over Sweden and other Scandinavian countries, to browse the bookstalls and attend a non-stop programme of readings, panel discussions and lectures. Every year the fair focuses on the literature of a single country and 2004 was the year of British writing. The British Council had assembled the largest contingent of writers from these isles ever to attend such an event. As at Edinburgh, I found myself thrust into a scene of public exposure, non-stop socialising and literary shop-talk when I least felt any appetite for it.

I had been aware for some time (and you, gentle reader, have no doubt made the same observation) that I had not only strayed into a zone of Jamesian ironies as a result of writing *Author, Author*, but I was in some measure re-enacting the story of my own novel. That was indeed the supreme irony, for me, of the Year of Henry James. Colm Tóibín was my Du Maurier, *The Master* his *Trilby*, and *Author, Author* was my *Guy Domville*. Like James I must suffer the pangs of professional envy and jealousy while struggling to conceal them. The correspondences were not, of course, exact – Colm was not a close friend of mine, his novel was in a different class from Du Maurier's and not a bestseller (*yet*, but if it won the Booker, it would bury mine under an avalanche of publicity and sales), and *Author, Author* was not a flop – but they were close enough to cause me some discomfort and dismay.

Four weeks later I sat in front of the TV at home and watched the Man Booker Prize programme, live coverage of the black-tie banquet at which the winning novel is announced and the cheque presented to its author. The BBC, which has been responsible for this programme for most of the last twenty-five years, has experimented with various formats without ever quite finding a satisfactory solution. Usually it is a combination of shots of the guests eating their dinners and quaffing their wine, recorded interviews with the short-listed authors and/or readings from their books, and comments and predictions from a panel of critics. This year they tried a new formula which I thought was disastrous. Kirsty Wark, one of the star presenters of *Newsnight* on BBC2, introduced the programme in a shimmering evening gown, standing on a dais high above the guests, looking like the goddess Athene, or that iconic female figure who is the trade-mark of Columbia movies, wielding her handmike as if it were the torch of learning. In her opening address, briefly surveying the year's crop of notable literary fiction, she mentioned 'a strange fascination with Henry James'. Later in the programme she descended to the floor and moved among the tables where the shortlisted writers were seated with their publishers, agents and friends, and in each case asked either the publisher or the agent to tell the hushed hall, and the TV audience, why they thought 'their' author should win, with this person sitting silently beside them in shot. It is hard to think of anything more likely to cause a writer acute embar-rassment, and it wasn't an easy assignment for the publishers and agents either. Peter Straus had obviously prepared care-fully for the occasion, and delivered a fluent panegyric on *The*

Master without apparently drawing breath. If he had been pleading before the judges, he might have been successful. In the opinion of most pundits, and the bookmakers, the contest in the last lap was between Alan Hollinghurst and David Mitchell, but Colm Tóibín was thought to be a strong challenger in third place. The winner had of course already been decided that afternoon, and it was Alan Hollinghurst. It would be hypocritical to pretend that I was not relieved when the announcement came, but recalling my own experience of being a 'losing' shortlisted author in 1984 and 1988, I could imagine how Colm would be feeling. However cool and calm you try to be on the night, however pleased you are to be shortlisted, you have to imagine yourself winning in order to prepare the few words of thanks that will be called for when the judges' decision is announced, so it is inevitably a let-down when the prize goes to somebody else.

The American edition of *Author, Author* was published by Viking in October. My previous three novels had received a more consistently favourable reception in the American press than in England, but the US reviews for *Author, Author* were deeply disappointing. Curiously, given the subject, the down-market papers *New York Newsday* and *People Magazine* were among the few that were enthusiastic, but they don't carry much literary weight. The *Boston Globe* was gratifying, and the *Washington Post* and the *New York Review of Books* were friendly, but the rest of the reviews in important publications were negative. Invariably they mentioned that the novel went over much of the same ground as *The Master*, published in the USA in June, and invariably they compared it unfavourably to Tóibín's book. There was in many of these reviews an implication that my novel was bound to be a loser simply by trailing after Tóibín's. Sophie Harrison struck this note at the outset of her piece in the *New York Times Book Review* (generally considered the most influential book pages in the USA): '*The Master* casts a terrible shadow over this book', and conjured up with relish the moment when I first heard about Tóibín's novel. 'It is hard not to imagine the awful emotions in the Lodge household at this point, the anguished telephone call: *He's written a what? About who?*' (Actually the imaginary dialogue is not very good – why would I say, '*He's written a what?*'?) *Entertainment Weekly* made the same point more sympathetically: 'Meet the year's unluckiest good novelist. Lodge . . . had the bright idea to fictionalise the life of Henry James . . . Then Colm Tóibín beat him to the finish line.'

Needless to say, these reviews did nothing to raise my spirits as I prepared for a brief US 'book tour' that had been arranged long ago. I had an invitation to speak at the Chicago Humanities Festival on the weekend of 6 November and Paul Slovak had suggested I should do readings in New York, Boston and Washington in the week following. The New York venue was the Poetry Center at the 92nd Street YMCA, the most prestigious place for such events in the city. In March he emailed me to say the Y had asked 'whether it might be possible to move your reading from Monday November 8 to Monday November 1'. This would mean ending instead of beginning my tour at Chicago. It had the advantage of bringing the events closer to the publication date of the novel, but he pointed out that Monday 1 November was the eve of the presidential election. It seemed to me that this was not a very auspicious time to be promoting a novel about Henry James (no doubt some other author slated for the 1st had come to the same conclusion about his book and asked for a different date). On the other hand the opportunity to observe the keenly contested and enormously important election at first hand was irresistible, so I went along with it. This decision, good audiences, and the fact that I had arranged to meet friends all along the line, made what might have been a gloomy trip actually very satisfying.

Alison Lurie had kindly agreed to introduce me at the Y, and she came down from Ithaca, where she teaches in the autumn semester at Cornell, to spend the weekend in New York. We spent an agreeable Sunday morning at the Metropolitan Museum, and strolled afterwards in the park, in unusually warm weather for the time of year, and sat on a bench in the sunshine while she counselled me wisely about managing my disappointment over the reception of *Author, Author*. The next day we went to the Neue Gallery of German and Austrian art, and ran into Joyce Carol Oates, who has had more than her fair share of rough treatment by the press. When I told her that *Entertainment Weekly* had called me the unluckiest good novelist of the year, she said dryly, 'Don't go around boasting about it. All the other writers will be jealous and say, "No, no, *I'm* the unluckiest good novelist of the year."'

The Y likes to have two authors for each event, and I was paired with Louis Auchinloss, a venerable figure well into his eighties but still writing indefatigably, author of more than forty novels and collections of short stories which in many ways continue the Jamesian tradition in American fiction. I had been reading one of them, *The Rector of Justin* (1964) on my journey, and told him sincerely that I was greatly enjoy-ing it when he joined me in the green room, tall, patrician, and immaculately suited, like one of his own characters. The Y readings are austerely theatrical: you walk out from the wings to the front of a large bare stage under bright lights,

99

THE YEAR OF HENRY JAMES

stand at a lectern, and address a darkened auditorium. There is no Q & A sequel – just a signing in the lobby afterwards. I read an extract from the chapter about the first night of *Guy Domville* – more or less the same as at Rye. After various experiments I had found that this reading worked best with audiences even if I had to impersonate all the characters myself, like Sloppy in *Our Mutual Friend* ('He do the police in different voices'). I always ended the reading at the moment when Henry James was booed and fled from the stage of the St James's, but at my next reading, in Cambridge Mass., I made an adjustment.

At every social gathering and encounter in New York that weekend, much of the talk was inevitably about the coming election. Most of the people I met were Democrats, passionately opposed to Bush, and immensely excited by signs of a last-minute surge by Kerry in the opinion polls. On election day I travelled by train to Boston, Kerry's home turf, and in the evening watched the early results on television with a friend who is a professor at Harvard and a number of her friends and colleagues. The party split up at about midnight when it was clear that the result would depend on the vote in Ohio, and the next morning it was evident that Bush had narrowly but decisively won. My 'escort', Sally, who came to my hotel to take me to a radio station to record an interview for a book programme, was devastated by the result, and said she and her husband were seriously thinking of emigrating. She told me her best friend was at home, unable to get out of bed, weeping uncontrollably. When she picked me up later to take me to the Harvard Bookstore for my reading she warned me that there might not be anybody there. Happily the rows of chairs were fully occupied when I walked in, but I had never seen so many glum, unsmiling faces at such an event. In the course of the day I had decided to modify my reading so that it ended at the very end of the chapter, a passage about Henry James walking home alone from the theatre after the debacle of the first night, a passage that begins: 'So it was over. He had come to the dead end of the road, the dry bottom of the well, the rock wall at the end of the tunnel. Failure.' It seemed to strike a chord.

Was *Author, Author* a failure? Well, no, not a world-class, total turkey, *Guy Domville*-type failure. But it was not the success I, or my publishers, had hoped for. The British reviews were about three to one in favour, and the good ones were very good indeed. *Author, Author* also did very well in those round-ups of people's 'Books of the Year' just before Christmas. But the number of hostile or unenthusiastic reviews was significant, and there were proportionally more of them in America. A novel about Henry James was bound to be controversial, and the existence of a competing novel gave opportunities for prejudicial comparisons which don't normally present themselves in reviewing fiction. The question of James's sexuality, for instance, was particularly sensitive, and those reviewers who objected to my presentation of James as a celibate bachelor by choice and inclination in middle life were able to invoke in contrast Tóibín's sympathetic rendering of James's homosexual yearnings. Commercially it is too soon to do a reliable audit, but at this time of writing sales of both the Secker and Penguin editions are substantially less than the sales of *Thinks...* at the same point after publication. This disappointing performance can be partly attributed to the resistance of readers to the subject of the book and its genre, both very different from anything my usual audience expects from me. But the publication of a highly praised novel on the same subject six months earlier must also have had some effect. It is perhaps relevant to record that when *L'Auteur! L'Auteur!* was published in France in January 2005, nine months before the French edition of *The Master*, it received almost unanimously favourable reviews, was on the bestseller list of *L'Express* for nine weeks, and sold (in the French equivalent of hardback) twice as many copies as Secker sold in the same period after publication. My novels are, however, surprisingly and gratifyingly popular in France, and the sales of this one were well below those of its predecessor, *Pensées Sécrètes (Thinks...)*, so no firm conclusions can be drawn.

'It's not a race, nor a contest. David Lodge's pitch-perfect bio-novel about Henry James and his crisis of the mid 1890s neatly complements Colm Tóibín's *The Master* and merits equal applause', Boyd Tonkin observed kindly in *The Independent*, when the paperback edition of my novel was published in the summer of 2005.[14] Well, it wasn't a race, but it *was* a contest, for reasons I have explained, though neither Colm Tóibín nor I had sought one; and it is pretty obvious that, in the Year of Henry James anyway, he won it. Exactly how critical was the order of publication of the two books, and what might have happened if it had been reversed, must remain matters of speculation.

Timing is not all, however, in the evaluation of literature. Time is all. Only time will tell whether *The Master* is a better book than *Author, Author*, or vice versa, or whether they are equally admirable in different ways, or equally negligible. Time will also tell when I have finally got over this episode in my professional life and feel able to put it behind me. It will be the moment when I decide I would

really like to read *The Master*. That will happen eventually
– but not just yet.

Birmingham, November 2005

Notes

1 Eve Kosofsky Sedgwick, 'Shame, Theatricality, and Queer
Performativity: Henry James's *The Art of the Novel*', in *Touching
Feeling: Affect, Pedagogy, Performativity* (2003), pp. 35–65.

2 Novick's main evidence is a passage in Henry James's notebooks,
written in California in March 1905, when he was gathering
material for *The American Scene* (1907) recalling his experiences
in the spring and summer of 1865 in Cambridge, Mass.: 'How
can I speak of Cambridge at all . . . The point for me (for fatal,
for impossible, expansion) is that I knew there, *had* there, in
the ghostly old C. that I sit and write of here by the strange
Pacific on the other side of the continent, *l'initiation première*
(the divine, the unique), there and in Ashburton Place . . . Ah,
the "epoch-making" weeks of the spring of 1865!' [Novick's
ellipses]. This certainly sounds as if it might refer to a sexual
experience, but in context James's heightened language could
equally well refer to his discovery of his literary vocation. No
convincing evidence is offered that Oliver Wendell Holmes was
James's lover.

3 *Guardian Review*, 2 April 2005, p. 30. Reviewing *Strangers:
Homosexual Love in the Nineteenth Century* by Graham Robb, in
the same journal, 22 November 2003, Alan Hollinghurst
observed: 'as gay studies started to take on the heft of a discipline, there were even bolder attempts to catch bigger writers

(Henry James being an eminently recalcitrant example) in what Robb calls "the elastic web of gay revisionism".'

4 'The Curse of Henry James', *Prospect*, September 2004, p. 66.

5 'The Haunting', *Daily Telegraph* (Books section), 13 March 2004.

6 There was a BBC adaptation as a single TV drama broadcast in 1975 which I did not see and about which I have no other information.

7 Philip Horne, *Henry James: A Life in Letters* (1999), p. 34.

8 Alfred Sutro, *Celebrities and Simple Souls* (1933), quoted in Simon Nowell-Smith, *The Legend of the Master* (1947), p. 135.

9 'Henry James and the Movies', in *Consciousness and the Novel* (2002), pp. 200–33.

10 Laurence Sterne, *The Life and Opinions of Tristram Shandy, Gentleman* (1759–67), Vol. IV, chap. xiii.

11 Colm Tóibín, *The Sign of the Cross: Travels in Catholic Europe* (1994), pp. 149–50.

12 Henry James described Flaubert passing his life 'in reconstructing sentences, exterminating repetitions, calculating and comparing cadences, harmonious *chutes de phrases*, and beating about the bush to deal death to the abominable assonance'. Peter Kemp, ed., *The Oxford Dictionary of Literary Quotations* (1999), p. 42.

13 'The Publishing Industry', *Guardian*, G2, 10 October 2005, p. 4.

14 *Independent*, 22 July 2005.

PART
TWO

HENRY JAMES:
Daisy Miller

Daisy Miller, first published as a magazine serial in the summer of 1878, has a very special place in the history of Henry James's literary career. It was by far his most successful work of fiction as measured by copies sold. A list of the estimated sales of his books in his lifetime in Britain and America gives a figure of 'above 30,000' for *Daisy Miller*, and the next highest is a mere 13,500 for *The Portrait of a Lady*.[1] It was the closest James came to writing a 'bestseller', though it predated the coinage of that word, and unfortunately he did not reap the monetary reward it usually implies. In those days it was necessary to publish a book in America, if only a few copies, to establish the author's copyright there, and James was too slow to prevent *Daisy Miller* from being pirated on a large scale before Harper published it in New York as a pamphlet in their 'Half-Hour' series. That edition sold 20,000 copies in a few weeks, but at a very low royalty-rate. In the summer of 1879 James wrote from England to his friend William Dean Howells, who had reported the fame of his story in America: 'Your account of the vogue of *D.M.* . . . embittered my spirit when I reflected that it had awakened no echo (to speak of) in my pocket. I have made 200$ by the whole American career of D.M. . . .'[2]

Nevertheless the literary status and celebrity James acquired from *Daisy Miller*, on both sides of the Atlantic, was a priceless asset. It is not an exaggeration to say that this modestly proportioned work, short enough to be read comfortably at a single sitting (though perhaps not, with appreciation, in half an hour), was the foundation of his distinguished subsequent career. Discerning readers had perceived the promise of his earlier fiction – the novels *Roderick Hudson* (1875) and *The American* (1877), and stories like 'Madame de Mauves' (1874) – but it was *Daisy Miller* which really impressed his name on the collective consciousness of the English and American reading public as a new star in the literary firmament, with a distinctive vision and voice. It was, as he wrote to his mother at the time, 'a really quite extraordinary hit'.[3] Above all, its success confirmed for the author himself that, in the social and cultural interaction of America and Europe, he had found a wonderfully rich seam of material for fictional exploitation. This is evidenced by his quickly following up *Daisy Miller* with the slightly longer tale 'An International Episode', serialised in the winter of 1878–9, which is a kind of reversal of the earlier one, sending a couple of rather dim upper-class Englishmen to America with ironic consequences; and then collecting these two stories, together with 'Four Meetings', the poignant account of an American school-mistress's frustrated desire to see Europe (she gets no further than Le Havre), in a book published by Macmillan in England in 1879. James consolidated his reputation with *The Portrait of a Lady* (1881), a full-length novel about a young American heiress 'affronting her destiny' in Europe, and he continued to compose variations on the 'international theme' throughout his career, including his late masterpieces, *The Wings of the Dove* (1902), *The Ambassadors* (1903) and *The Golden Bowl* (1904).

It was subject matter he was uniquely fitted to explore by the circumstances of his life. He was born in New York in 1843, the second son in a family of four sons, the eldest of whom, William, became an eminent philosopher and psychologist, and one daughter, Alice. Their father, Henry James Sr, was a man of strong, unorthodox opinions on education, which his inherited income allowed him to indulge. He believed that his children would benefit from being exposed to the influence of European culture from an early age, and with this aim took them on frequent extended visits to England and the Continent, where for periods they were put to school. The consequence, especially for the two eldest and most gifted brothers, was a somewhat disjointed education which retarded their discovery of their true vocations, and Henry came to believe that the restless, itinerant nature of his early life had alienated him from his native country and led him to make his literary career in Europe (for a time in France, and then permanently in England, where he settled in 1876). But if some personal and psychological loss was involved in this expatriate existence, there was an immense gain for literature, which *Daisy Miller* was the first of his works to demonstrate to a large audience.

Every fictional story has its moment of conception, when the basic idea, or 'germ' as Henry James called it, is first planted in the writer's imagination. For James this was often something told to him in casual conversation, as in the case of *Daisy Miller*. In the Preface to Volume XVIII of the New York Edition of his *Novels and Tales*, which included an extensively revised text of the story* some thirty years after its original publication, he recalled:

> It was in Rome during the autumn of 1877; a friend then living there . . . happened to mention – which she might perfectly not have done – some simple and uninformed American lady of the previous winter, whose young daughter, a child of nature and of freedom, accompanying her from hotel to hotel, had 'picked up' by the wayside, with the best conscience in the world, a good-looking Roman, of vague identity, astonished at his luck, yet (so far as might be, by the pair) all innocently, all serenely exhibited and introduced: this at least till the occurrence of some small social check, some interrupting incident, of no great gravity or dignity, and which I forget.[4]

Out of this slight, almost trivial, anecdote James wove a story which dramatises profound differences of manners between America and Europe, and more importantly between different classes of Americans who meet in Europe. For the principal opposition in the action of *Daisy Miller* is not between Americans and Europeans (as it was in *The American*, for instance) but between two kinds of Americans in Europe: the upper-class, regular visitors and residents like Mrs Costello and Mrs Walker, who scrupulously observe the proprieties of

* All quotations from *Daisy Miller* in this essay are from the text of the first version of the story published in book form by Macmillan in 1879, unless otherwise indicated. Differences between the two versions, both of which are available in modern reprints, are discussed below.

'good' society in the Old World (which also serves as their model in the New), and the less cultivated, more provincial, *nouveaux riches* American tourists, like the Millers, who behave exactly as they do at home. Henry James was one of the first novelists to perceive the social significance of tourism, as an activity accessible to anyone affluent enough to take advantage of the ease of travel in the industrial age. In America – certainly in the 'minutely hierarchical' society of New York – the snobbish Costellos and Walkers would have avoided any social contact with the Millers; in Europe, however, the latter must be either assimilated or ostentatiously excluded. Mrs Costello, who defines herself as 'very exclusive', and is naively admired by Daisy for that attribute, is determined to freeze out the Millers from the beginning: 'They are very common . . . They are the sort of Americans that one does one's duty by not – not accepting.' Mrs Walker offers Daisy the opportunity to be assimilated, but is rebuffed, with fatal consequences. It is the European context which raises the stakes in this conflict of manners, and at the centre of the conflict, trying to interpret it, taking part in it, and having a personal interest in the outcome, is a young man who is American by birth but has lived most of his life in Europe, and does not fully belong to either society: Winterbourne. There was no such person in the anecdote which provided James with his 'germ'; he is entirely James's invention, and a crucial one, for the story is as much about Winterbourne as it is about Daisy Miller.

James also added to his source-story an earlier episode in a different setting: Winterbourne first meets Daisy Miller in the little resort of Vevey on the shores of Lake Geneva, and is both charmed and confused by her uninhibited friendliness, while his aunt is scandalised by her readiness to make an unchaperoned excursion with him to the Castle of Chillon. When Winterbourne catches up with Daisy in Rome some months later he is disconcerted to find that she has acquired an Italian escort, Mr Giovanelli, a handsome young man of dubious social status, thought to be a fortune-hunter, whom she insists on introducing to the exclusive circle presided over by Winterbourne's friend, Mrs Walker. The way Daisy conducts herself with this admirer without apparently being engaged to him causes her to be ostracised by Mrs Walker's set, to which Daisy responds by flouting the conventions still more openly. When Winterbourne encounters her alone with Giovanelli in the Colosseum by moonlight he finally decides that 'she was a young lady whom a gentleman need no longer be at pains to respect'. Daisy catches the 'Roman fever' (malaria) as a result of this rash adventure, and dies shortly afterwards.

Daisy Miller begins as a comedy of manners and ends as a tragedy of manners. As James himself said to a correspondent two years after its first publication, 'The whole idea of the story is the little tragedy of a light, thin, natural, unsuspecting creature being sacrificed as it were to a social rumpus that went on quite over her head and to which she stood in no measurable relation.'[5] It may be difficult for readers in the twenty-first century to understand that a rumpus about manners could have such grave consequences, but in the nineteenth century 'manners' in the sense of 'social behaviour' still retained some of the older meaning of 'morals'. The conduct of Daisy and her family violates the code of manners to which Mrs Costello and Mrs Walker subscribe in several ways, some of which are explicitly noted, others merely implied in the narrative. The Millers are, for instance, much too familiar with their courier, transgressing the order of the European class-system. They do not conform to the authoritarian structure of the traditional patriarchal family: Mr Miller is at home in Schenectady, earning the money that sends his womenfolk unprotected to Europe, and Mrs Miller is a weak, unintelligent mother, unable to counsel her daughter or control her obstreperous young son. They are largely ignorant of European culture and history, and their speech lacks elegance and polish. The main issue, however, on which the whole story turns, is the proper conduct of a young unmarried woman in relation to the opposite sex.

At the time and place in which the story is set a respectable unmarried young lady was not supposed to be in the company of a man without the presence of a chaperone. The code implied a 'double standard' of sexual morality, assuming that men were irrepressible sexual predators who could only be prevented from seducing every available virgin by the watchful guardianship of older women. In practice a young woman could forfeit respectability merely by violating the rule, even if nobody really suspected her of having illicit sexual intercourse. This code was enforced with varying degrees of rigidity in different classes and contexts. In the upper echelons of European society, where marriages were contracts involving the redistribution of inherited wealth and property, and the perpetuation of perhaps historic family names, the guaranteed purity of brides was a high priority and the observance of the code correspondingly strict; but in the more democratic and less cynical society of America the rules were more relaxed. In 'Lady Barberina', a story Henry James wrote a few years after *Daisy Miller*, a rich young American doctor is attracted by the beautiful daughter of an English aristocratic family but is baffled by the difficulty of getting to know her before asking for her hand in marriage (and, indeed, even after doing so). Having managed to take her aside at a party, he says:

> 'How do people who marry in England ever know each other before marriage? They have no chance.'
> 'I am sure I don't know,' said Lady Barberina. 'I never was married.'
> 'It's very different in my country. There a man may see much of a girl; he may come and see her, he may be constantly alone with her. I wish you allowed that over here.'

Daisy Miller has obviously enjoyed such freedom, as she makes clear to Winterbourne in their first conversation:

> 'In New York I had lots of society. Last winter I had seventeen dinners given me; and three of them were by gentlemen,' added Daisy Miller . . . she was looking at Winterbourne with all her prettiness in her lively eyes and in her light, slightly monotonous smile. 'I have always had,' she said, 'a great deal of gentlemen's society.'

By delaying Daisy's final declarative sentence with a description of her attractive appearance, and then delaying its conclusion further with the inserted speech tag, 'she said', James makes us feel its effect on the young man before he tells us: 'Poor Winterbourne was amused, perplexed, and decidedly charmed.' Winterbourne does not know how to interpret the manners of this young woman from Schenectady. He has 'never yet heard a young girl express herself in just this fashion' except where it revealed 'a certain laxity of deportment'.

Was she simply a pretty girl from New York State – were they all like that, the pretty girls who had a good deal of gentlemen's society? Or was she also a designing, an audacious, an unscrupulous young person?

This is the question that torments Winterbourne for the duration of his acquaintance with Daisy. Is she a new type of fearless, independent but virtuous American womanhood, or is she a shameless coquette who exploits the relative freedom apparently permitted to young people in America? His aunt tells him he is unqualified to judge correctly.

'You have lived too long out of the country. You will be sure to make some great mistake. You are too innocent.'
'My dear aunt, I am not so innocent,' said Winterbourne, smiling and curling his moustache.

Facial hair is a physical index of male sexual maturity and moustaches function in this story as metonymic symbols of virility. Winterbourne is jealous when he later discovers Daisy in Rome 'surrounded by half-a-dozen wonderful moustaches'. So in curling his moustache as he denies being 'innocent' he is hinting (or pretending) that he is sexually experienced – enough, at least, to judge whether Daisy is morally 'innocent'. But in fact he cannot make up his mind about her behaviour, much to his own annoyance. Not until his final encounter with Daisy, in the Colosseum, does he condemn her unequivocally – only to discover later that he was mistaken. (He has in fact made precisely the opposite 'great mistake' to the one his aunt predicted.[6]) At Daisy's funeral Giovanelli assures him that she was 'the most innocent' young lady he had ever known, and Winterbourne realises, too late, that she might have returned his love – or as he puts it to his aunt, in his prim way, 'she would have appreciated one's esteem'.

Henry James was arguably the first among English and American writers to understand, analytically as well as intuitively, the importance of 'point of view' in telling a story. From whose perspective should it be told – one character's, several characters', the omniscient author's, or a combination of these methods (as in the classic Victorian novel)? This fundamental choice by the writer determines the meaning and effect of any story. *Daisy Miller* is an early example of James's mastery of the single, limited and fallible point of view. The title implies that Daisy is the subject of the tale, but everything we know about her, as readers, is filtered through the consciousness of Winterbourne. We see her only through his eyes; we acquire only information about her that is passed to him. Therefore, in making up our own minds about Daisy's character we are simultaneously having to make up our minds about Winterbourne's, and about the reliability of his perceptions and judgements.

There is an authorial narrator, who on a few occasions refers to himself as 'I'. He sets the scene at the opening of the story, and conveys certain facts about Winterbourne (though never directly about Daisy); but for the most part his persona is unobtrusive and self-effacing, very unlike the expansive, judgemental authorial narrators of, say, Dickens's novels, or George Eliot's. Many of Winterbourne's private thoughts about Daisy are rendered in free indirect style, transposing what he is saying to himself, or asking himself, into a third-person/past-tense discourse, so that we have the illusion of direct access to his mind. An example would be the sentence just quoted above: 'Was she simply a pretty girl from New York State – were they all like that, the pretty girls who had a good deal of gentlemen's society?' (This is in fact a particularly subtle application of the technique, since it includes a slightly patronising recall of Daisy's own words.) Even when his thoughts are reported in a more straightforward way, there is so little difference between the style of the authorial voice and Winterbourne's own diction that we have very little sense of moving outside his consciousness. To take an example from the same place, in 'Poor Winterbourne was amused, perplexed, and decidedly charmed' the authorial epithet, 'Poor', expresses an amused sympathy with the young man's bafflement, and the other words are exactly those he would have used about himself.

This authorial narrator is certainly not omniscient. 'I hardly know,' he says, after the opening description of Vevey, comparing its hotels to those of American resorts, 'whether it was the analogies or the differences that were uppermost in the mind of a young American, who, two or three years ago, sat in the garden of the Trois Couronnes . . .' The narrator tells us very little about the background and past history of this young man, and the most interesting information is notably ambiguous:

> When certain persons spoke of him they affirmed that the reason of his spending so much time at Geneva was that he was extremely devoted to a lady who lived there – a foreign lady – a person older than himself. Very few Americans – indeed I think none – had ever seen this lady, about whom there were singular stories.

The ambiguity is, pointedly, never resolved. At the end of the story Winterbourne returns to live in Geneva, 'whence there continue to come the most contradictory accounts of his motives of sojourn: a report that he is "studying" hard – an intimation that he is much interested in a very clever foreign lady'.

Since Winterbourne's interest in Daisy is at least partly sexual, the question of his own sexuality is highly relevant to our interpretation of his speculations about her character. His surname (foregrounded by the fact that we never learn his Christian name)* suggests 'born of winter', or one who has a wintry life ahead of him, 'bourn' being an archaic word for destination. These connotations do not encourage belief that he is conducting a passionate love affair in Geneva, and his general behaviour, thoughts and speech present him as a young man who, though superficially sophisticated, is in fact sexually diffident and probably inexperienced. He is attracted to Daisy's pretty looks and vitality at their first meeting, and he is excited by her availability, living as he does in a society where 'nice' girls are unapproachable except under very strict surveillance. When she invites him on the spur of the moment to take her out on the lake in a boat at night he begs her mother 'ardently' to let her go, for 'he had never yet enjoyed the sensation of guiding through the summer starlight a skiff freighted with a fresh and beautiful young girl'. But the appearance of the courier puts paid to this scheme. 'I hope you are disappointed, or disgusted, or something!' Daisy says skittishly, bidding him goodnight. Winterbourne says only: 'I am puzzled.'

> He lingered beside the lake for a quarter of an hour, turning over the mystery of the young girl's sudden familiarities

* In the revised text of the story he introduces himself to Daisy and her mother in Section II as 'Mr Frederick Forsythe Winterbourne', but is referred to elsewhere by his surname alone.

and caprices. But the only very definite conclusion he came to was that he should enjoy deucedly 'going off' with her somewhere.

He manages to take Daisy to Chillon unchaperoned, and as she comes down the hotel stairs to meet him 'he felt as if there were something romantic going forward' and 'could have believed he was going to elope with her', but he is so preoccupied with observing and analysing her behaviour on the trip that he doesn't fully enjoy her company – at least, Daisy asks him, 'What on *earth* are you so grave about . . . you look as if you were taking me to a funeral.' When he tells her that he must leave Vevey and return to Geneva the next day, she expresses her disappointment so emphatically that 'Poor Winterbourne was fairly bewildered; no young lady had as yet done him the honour to be so agitated by the announcement of his movements'. The prissy diction here betrays a certain alarm that Daisy is forcing the pace of their relationship. As she accuses him of being in thrall to some female 'charmer' in Geneva (whose existence he denies) she seems to him 'an extraordinary mixture of innocence and crudity'. Later, in Rome, her conduct with Giovanelli strikes him as 'an inscrutable combination of audacity and inno- cence'. Is she really 'nice' or a coquette? Is her 'flirting' harm- less or dangerous? Should he court her with respect, or 'treat her as the object of one of those sentiments which are called by romancers "lawless passions"'? He ends up doing neither, because of

his want of instinctive certitude as to how far her eccen- tricities were generic, national, and how far they were personal. From either view of them he had somehow missed

her, and now it was too late. She was 'carried away' by
Mr Giovanelli.

The discomfort of his situation, tugged back and forth by
conflicting loyalties to both sides in the war of manners, is
subtly dramatised in the sequence when he escorts Daisy to
the Pincio Gardens. Having given her his protection through
the Roman streets, he is obliged to hand her over to a rival
whom he suspects and despises; then, when Daisy refuses
Mrs Walker's insistent invitation to get into her carriage,
Winterbourne is ignominiously compelled to get in himself,
under the threat of banishment if he does not, and to watch
Daisy walk away with Giovanelli. When he gets out of the
carriage and goes in pursuit of Daisy and 'her cavalier', the
intimacy of their posture, half concealed by a parasol, stops
him in his tracks, and he walks – 'not towards the couple
with the parasol; towards the residence of his aunt,
Mrs Costello'.

Winterbourne is one of several young men in James's
early novels and stories who are attracted to certain women
but restrained by various doubts and inhibitions from seeking a full sexual relationship with them, and are left at the
end of the story with no prospect of any other. The
American hero of 'Madame de Mauves', for instance,
Longmore (a name as obviously symbolic as Winterbourne),
falls in love with the unhappily married eponymous heroine
(another American expatriate), and is encouraged by her
cynical French husband and sister-in-law to become her lover,
but Longmore's moral scruples and Madame de Mauves's
perverse devotion to the role of the wronged wife lead him
to take the path of renunciation and go back to America.
Some time later the husband commits suicide, and

Longmore's first instinct is to return to Europe. But, says the narrator in the last words of the story:

> Several years have passed, and he still lingers at home. The truth is, that in the midst of all the ardent tenderness of his memory of Madame de Mauves, he has become conscious of a singular feeling, – a feeling for which awe would be hardly too strong a name.

'Fear' might be too strong, but not altogether wide of the mark. One of the most interesting interpolations of the narrator of *Daisy Miller* about Winterbourne concerns the latter's puzzled perception of her relaxed and inclusive friendliness:

> He could hardly have said why, but she seemed to him a girl who would never be jealous. At the risk of exciting a somewhat derisive smile on the reader's part, I may affirm that with regard to the women who had hitherto interested him it very often seemed to Winterbourne among the possibilities that, given certain contingencies, he should be afraid – literally afraid – of these ladies. He had a pleasant sense that he should never be afraid of Daisy Miller.

Instead of following up this 'pleasant sense' in order to enjoy Daisy's company more, however, Winterbourne perversely interprets her inclusive friendliness as a sign of moral weakness. The passage continues:

> It must be added that this sentiment was not altogether flattering to Daisy; it was part of his conviction, or rather of his apprehension, that she would prove a very light young person.

So there is a sense in which Winterbourne *is* afraid of Daisy, or at least of the temptation to 'lawless passions' which, in one aspect, she represents for him.

'"Frederick Winterbourne, c'est moi," [Henry James] might have said,' observes a modern critic, echoing Flaubert's famous remark about Madame Bovary.[7] That is probably an overstatement, but it is likely that he put a good deal of himself into the portrayal of Winterbourne and similar characters. It is the view of his most authoritative biographer, Leon Edel, that James both worshipped and feared his mother and that this ambivalence was carried over into his adult relationships with women.[8] He was attracted to many women in his life, and had intimate friendships with several, but he always backed off when there seemed any risk of being drawn into marriage or other kind of sexual relationship. By the mid-1870s, not long before he wrote *Daisy Miller*, he had decided that he would not marry. How far this decision was due to his determination to dedicate himself fully to his art, and how far to a growing awareness of the ambiguity of his own sexual nature, is hard to say. Edel, and the majority of his other biographers, believe that he never had a physical relationship with anyone of either sex, but in the last analysis they must admit that it is impossible to be certain on such matters, and leave further speculation to novelists. There was certainly a homosexual element in James's make-up, which became more obvious in late middle age, but he was not a closet gay writer, like, say, E. M. Forster, who had no real empathy with heterosexual love and was obliged to fake the representation of it in his fiction. The man who wrote, 'he had never yet enjoyed the sensation of guiding through the summer starlight a skiff freighted with a fresh and beautiful young girl', was not a stranger to 'straight' romantic attraction. Henry James wrote some of the greatest novels in modern literature about love, and the betrayal of love, between men and women, and no one has written better about marriage this side of the bedroom door. But he was also able to draw on his own experience and temperament to create memorable portraits of repression, inhibition, diffidence and regret in the affective life of men like Winterbourne. In a way, these troubled, self-doubting, eternally celibate heroes are surrogates for the writer himself. Like him they observe life rather than participate fully in it, but without enjoying the compensating creative fulfilment of the artist.

When it was first published, *Daisy Miller* was subtitled 'A Study', an interestingly problematic term. In the late nineteenth century it could mean 'A discourse or literary composition devoted to the detailed consideration of some question, or the minute description of some object' or 'a literary work executed as an exercise or an experiment in some particular style or mode of treatment'. Although these meanings are not entirely irrelevant to *Daisy Miller*, they do not apply exactly. James's subtitle is therefore usually interpreted as a metaphor drawn from the visual arts; but even in that context 'a study' can mean several different things, from 'a careful preliminary sketch for a work of art', or 'an artist's pictorial record of his observation of some object, incident, or effect, or of something that occurs to his mind, intended for his own guidance in his subsequent work', to 'a drawing, painting or piece of sculpture aiming to bring out the characteristics of the object represented, as they are revealed by especially careful observation'.[9] Leon Edel maintains that James was implying by the word 'study' that 'he had written the equivalent of a

pencil-sketch on an artist's pad rather than a rounded character',[10] and quotes in support a remark in the Preface to the
revised version of the story in the New York Edition of 1909.
James dropped the subtitle in this edition, and professed not
to remember the reasons why he had originally appended it,
'unless they may have taken account simply of a certain flat-
ness in my poor little heroine's literal denomination'. This
itself is, however, a somewhat cryptic explanation (it is not
obvious that 'Daisy Miller' is a particularly 'flat' name). In any
case the Preface is a deceptive guide to the story, and needs
to be treated with caution. There is an obvious sense in which
the last of the dictionary definitions of 'study' cited above is
metaphorically applicable to *Daisy Miller*. As Philip Horne[11]
and other critics have pointed out, throughout the story
Winterbourne is continually, almost obsessively 'studying'
Daisy, both as a type and as an individual. He is immediately
attracted by her pretty appearance, but his first reaction clas-
sifies her generically: '"How pretty they are!" thought
Winterbourne, straightening himself in his seat.' 'They'
means 'American girls', though we are able to infer this only
because of the narrator's introductory remarks about the in-
vasion of the Swiss hotel by American tourists, and the
'flitting hither and thither of "stylish" young girls' who make
Vevey seem like Newport or Saratoga. We are told that
Winterbourne 'had a great relish for feminine beauty; he was
addicted to observing and analysing it'. He soon becomes
addicted to observing and analysing every aspect of Daisy's
person and behaviour, long after Mrs Walker's circle have
made up their minds about her.

> They ceased to invite her, and they intimated that they
> desired to express to observant Europeans the great truth

that, though Miss Daisy Miller was a young American lady, her behaviour was not representative – was regarded by her compatriots as abnormal.

On one level – the level of character psychology – Winterbourne's treatment of Daisy as an object of 'study' is a way of displacing or suppressing his own erotic interest in her. As Philip Horne astutely observes: 'a secure state of knowledge about her even becomes at certain points, perversely, more desirable to him than Daisy's virtue'.[12] But there is no doubt that the anthropological or sociological aspect of the story contributed very largely to its popularity. The question of whether Daisy was an accurate portrait of a recognisable type of young American girl, or 'an outrage on American girlhood',[13] and the related question of whether she was an innocent victim of social prejudice or the author of her own misfortunes, were fiercely debated, especially in America. W. D. Howells reported to his and James's mutual friend James Russell Lowell, then resident in England:

HJ waked up all the women with his *Daisy Miller*, the intention of which they misconceived. And there has been a vast discussion in which nobody felt very deeply, and everybody talked very loudly. The thing went so far that society almost divided itself into Daisy Millerites and anti-Daisy Millerites.[14]

If this suggests a prejudice against James's heroine among genteel American women, there were nevertheless enough female admirers to make 'Daisy Miller' hats fashionable for a while.[15] In the longer term, 'Daisy Miller' entered the language as a generic term for a certain type of attractive but forward and uncultivated young American girl at large in Europe.

Henry James was not altogether pleased by the proverbial status his creation acquired. It irritated him that throughout his career he was best known and remembered by the general public as the author of this early and comparatively slight work, while his much more ambitious and complex later fictions were neglected. His last secretary, Theodora Bosanquet, compared his feelings to those of 'some *grande dame* possessing a jewel-case richly stocked with glowing rubies and flashing diamonds, but condemned by her admirers always to appear in the single string of moonstones worn at her first dance'.[16] This helps to explain the somewhat deprecatory tone of James's remarks about the story in the 1909 Preface, and the curious discussion of it with two friends which he claims to have had some time after its original publication. Although there was no doubt a factual basis for this anecdote, one can hardly avoid the conclusion that James improved it in the telling for his own purposes. The three friends are observing the indecorous behaviour of a pair of young American girls on the water-steps of a hotel in Venice, and one describes them as 'a couple of attesting Daisy Millers' (meaning that they prove the representativeness of James's character). The other companion, his 'hostess', protests against this application of the name, and then addresses the author in a long speech of such syntactical and rhetorical complexity, flattering him under the appearance of chiding him, that only Henry James himself could have composed it, and no human being could possibly have recalled it verbatim after an interval of years. The essential gist of her accusation is that James, having started out with a character who was a recognisable and generally deplorable 'type', invested her with such irresistible charm and pathos as to make her quite exceptional, so that paradoxically the two young Americans 'capering' before them are the 'real little Daisy Millers' while James's heroine is not. James meekly concedes that 'my supposedly typical little figure was of course pure poetry, and had never been anything else . . .'

By this devious means Henry James sought to correct the received view of *Daisy Miller* as a realistic 'study' of a certain kind of young American woman, and to present it as a work of imagination which transcends the limits of empirical verisimilitude. At the time when the story first appeared, James was often linked with Howells as an exponent of a new kind of social realism in post-Civil War American fiction, but it was a classification that proved less and less appropriate as his work developed. The 'solidity of specification' which characterised his earlier novels and tales, and which he still insisted was an essential requirement of the 'Art of Fiction', in his 1884 essay of that title,[17] gave way to a more impressionistic, ambiguous and subjective rendering of experience in the later ones. In the late 1890s and the early years of the twentieth century James's fiction took a direction that could indeed be described as 'poetic', entailing the use of iterative symbolism and a highly wrought style permeated with metaphor. The very titles of some of the key works of his 'major phase' – *The Turn of the Screw*, *The Wings of the Dove*, *The Golden Bowl*, 'The Beast in the Jungle' – illustrate the point, contrasting with the simple referential titles characteristic of the earlier ones: *Roderick Hudson*, *The American*, 'Madame de Mauves', *Daisy Miller*. In the 1909 Preface, therefore, James was trying to present *Daisy Miller* as a kind of minor precursor of his mature art, playing down the very qualities that had made it so popular on its first appearance. And the changes and additions he made to the text in the 1909 version were, consciously or unconsciously, motivated by a desire to make it (as far as was possible without completely rewriting it) stylistically consistent with his later work, and to encourage a view of the heroine as exceptional rather than typical.

It has been estimated that James modified 90 per cent of the sentences of the original text in the New York Edition (NYE), and added some 15 per cent to its length.[18] Many of the revisions are trivial, and none of them alters the structure of the story; but cumulatively they have a considerable effect on the way the reader receives it. The most significant fall into one of three categories: (1) expanded descriptions of Winterbourne's thoughts about Daisy; (2) the replacement of simple speech-tags, like 'he/she said/declared/exclaimed', with more elaborately descriptive phrases (which also reflect Winterbourne's perceptions); and more rarely, (3) emendations of the dialogue itself, which generally add emphasis rather than changing the original meanings. The 1909 text contains more information than the 1879 text, but because this additional information is nearly all about Winterbourne (since nearly everything is narrated from his point of view) it actually unbalances the story, in my opinion, and spoils the quality which W. D. Howells very perceptively singled out for special praise, when he wrote to James in 1882, three years after its first publication:

> That artistic impartiality which puzzled so many in the treatment of Daisy Miller is one of the qualities most valuable in the eyes of those who care how things are done . . . this impartiality comes at last to the same result as sympathy.[19]

What Howells meant by 'artistic impartiality' was James's refusal to judge his heroine. Instead, he shows Winterbourne judging her, and leaves it to the reader to decide how justly. Judging Daisy entails judging Winterbourne; this complicates the interpretive process and involves the reader in the active production of the text in a way more characteristic of modern fiction than the classic Victorian novel. Both versions of the story make this demand on the reader, but in the 1909 text the disparity between the 'objective' reality of Daisy and Winterbourne's subjective responses to her, between the transparency of her speech and the 'logic-chopping' complexity of his inner dialogue with himself, is more marked and insistent. Philip Horne, who has made a scrupulous comparison of the two texts, observes that 'whereas the first edition offers strong intermittent hints that we should doubt Winterbourne's conclusions, the NYE works the doubts far more closely into the texture of the narration', and 'in the revised version the speeches stand out from the interpretive framework Winterbourne progressively tries to fit them into'.[20] By making us, as readers, less likely to trust Winterbourne, the 1909 text correspondingly makes us more likely to sympathise with Daisy, but as Howells observed, the 'impartiality' of the 1879 text is not incompatible with 'sympathy' for her; it merely makes the reader work harder to achieve it. The impartiality also extends to the characterisation of Winterbourne, generating more sympathy for him than he seems to deserve in the 1909 version, so that we end the story with a feeling of regret for his unfulfilled life as well as sadness at the untimely end of Daisy's.

Although the 1879 text is shorter, sparer, and stylistically simpler than the 1909 text it is paradoxically richer in meaning – but the meaning inheres as much in what is implied as in what is stated. One might almost say that in *Daisy Miller* James anticipated Ernest Hemingway's theory of the short story: that 'you could omit anything if you knew what you omitted, and the omitted part would strengthen the story and make people feel something more than they understood'.[21] Indeed William James (often a severe critic of his brother's work) praised another, earlier story of Henry's in precisely those terms:

> You expressly restrict yourself, accordingly, to showing a few
> external acts and speeches, and by the magic of your art
> making the reader *feel* back of these the existence of a body
> of being of which these are casual features.[22]

Not a word in *Daisy Miller* is redundant. Where there is repetition, the repetition is functional (notably in the artless speech of the Miller family, whose members characteristically employ the same keyword or phrase again and again, contrasting with the elegant variation in the Europeanised characters' dialogue) and the silences are eloquent.

Comparison with the revised text helps to bring out the qualities of the original story. Consider, for example, the first scene. 'Scene' is a particularly appropriate term because the whole story unfolds in a sequence of dramatic encounters between the characters as they might be presented in a good play or film, where every line of dialogue (however banal), every bit of body language, every glance and pause, signifies. 'Dramatise, dramatise!' was James's habitual injunction to himself as a novelist, and he was always much more successful in applying the lessons of drama to narrative than he was in writing for the theatre, including his

early attempt to adapt *Daisy Miller* for the stage.*
Winterbourne is seated on the terrace of the hotel, enjoying a coffee and a cigarette, when he is accosted by young
Randolph Miller, asking for a lump of sugar from his table.
Randolph, who was not in James's source-anecdote, is a brilliant comic creation. He is a little American barbarian, who
affronts European standards of decorum in both speech and
behaviour much more blatantly than his sister or mother –
refusing to go to bed at an appropriate hour, eating what
he fancies, doing what he likes, despising Europe and boasting about his native country; but he does it all with such
self-assurance and amusing candour, combining youthful
indiscretion with a certain knowingness, that he functions
in the story as a kind of jester or wise fool, exposing the
tensions and contradictions in the adult social world. In this
first scene, he takes three lumps of sugar from
Winterbourne, and bites one of them.

'Oh, blazes, it's har-r-d!' he exclaimed, pronouncing the
adjective in a peculiar manner.

---

* After describing the anecdotal source of *Daisy Miller* in the Preface, James observes
that it was the very absence of detailed information about the American mother
and daughter 'that left a margin for the small pencil-mark inveterately signifying, in
such connexions, "Dramatise, dramatise!"' The feature film of *Daisy Miller* released
in 1975, directed by Peter Bogdanovich, with a script by Frederic Raphael, was not
entirely satisfactory, but showed how few changes were necessary to adapt the story
for performance.

James adapted *Daisy Miller* in 1882 for a New York theatre whose manager rejected
it as 'too literary'. In fact, in trying to cater to the rather coarse theatrical taste of
the time, James produced a vulgar travesty of the original story, including a contrived
'happy ending'. He subsequently published the playtext, but, not surprisingly, it was
never performed. He incorporated one or two details from it, including
Winterbourne's given names, into the NYE text.

The NYE reads as follows:

> 'Oh, blazes, it's har-r-d!' he exclaimed, divesting vowel and
> consonants, pertinently enough, of any taint of softness.

The verbal phrase in the second version is stylistically typical
of late James, playing on the word 'hard' and opposing it to
'softness' (he loved figures of antithesis) and using muted
metaphor in 'divesting' and 'taint'; but one has to ask whether
this rhetorical flourish serves any purpose other than to
emphasise the obvious cultural distance between
Winterbourne and Randolph, and to make the former seem
rather too pleased with his own wit. In the original text he is
much more interested in the boy. 'Peculiar' there has the
meaning of 'distinctive' and leads more logically to the next
sentence, which is almost the same in both versions:

> Winterbourne had immediately perceived that he might have
> the honour of claiming him as a fellow-countryman. ['coun-
> tryman' in NYE]

There follows a droll speech from Randolph in which he
blames the chronic loss of his milk-teeth on Europe and its
hotels, and then a conversation about the relative merits of
American and European candy, boys – and men. 'Are you an
American man?' Randolph asks. On receiving an affirmative
answer, 'American men are the best,' he declares ('with assurance' the NYE redundantly adds) and then, 'Here comes my
sister! . . . She's an American girl you bet.' To which
Winterbourne, seeing a beautiful young lady advancing,
'cheerfully' replies: 'American girls are the best girls.' Because
Winterbourne has to adopt the simple directness of the child's

speech, the conversation highlights issues which will be crucial to the story. Is Winterbourne a real American? Is he a real man? Is Daisy the best kind of girl?

The first encounter between Winterbourne and Daisy is beautifully handled and full of subtle implication. We sense Winterbourne's immediate interest in and attraction to her, and also his uncertainty about how to proceed. He is constrained by a code of manners which requires that a gentleman be introduced to a lady before he speaks to her. According to the same code, Daisy should either find a gracious way of overcoming this difficulty, perhaps by employing Randolph, or remove herself and her brother promptly from the stranger's presence, but Daisy seems disinclined to either course of action. She reproves Randolph for 'scattering the pebbles about Winterbourne's ears' without acknowledging the young man's existence at all. Winterbourne addresses a remark to Randolph, who tells his sister 'He's an American man,' but 'the young lady gave no heed to this announcement' (the NYE has 'this circumstance' which is weaker, departing from the 'introduction' subtext). '"Well, I guess you had better be quiet," she simply observed.' Winterbourne then presumes to treat Randolph's remark as an introduction and addresses Daisy directly. She glances at him but says nothing and looks over the parapet at the lake and the mountains.

> While he was thinking of something else to say, the young lady turned to the little boy again.
> 'I should like to know where you got that pole,' she said.

The NYE has '. . . the young lady turned again to the little boy, whom she addressed quite as if they were alone together'. The additional clause is not really necessary, and indeed the scene works much better if we sense the unconventionality of her behaviour without having the reasons spelled out. 'I bought it!' responded Randolph. The NYE has 'Randolph shouted'. It's a trivial change, but makes Randolph seem ruder and less 'smart' – to me, a loss of subtlety.

'You don't mean to say you're going to take it to Italy!'
'Yes I am going to take it to Italy!' the child declared.

The NYE has: '"Yes, I'm going to take it t'Italy!" the child rang out.' The contraction 'I'm' in the revised text perhaps sounds more natural (though 'I am' could be Randolph's way of asserting his independence). The contraction 't'Italy' is less convincing. In later life Henry James became increasingly disturbed by the slovenliness of American demotic speech – a concern he explicitly voiced in a 1905 lecture called 'The Question of Our Speech' – and one can't help suspecting that this affected his revision of the dialogue in *Daisy Miller*. The NYE, for instance, has Daisy saying of Randolph, a little later in this scene, 'He don't like Europe,' instead of the 1879 text's 'He doesn't like Europe.' One would trust Henry James's ear for how a young girl like Daisy would speak in the mid-1870s in the earlier text rather than the later. (An early American reviewer said he 'had succeeded to admiration in the difficult task of representing the manner in which such people as Mrs and Miss Miller talk'.[23]) As for the metaphorical 'rang out', it belongs to a whole series of elegant variations in the NYE on the basic speech-tags of the original story which make the prose more 'poetic'. There are further examples shortly afterwards in the reworking of this passage:

The young girl glanced over the front of her dress, and smoothed out a knot or two of ribbon. Then she rested her eyes upon the prospect again. 'Well, I guess you had better leave it somewhere,' she said, after a moment.

The NYE has 'gave her sweet eyes to the prospect', which seems too fondly sentimental at this early stage of Winterbourne's acquaintance with the girl, and loses the sense of Daisy's completely relaxed manner; and it has 'she dropped' instead of 'she said'. A few lines later there is an unfortunate repetition of 'drop' in the NYE when '"Are you – a – going over the Simplon?" Winterbourne pursued, a little embarrassed' becomes: '"And are you – a – thinking of the Simplon?" he pursued with a slight drop of assurance.' It is unfortunate because obviously unintended: when elegant variation is the rule, then unmotivated repetition becomes intrusive. James may have looked for an alternative to 'a little embarrassed' because the word 'embarrassed' occurs twice not long afterwards in the original text – although there the repetition is motivated:

. . . Winterbourne presently risked an observation upon the beauty of the view. He was ceasing to be embarrassed, for he had begun to perceive that she was not in the least embarrassed herself.

Admittedly, a few of James's revisions were genuine improvements. When, for instance, Daisy tells Winterbourne at their penultimate meeting in Rome that she is engaged and immediately adds, 'You don't believe it!' the 1879 text has:

He was silent a moment; and then, 'Yes I believe it!' he said.

The NYE has:

> He asked himself, and it was for a moment like testing a
> heart-beat; after which,
>   'Yes, I believe it!' he said.

The simile is very effective, partly because the word 'heart' is closely associated with the emotion of love as well as with life. But many of the revisions make one wonder what James thought he had gained by them. In their penultimate meeting, when Winterbourne is trying to convey to Daisy the disapproval of Mrs Walker's circle, he asks her if she has not noticed anything, and she replies, in the 1879 text: 'I have noticed you. But I noticed you were as stiff as an umbrella the first time I saw you.' This homely simile is vivid and (like 'heart-beat') it has a contextual appropriateness: Winterbourne is just the kind of man, prudent and correctly dressed, to carry with him a tightly furled umbrella – and it is a *furled* umbrella that is evoked by 'stiff'. The epithet is one Daisy often applies pejoratively to Winterbourne in the course of the story. (When he tells her in the Pincio Gardens that she should get into Mrs Walker's carriage, she says, 'I never heard anything so stiff,' and when on another occasion he says he can't dance, she says, 'Of course you can't, you're too stiff.') In the NYE this speech becomes: 'But I noticed you've no more "give" than a ramrod the first time ever I saw you.' 'Ramrod' has military associations which make this an unlikely figure of speech for Daisy to use, and inappropriate to describe Winterbourne; and the echo of Daisy's previous complaints about Winterbourne's 'stiffness' is lost. There is a danger, when a writer revises his work after a very long interval, of disturbing, for the sake of a local effect, delicate relationships of sameness and difference between the component parts of the text that, even with an artist as self-conscious as Henry James, evolved organically and intuitively in the original creative process.

I have tried to show how the surface simplicity and economy of the story's style and narrative method actually generate a great density of meaning and implication. These qualities are by no means completely effaced in the New York Edition, but they are more consistently present in the original text, right up to its beautifully understated conclusion. Imagine what a sentimental meal a Victorian novelist would have made of Daisy Miller's last illness! There are no deathbed histrionics in this story. Winterbourne never sees Daisy after the scene in the Colosseum, and James conveys the pathos and finality of her death by the almost brutal brevity with which he reports it, 'cutting' (like a film maker) quickly to the funeral. Daisy sends him a message through her mother to say that she was not engaged to Giovanelli:

'I don't know why she wanted you to know; but she said to me three times – "Mind you tell Mr Winterbourne." And then she told me to ask if you remembered the time you went to that castle, in Switzerland. But I said I wouldn't give any such messages as that. Only, if she is not engaged, I'm sure I'm glad to know it.'

But, as Winterbourne had said, it mattered very little. A week after this the poor girl died; it had been a terrible case of the fever. Daisy's grave was in the little Protestant cemetery . . .

The phrase 'it mattered very little' is not quite as callous as it sounds out of context. It takes us back by a direct echo to the climactic scene in the Colosseum. As Giovanelli goes off to see to the carriage, Daisy chatters defiantly about the beauty of the moonlit scene. When she wonders why Winterbourne is silent he merely laughs, and she asks: '*Did* you believe I was engaged the other day?'

'It doesn't matter what I believed the other day,' said Winterbourne, still laughing.

'Well, what do you believe now?'

'I believe it makes very little difference whether you are engaged or not.'

There is a double implication here: that if Daisy were engaged to Giovanelli it would not affect the impropriety of her being alone with him at that hour in such a place, and that for the same reason Winterbourne is no longer interested in whether her affections are engaged or not. He is in a state of shock, and there is a touch of hysteria about his laughter. But of course the question *does* matter to Daisy, because she really cares for him, as she later reveals by the message she sends him through her mother.

The sentence, 'But, as Winterbourne had said, it mattered very little', is charged with emotions carried over from the previous scene. The 1909 text, 'But as Winterbourne had originally judged, the truth on this question had small actual relevance', contains the same information, but loses the echo of the dialogue in the Colosseum, and makes Winterbourne sound coldly forensic – assuming we attribute this reflection to him rather than to the narrator. It is in fact hard to distinguish between them in either version. We can but guess at

the conflicting emotions Winterbourne must be feeling about
Daisy's death. Only after the funeral, when Giovanelli assures
him that Daisy really was 'innocent', and that he had no hope
of marrying her, do they resolve themselves into real grief
and regret:

> 'Why the devil,' he asked, 'did you take her to that fatal
> place?'
> Mr Giovanelli's urbanity was apparently imperturbable.
> He looked on the ground for a moment, and then he said,
> 'For myself, I had no fear; and she wanted to go.'

In the NYE he says: 'For myself I had no fear; and *she* – she
did what she liked.' One might speculate that James thought
that the phrase, 'she did what she liked', sounded more like
an epitaph on Daisy Miller's life than 'she wanted to go', and
he set it up accordingly with Giovanelli's somewhat histrionic
'*she* – she'. But for the attentive reader – and surely for
Winterbourne – the phrase, she wanted to go, evokes
poignant echoes of the hero and heroine's first two meetings
by the lakeside at Vevey, scenes in which the verb 'to go' is
constantly in use, as the question is debated and pondered
whether Daisy will go to Chillon, and how, and with whom.

It is interesting that neither Giovanelli nor Winterbourne
seems to fear catching the 'Roman fever' in the Colosseum.
If the former, as a native, was less vulnerable, Winterbourne
would surely have been at risk; but in the story the fever
seems to be a lethal threat exclusively to women. It operates as a symbol, or what T. S. Eliot called an 'objective
correlative',[24] of Daisy's jeopardy as a woman who refuses

to abide by the rules, designed for her protection, of the society in which she finds herself. Because Daisy merely claims the kind of freedom that a young woman today would take for granted, it is tempting to regard her as a kind of proto-feminist heroine, defying patriarchal society, but there is nothing ideological in her rebellion against the stuffy ethos of the Mrs Walkers and Mrs Costellos. On the other hand it would be a great mistake to interpret the fever as some kind of providential punishment or poetic justice for mis-behaviour. Daisy is indeed partly responsible for her own fate by recklessly ignoring warnings about the fever; but it is the disapproval of the Europeanised Americans, and Winterbourne's chilly reserve in Rome, that push her into more and more extreme demonstrations of her independ-ence and of her determination to enjoy herself, culminating in the fatal visit to the Colosseum. Henry James's comments about Daisy's motivation, two years after the story's first appearance, in a letter already quoted, make this clear – indeed, almost too clear:

> Poor little D.M. was (as I understand her) above all things *innocent*. It was not to make a scandal – or because she took pleasure in a scandal – that she 'went on' with Giovanelli. She never took the measure, really, of the scandal she produced, and had no means of doing so: she was too ignor-ant, too irreflective, too little versed in the proportions of things . . . She was a flirt – a perfectly superficial and un-malicious one; and she was very fond, as she announced at the outset, of 'gentlemen's society.' In Giovanelli she got a gentleman who to her uncultivated perception was a very brilliant one . . . and she enjoyed his society to the largest possible measure. When she found that this measure was

thought too large by other people – especially Winterbourne – she was wounded; she became conscious that she was accused of something of which her very comprehension was vague. This consciousness she endeavoured to throw off; she tried not to think of what people meant and easily succeeded in doing so; but to my perception she never really tried to take her revenge upon public opinion – to outrage it and irritate it . . . The keynote of her *character* is her innocence – that of her *conduct* is of course that she had a little sentiment about Winterbourne that she believed to be quite unreciprocated . . .[25]

There is a danger that we will take that statement as the last, authoritative word on the story. But James was careful to qualify his analysis of Daisy with the phrases 'as I understand her' and 'to my perception', allowing the possibility of understanding and perceiving her differently. Certainly the narrative method he used so skilfully in the story allows for a wide range of emphasis in its interpretation, and makes it infinitely rereadable.

Notes

1 Graham Clarke, ed., *Henry James: Critical Assessments: 1: Memories, views and writers* (1991), p. 41.

2 Philip Horne, ed., *Henry James: A Life in Letters* (1999), p. 111.

3 Leon Edel, ed., *Henry James Letters* (1974–84) Vol. 2, p. 213.

4 Preface to the New York Edition of *The Novels and Tales of Henry James*, Volume XVIII (1909).

5 Letter to Mrs Eliza Lynn Linton, 6 October 1880, in Horne, *Henry James: A Life in Letters*, p. 122.

6 A point made by Millicent Bell, *Meaning in Henry James* (1991), p. 65.

7 Vivian R. Pollack, ed., *New Essays on Daisy Miller and The Turn of the Screw* (1993), Editor's introduction, p. 5.

8 Leon Edel, *The Life of Henry James* (Penguin edn, 1977), Vol. I, pp. 47–9.

9 All definitions are from the *Oxford English Dictionary*.

10 Edel, *The Life of Henry James*, Vol. I, p. 517.

11 Philip Horne, *Henry James and Revision: the New York Edition* (Oxford: Clarendon Press, 1990), p. 235.

12 Ibid.

13 The words are those of Leslie Stephen. James recounts in the Preface that he first submitted the story to the editor of *Lippincott's Magazine*, based in Philadelphia, who promptly rejected it without explanation, and a 'friend' (actually Leslie Stephen, who accepted it for the English *Cornhill Magazine*) suggested that this was the reason.

14 Roger Gard, ed., *Henry James: The Critical Heritage* (1968), p. 74.

15 Edel, *Life*, Vol. I, p. 521.

16 Quoted by Jean Gooder, ed., *Henry James: Daisy Miller and Other Stories* (1985), p. xiv.

17 Henry James, *The Future of the Novel: Essays on the Art of Fiction*, ed. Leon Edel (New York: Vintage Books, 1956), p. 14.

18 Jean Gooder, ed., *Henry James: Daisy Miller and Other Stories*, p. xxix.

19 Quoted by Horne, *Henry James and Revision*, p. 264.

20 Ibid., pp. 234 and 258.

21 William Carlos Baker, *Ernest Hemingway* (1972), p. 165.

22 Quoted by Horne, *Henry James and Revision*, p. 229. William James was commenting on the story, 'A Most Extraordinary Case', first published in 1868.

23 Clarke, ed., *Henry James: 1: Memories, views and writers*, p. 81.

24 'The only way of expressing emotion in the form of art is by finding an "objective correlative"; in other words, a set of objects, a situation, a chain of events which shall be the formula of that *particular* emotion . . .' T. S. Eliot, *Selected Essays* (1951), p. 145.

25 Letter to Mrs Eliza Lynn Linton, 6 October 1880, in Horne, *Henry James: A Life in Letters*, p. 122.

H. G. WELLS

Kipps: The Story of
a Simple Soul

The early novels and tales of H. G. Wells fall into two quite different and distinct categories. He first made his name as the author of 'scientific romances' like *The Time Machine* (1895), *The Island of Dr Moreau* (1896), *The War of the Worlds* (1898) and *The First Men on the Moon* (1901), classics of what is now called science fiction. In these works he explored the implications of recent discoveries about evolution and cosmology in thrilling yarns which tapped into deep sources of anxiety and wonder in the collective unconscious. Over the same period he was also writing more conventional realistic novels about contemporary social life: *The Wheels of Chance* (1896), *Love and Mr Lewisham* (1901), and *Kipps: The Story of a Simple Soul*, which was completed and published in 1905, but begun much earlier. All three books have as their central character a young man of humble background and limited horizons who glimpses the possibility of a richer and more fulfilling existence but is unable to seize the opportunity and in the end resigns himself to a life more ordinary. All three stories contain a significant autobiographical element. Hoopdriver (the hero of *Wheels of Chance*) and Kipps are drapers' assistants, as was Wells for two miserable years in youth; and Mr Lewisham is a teacher, as Wells was before he became a professional writer.

It was his literary genius that allowed Wells to throw off the chains of wage-slavery and become a free spirit and a rich and famous man. That blessing is not vouchsafed to the heroes of these novels, though the possibility is briefly and rather absurdly entertained by Kipps ('he let it be drawn from him that his real choice in life was to be a Nawther'). As Wells's biographers, Norman and Jean Mackenzie, observe: 'The "little men" to whom Wells gave his best writing as a novelist . . . are not fated to escape into their wish-fulfilments. They are nostalgic figures and, unlike their author, they are not permitted to cross the frontier of success. They are not fit to become supermen.'[1] By 'nostalgic' the Mackenzies indicate that in creating these characters Wells drew deeply on memories of his early life and the emotions associated with it; but at the same time he celebrated his own escape from its limitations, humiliations and privations, by placing himself as author at a comic distance from his heroes. This is especially true of *Kipps*, probably the funniest of all his novels.

Herbert George Wells was born in 1866, the fourth child of his parents, who had met when his mother was a lady's maid and his father a gardener at a large country house. By the time of Herbert's birth they were running a rather unsuccessful shop, grandiloquently called Atlas House, in the high street of Bromley, Kent, selling chinaware and cricket equipment.

Joseph Wells was a professional county cricketer of some note, and his earnings from this source usefully supplemented their meagre business income. The family lived above and behind the shop, in dark, cramped and insanitary accommodation which made an indelible mark on the consciousness of young Bertie (as he was known in the family) and gave him a life-long obsession with domestic architecture. His parents clung to the very lowest rung of the lower middle class, sending their son to a cheap and badly managed private school to avoid the stigma of a state 'board school'. In fact Wells largely educated himself, making good use of a long period of conva-lescence at the age of seven to develop a precocious enthusi-asm for reading, which his parents did their best to discourage. When his father broke his leg and was forced to retire from cricket the family fortunes declined steeply. His mother took the position of housekeeper at Uppark, in Sussex, the stately home where she had formerly been employed, and young Bertie's occasional sojourns in this establishment gave him a valuable insight into the upper reaches of the English class system and the place of the landed aristocracy and gentry in English social history.

It was Mrs Wells's intention that Bertie should, like his two older brothers, be apprenticed as a draper's assistant when he left school at the age of fourteen. Wells put up some resistance to this plan, and contrived to get dismissed by his first employer within a few weeks, but after short spells as a pupil teacher and chemist's assistant he finally submitted to becoming a draper's apprentice at Southsea, a seaside district of Portsmouth in Hampshire, in June 1881. Recalling that experience in his *Experiment in Autobiography* he wrote, 'I recall those two years of my incarceration as the most unhappy hopeless period of my life',[2] but it qualified him to write, in the early chapters of

Kipps, one of the most vivid accounts in English fiction of the lives of workers in the retail trade. In his second year a new apprentice took over some of Wells's more menial duties, but also the errands that had provided occasional relief and escape from the shop's boring routine and petty restrictions. 'He had by the bye,' Wells recalled, 'an amusing simplicity of mind, a carelessness of manner, a way of saying "Oo'er," and a feather at the back of his head that stuck in memory, and formed the nucleus which grew into *Kipps* . . .'[3]

When he could bear the ignoble servitude of the Southsea Drapery Emporium no longer, Wells abandoned his apprenticeship and returned to Midhurst, the nearest town to Uppark, to work as an unqualified teaching assistant. This was another kind of wage-slavery, but more congenial, and it provided a platform from which the talented young man was able to propel himself into higher education. He won a scholarship to the Normal School of Science in South Kensington (later to become Imperial College) where he studied a range of subjects, including biology under the instruction of Professor Thomas Huxley, and eventually took a first-class degree in zoology. Wells's interest in and aptitude for the physical sciences was an unusual preparation for a literary career but, combined with a natural gift for verbal expression nourished on voracious reading, it was precisely what gave him 'competitive edge' when in the early 1890s he began to supplement his earnings as a tutor in a correspondence college with freelance journalism and, in due course, fiction. He bridged the gap between 'the two cultures' long before that phrase was coined by C. P. Snow.

Wells badly needed the extra money at this time, because of the complications of his personal life. In spite of indifferent physique, and a history of illness and serious accidental injuries, the young Wells was very interested in sex and very frustrated by the repression and prudery that inhibited relations between men and women in late Victorian England. In 1891 he married his cousin Isabel but quickly discovered that they were sexually and emotionally ill-matched. Soon he was conducting an affair with one of his adult students, Amy Catherine Robbins – whom he later renamed 'Jane' – and lived with her in what was then known as sin until he obtained a divorce in 1895 and was free to marry her. Curiously she seemed no more capable of satisfying his erotic needs than her predecessor, but she was more tolerant of his tendency to seek satisfaction with other women, and she remained his faithful, supportive and more or less complaisant wife until her death in 1927. It is probably not coincidental that both Kipps and Lewisham find themselves compromised by conflicting ties and obligations to two women; but the urgency of Wells's own sexual desires finds little expression in *Love and Mr Lewisham*, and none at all in *Kipps*, whose hero has a childlike innocence in this as in every other respect.

The composition of the latter novel had a long and complicated history. We can date its inception very precisely. In his earlier years Wells was in the habit of drawing little cartoon-sketches which he called 'picshuas' as a kind of visual diary, and one of these, dated 5 October 1898, shows Wells as an authorial chicken who has just hatched an egg from which has emerged a diminutive figure named 'Kipps'.[4] He and Jane were at this time living in a rented cottage by the edge of the sea at Sandgate, a few miles to the west of Folkestone, and he was to situate his new hero in the same part of England, where the Romney Marshes meet the cliffs of Folkestone. In July of that year the young couple had set out on a cycling tour of the south coast, but at Seaford in Sussex

Wells became seriously ill, with acute pain in the kidney which had been damaged in a football injury some years earlier. Luckily he was able to consult a very able and sympathetic doctor, Henry Hick, whom he had met through George Gissing, and who lived in the little town of New Romney. Hick generously took the invalid and his wife into his own house and nursed him there. While he was convalescing Henry James cycled over from Rye with Edmund Gosse, who was staying at Lamb House, and met Wells for the first time, commencing a literary friendship which began in mutual esteem but ended unhappily some seventeen years later. In the autumn of 1898 Gosse and James were covertly checking out Wells's possible need of a grant from the Royal Literary Fund, but they discovered that the young writer's finances were in good order and that he was already planning to build himself a house in the locality with an en suite bathroom for every bedroom – which in due course materialised as Spade House, Sandgate. Meanwhile he rented the aptly named Beach Cottage in the same place, where he finished *Love and Mr Lewisham* and began the story of Arthur Kipps, a humble draper's assistant who inherits a fortune and is suddenly promoted into the bourgeoisie.

Originally, however, the novel was entitled *The Wealth of Mr Waddy*, and apart from a brief 'Prelude' Kipps himself did not figure in the early chapters. Wells worked hard on the book in late 1898 and submitted a draft of the first 35,000 words, with an additional 15,000 words of notes indicating the intended development of the story, to his agent J. B. Pinker in January 1899. As Pinker endeavoured without success to interest publishers and magazine editors in the project, Wells added further passages to the typescript, but towards the end of 1899 he abandoned the novel on the grounds that it had grown too big and unwieldy in scale. Later he returned to the story, focusing more narrowly on the character and fortunes of Arthur Kipps, but he still had difficulty in bringing it to a conclusion that was aesthetically and thematically satisfying, for reasons that will be examined later.

The sizeable fragment of *The Wealth of Mr Waddy*, which Wells himself believed to be lost, in fact survived and was published posthumously.[5] It is well worth reading on its own merits as well as for the fascinating glimpses it affords into the workshop of Wells's imagination and the light it throws on his development as a novelist. As its editor, Harris Wilson, observes, it supports 'the contention of some critics that the early Wells was much "darker" than the later'.[6] Mr Waddy, who is only briefly mentioned in the published novel as the source of Kipps's legacy, dominates the early chapters of the earlier version – a monster of egotism and misanthropy who provokes a kind of appalled laughter in the reader. Selfish and irascible by nature, he is further embittered by being crippled in a cycling accident just as he inherits a fortune, and condemned to spend the rest of his life in a wheelchair. He has no compassion for those similarly afflicted but more needy. 'Convalescent Homes indeed! Lethal chambers are what we want,' is his typical reaction to a request for a charitable dona-tion. Residing in Folkestone, he tyrannises over a little group of servants and hangers-on, who include Chitterlow and his wife Muriel. An ill-fated attempt to make their son Harry ingratiate himself with Waddy in the manner of Little Lord Fauntleroy so enrages the misanthropic invalid that he loses control of his wheelchair on the Folkestone Leas and careers down a path that leads to the cliff-edge, to be saved from certain death by the chance intervention of Kipps. Waddy dies shortly afterwards from shock, but not before he has left all his fortune to Kipps, as much to spite his retainers as out of gratitude to his rescuer.

The retrospective account that follows of Kipps's character, background and apprenticeship as a draper is very similar to the corresponding passages in the published novel, though more condensed. Wells's notes indicate that the rest of the plot was to develop along essentially the same lines as in *Kipps*, and the characters of Ann, Helen and Coote (a little younger) were already in place, as well as the Chitterlows. So his declared reason for abandoning *Mr Waddy*, and starting afresh – that it had been planned on 'too colossal a scale'[7] – doesn't quite ring true. Perhaps Pinker's failure to find a publisher made him think its comedy was too black to have popular appeal, for he was always desirous of commercial success as well as critical acclaim. The characters, apart from Kipps himself, are greedy, predatory and unscrupulous, with not a redeeming feature between them, whereas in *Kipps* they are treated more gently, their behaviour being expressive of what is wrong with society in general rather than manifestations of personal malevolence.

The model for both versions was pre-eminently Dickens, as Wells himself frankly acknowledged. He wrote to his father about *Mr Waddy* in December 1898, 'I am writing rather hard . . . at a comic novel in the old-fashioned Dickens line',[8] and seven years later he wrote to his publisher Macmillan about the finished *Kipps*: 'I've been aiming at the interest of character, the same interest that gives Dickens his value . . .'[9] The very names 'Chitterlow', 'Coote' and 'Kipps' have a Dickensian ring. In some ways the discarded character of Mr Waddy was the most Dickensian of all, a comic villain with something of the demonic energy and eloquence of Quilp or Fagin, but Chitterlow has an obvious ancestry in Jingle,

Micawber and other plausible, unreliable good fellows in Dickens's corpus, while the orphaned and repressed childhood of Kipps occasionally reminds one of the young David Copperfield and of Pip in *Great Expectations*. The opening pages of *Kipps* are particularly reminiscent of the beginnings of those two novels, and the allusion to *Barnaby Rudge* on the first page (Kipps's mother wears a 'Dolly Varden hat' in the only image of her that survives) may be a conscious acknowledgement by Wells of his debt to Dickens. The two writers had indeed much in common – a penurious lower-middle-class background, an indifferent education, and the talent, energy and ambition to overcome these handicaps. Both men were scornfully critical of what they perceived as a corrupt and ossified social system which privileged the undeserving few and stifled the potential of most of its members; and just as Dickens drew on the emotional trauma of being made to work in a blacking factory at the age of twelve to give an authentic pathos to his representations of loneliness, unhappiness and oppression, so Wells drew on his miserable existence as a draper's apprentice to similar effect.

But the most important debt Wells owed to his great precursor was in the use of the authorial voice. In *Kipps*, as in the novels of Dickens, it is the authorial voice that brings the characters to life, moralises on the story, and provides most of the humour. The early chapters about Kipps's friendship with Sid Pornick exploit the Dickensian trick of describing the naiveties of the young in a knowing adult voice: '[Sid] produced a thumbed novelette that had played a part in his sentimental awakening; he proffered it to Kipps, and confessed there was a character in it, a baronet, singularly like himself.' The ironic distance between the teller and the tale persists into the narrative of the hero's adult life. Kipps is a 'simple soul', unable to

articulate his anxieties and longings, while the other characters, blinkered by the prejudices of their class or their own
selfish egos, communicate in clichés, platitudes and stock
responses which Kipps can only parrot. The narrator alone is
allowed to be truly eloquent – with a few exceptions, as when
Minton, the senior apprentice at the Folkestone Drapery
Bazaar, memorably declares to Kipps, 'I tell you we're in a
blessed drain-pipe, and we've got to crawl along it till we die.'
But it is the narrator who describes the effect of this bleak
pronouncement on the hero:

> There were times when Kipps would lie awake, all others in
> the dormitory asleep and snoring, and think dismally of the
> outlook Minton pictured. Dimly he perceived the thing that
> had happened to him, how the great stupid machine of retail
> trade had caught his life into its wheels, a vast, irresistible
> force which he had neither strength of will nor knowledge
> to escape. This was to be his life until his days should end.
> No adventures, no glory, no change, no freedom. Neither
> though the force of that came home to him later – might
> he dream of effectual love and marriage.

The full hopelessness of Kipps's plight strikes him when he
falls in love with the unattainable cultured beauty who is his
art teacher, Helen Walshingham, and then, as a result of
Chitterlow's reckless irruption into his life, is dismissed from
his place. He goes down into the basement of the shop, deliberately upsets a box of window tickets 'and so, having made
himself a justifiable excuse for being on the ground with his
head well in the dark, he could let his poor bursting little heart
have its way with him for a space'.
From this lowest point in his fortunes he is rescued by the

legacy from Waddy (now an offstage character who, we are told, prevented his son, Kipps's father, from marrying Kipps's mother, and repented of this action). This was a plot device often used by Victorian novelists to bring a story to a happy conclusion. In *Kipps*, however, it triggers the main action, giving the hero a chance to achieve happiness and fulfilment which he fails disastrously to seize (until the author takes pity on him and rescues him with another *deus ex machina* in the form of Chitterlow's hit play). Although money is necessary to Kipps's happiness, it is not sufficient, because he doesn't know how to conduct himself as a 'gentleman', a consequence partly of his impoverished education and upbringing, but also of the limitations of his own character and intelligence. He is sponged on by Chitterlow, exploited by the Walshinghams, and brainwashed by Coote, his self-appointed mentor. Most of the time among his new friends he feels embarrassed and ill at ease, overdressed and underbred. His wealth allows him to form the attachment to Helen that had seemed an unrealisable dream, but 'He had prayed for Helen as good souls pray for heaven, with as little understanding of what it was he prayed for'. In her company he is mainly conscious of his own inadequacy. She looks at him 'with an eye of critical proprietorship', noting his deficiencies 'as one might go over a newly taken house'. Their engagement is entirely lacking in sexual passion – he is too intimidated even to attempt to kiss her. When he meets his old childhood sweetheart, Ann, he feels no such inhibition, but then finds himself in a moral and emotional dilemma from which he simply runs away – to London.

Kipps's adventures in London constitute the comic highpoint of the novel. His prolonged and unsuccessful struggle to master the protocol of the luxury hotel where he is staying anticipates the farcical misadventures of Rowan Atkinson's Mr Bean, but it also reinforces the moral of the story, that class and culture are stronger social forces than mere wealth. On his first day in the capital Kipps goes hungry because, although he has plenty of money, he can't find a dining place in which he would feel comfortable, and only a chance meeting with Sid Pornick, who takes him home for a cosy family meal, saves him from fasting. 'There were no serviettes and less ceremony, and Kipps thought he had never enjoyed a meal so much.' The humiliating experience of eating next day among disdainful waiters and plutocratic diners in the hotel restaurant is enough to convert him temporarily to socialism – a concept to which he has just been introduced by Sid and the latter's lodger, Masterman.

> The mental change Kipps underwent was, in its way, what psychologists call a conversion. In a few moments all Kipps' ideals were changed. He who had been 'practically a gentleman,' the sedulous pupil of Coote, the punctilious raiser of hats, was instantly a rebel, an outcast, the hater of everything 'stuck up,' the foe of Society and the social order of today. Here they were among the profits of their robbery, these people who might do anything with the world . . .

This of course is an ironic overstatement of Kipps's change of attitude. He continues to try to conform to the social code of the hotel, and continues to fail. His efforts to purchase the respect of the staff by extravagant tipping merely make him ridiculous – though it is only the reader, by courtesy of the authorial voice, who perceives just how ridiculous. 'At his departure, Kipps, with a hot face, convulsive gestures, and an embittered heart, tipped everyone who did not actively resist, including an absent-minded South African diamond merchant who was waiting in the hall for his wife.' But he does return to Folkestone to some extent a changed man – or at least a desperate and determined one. When Ann reappears in his life, as a maid at one of the bourgeois establishments where he is submitted to further social torture, for once in his life he takes control of his own destiny and persuades her to marry him. In this part of the story Wells makes deft use of the conventions that divided middle-class people from their servants to dramatise the transgressive nature of Kipps's action – Ann, for instance, will not speak to him about personal matters at the front door of the house where she works, only in the 'basement after nine. Them's my hours. I'm a servant, and likely to keep one. If you're calling here, what name please?'

Even when he is married to a woman whom he really loves, Kipps has difficulty finding a style of life that coincides with his desires because of his ambiguous social status. When he tries to get a house built he is bullied by the architect into commissioning an absurdly ostentatious and impractical dwelling (Wells's hobby horse about domestic architecture gets a thorough airing in this sequence), and Ann causes problems by refusing to employ a proper complement of servants. In a poignant scene, she confesses that she pretended to be her own servant when some respectable visitors caught her painting the floor of their temporary home. Kipps's reproachful dismay reveals that he is far from being liberated from bourgeois aspirations, and causes their first matrimonial tiff. This, however, is swamped by a far greater catastrophe, when Helen Walshingham's brother embezzles Kipps's fortune.

At this point the story seems to have reached its final reversal, with Kipps stripped of most of his wealth, and perhaps happier for its absence. He is not quite back where he started. There is just enough value in the villa he inherited from Waddy and his own half-built house to save him from bankruptcy and enable him to open a little shop – something he had always secretly wanted to do, but felt was incompatible with being a gentleman. Ann embraces the plan enthusiastically: 'A certain brightness came into Ann's face. "Nobody won't be able to come leaving cards on us, Artie, now, any more. We are out of *that!*"' The shop, surprisingly and inauspiciously in view of Kipps's limited education, is a bookshop, belonging to a chain called the Associated Booksellers' Trading Union, a new speculative venture which the narrator tells us would soon fail. Kipps, however, is protected by the handsome, unexpected return on his investment in Chitterlow's play, *The Pestered Butterfly*, and thus able to run his little bookshop in Hythe as a kind of hobby. There, the narrator archly and unconvincingly observes,

you may see him for yourself and speak to him and buy this book of him if you like . . . He has it in stock, I know. Very delicately I've seen to that. His name is not Kipps . . . but everything else is exactly as I have told you . . . (Of course you will not tell Kipps that he is 'Kipps' or that I have put him in this book. He hasn't the remotest suspicion of that . . .)

The sudden changes of direction and shifts of tone in the concluding chapters of *Kipps* suggest that Wells was not at all certain how to end the story, and he himself confessed to Pinker that Book III was 'scamped . . . a thing of shreds and patches, but it is quite handsomely brought off'.[10] To understand Wells's difficulties with this part of the novel it is helpful to look at his political views. Political issues were at the forefront of his mind when he was striving to finish *Kipps*, because of his involvement in the Fabian Society, founded in 1884, by George Bernard Shaw among others, as a kind of think-tank and talking shop for left-wing, middle-class intellectuals who espoused the gradual evolution of modern society towards socialism but rejected class struggle and violent revolution on the Marxist model. H. G. Wells was a natural recruit to the Fabians. His non-fiction books and articles called for a radical transformation of British society by the application of rational planning and new technology, sweeping away unearned privilege and opening up a decent quality of life to the masses. The Fabians hoped he would bring a new energy and eloquence to their programme and make it more appealing to the young. Wells himself was flattered to be introduced into this high-minded and exclusive intellectual milieu, and in 1903 he was elected, sponsored by G. B. Shaw and Graham Wallas.

Very soon, however, there were clashes of opinion and style between the Old Guard of the society and the new recruit. Wells felt the society had achieved too little in its twenty years of existence, and that it needed a thorough shake-up of its policies and executive officers. In this he was probably right, but his manner of proceeding was abrasive and caused considerable offence. He instigated the setting-up of a committee to consider the reform of the society and a series of dramatic and divisive debates ensued which ended in 1906 when Wells was procedurally outmanoeuvred and defeated by Shaw, after which his active involvement rapidly diminished and eventually ceased. In the *Autobiography* he declared: 'no part of my career rankles so acutely in my memory with the conviction of bad judgment, gusty impulse and real inexcusable vanity, as that storm in the Fabian tea-cup.'[11] Though he blames himself for the debacle, a parting of the ways was inevitable. Wells's 'socialism' was not at heart democratic, but meritocratic – even, in some respects, autocratic. Early in 1905 he published *A Modern Utopia*, in which he envisaged a world run by an elite of wise and clever men (called rather revealingly Samurai) for the benefit of all – but an 'all' purged of antisocial and unproductive elements by a chilling eugenic policy. The latter part of *Kipps* (which was completed in 1904, and published in the autumn of 1905) shows signs, particularly in the characterisation of Sid Pornick's lodger, Masterman, of the intellectual strain Wells was under as he struggled to define his political philosophy and to reconcile it with Fabianism.

Surviving drafts of the novel show that originally Masterman was given several opportunities to expound the doctrine of socialism to Kipps, who was to be genuinely converted and resolve to bring up his son by its light.[12] In the finished novel Masterman is given much less scope, and is a much more ambiguous character, a malcontent rather than a genuine reformer, embittered by his ill-health and other misfortunes, raging against the injustices and corruption of the social system and anticipating its imminent self-destruction with gloomy relish. He seems to be something of a parasite on the Pornicks, and Sid's awed regard for him is portrayed as naïve. Kipps's own verdict is, 'Bit orf 'is 'ead, poor chap.' This unsympathetic portrayal is all the more puzzling because the character was partly based on George Gissing, whom Wells regarded as a good friend, and whose death in December 1903 had upset him very much. Perhaps in a clumsy effort to disguise the model for his fictional character, Wells gave him the name of another writer and politician of radical views, C. F. G. Masterman, who was not amused, though he reviewed the novel favourably and later became a good friend and supporter of Wells.

What seems to have happened, then, is that in the process of writing Masterman's exposition of socialist theory Wells concluded that he didn't really believe in it himself, and so couldn't in good faith show his hero embracing it. Therefore in the final version of the novel the character of Masterman was reduced in stature, to such an extent that he hardly has any function at all. Kipps's rebellion against bourgeois values is not ideological in motivation, but personal, emotional and opportunistic. Just how tenuous it is, is revealed when he quarrels with Ann over a trivial breach of social decorum, provoking an exasperated outburst from the author:

> The stupid little tragedies of these clipped and limited lives!
>   As I think of them lying unhappily there in the darkness, my vision pierces the night . . . Above them, brooding over them . . . there is a monster, a lumpish monster . . . It is matter and darkness, it is the anti-soul, it is the ruling power of this land, Stupidity. My Kippses live in its shadow . . . I have laughed, and I laugh at these two people; I have sought to make you laugh . . .
>   But I see through the darkness the souls of my Kippses as they are . . . as things like the bodies of little, ill-nourished, ailing, ignorant children – children who feel pain, who are naughty and muddled and suffer, and do not understand why. And the claw of this Beast rests upon them!

In this remarkable passage Wells comes perilously close to scuttling his own novel. He renounces the stance of genial comic detachment which he has adopted as narrator up to this point, and adopts a prophetic, even apocalyptic, tone. The lives of Arthur and Ann Kipps are seen as tragic rather than comic, but they are 'stupid little tragedies', mere symptoms of a much bigger and all-embracing malaise. One senses that the author would like to sweep away the whole social system to which his characters (and the masses of people like them) belong, in order to create his model state – and too bad if they perish in the process. But the author relents, the genial comic mask is quickly replaced, the story of the Kippses is resumed and brought to a happy conclusion – represented by, of all things, a shop, an idealised instance of 'the great stupid machine of retail trade' that had formerly oppressed and enslaved the hero.

Though he privately acknowledged its flaws, Wells had faith in his book and was determined that it should be a success when it was finally published, in October 1905. He wrote to his publisher, Macmillan, in August:

> It is, I feel, the most considerable book (from the point of view of a possible popularity) that you have so far published for me, and I think that now is the time for a very special effort to improve my position with the booksellers and book-buyers . . . I look to you for some able and sustained advertisement and I will confess that I shall feel it is you and not me to blame if Kipps is not carried well over 10,000 copies.[13]

The eminent publisher was not used to being hustled by his authors in this fashion and did not take kindly to it, but Wells pestered him both in person and by letter after publication with schemes to promote the novel: men with sandwich boards parading the streets, advertisements in theatre programmes, leaflets for subscribers to the *Times* Book Club, and even posters at Portsmouth & Southsea Station saying 'KIPPS WORKED HERE'. How many of these suggestions were adopted is not known, but the authorial pressure seems to have had some effect, for, after a sluggish start, sales improved steadily in November and December and by Christmas 12,000 copies of *Kipps* had been sold – the best Wells had so far achieved with any book.[14] By 1910 it had sold 60,000 in a cheaper edition, and it has always been one of the most popular of his novels.

The reviews at the time of publication were generally excellent, but probably none of them gave Wells as much pleasure as a private letter from Henry James:

What am I to say about Kipps but that I am ready, that I am compelled, utterly to *drivel* about him? He is not so much a masterpiece as a mere born gem – you having, I know not how, taken a header straight down into the mysterious depths of observation and knowledge, I know not which and where, and come up again with this rounded pearl of the diver. But of course you know yourself how immitigably the thing is done – it is of such a brilliancy of *true* truth. I really think that you have done, at this time of day, two particular things for the first time of their doing among us. (1) You have written the first closely and intimately, the first intelligently and consistently ironic or satiric novel. In everything else there has always been the sentimental or conventional interference of which Thackeray is full. (2) You have for the very first time treated the English 'lower middle class', etc. without the picturesque, the grotesque, the fantastic and romantic interference, of which Dickens, e.g., is so misleadingly, of which even George Eliot is so deviatingly, full. You have handled its vulgarity in so scientific and historic a spirit, and seen the whole thing all in its *own* strong light.[15]

James continues for many more lines in the same vein. His rapturous and unqualified praise is, it must be admitted, something of a surprise. One would have expected that the flaws in the novel, of which Wells himself was well aware, would have been recognised by James, who set himself and others such high standards of formal elegance and consistency in the art of fiction. One almost wonders whether he actually read *Kipps* with close attention to the very end, since it is the third section of the novel that is weakest. But there are other explanations for the somewhat extravagant tenor of his tribute. He was writing privately to a friend and East Sussex neighbour, to a younger writer whose talent he appreciated all the more because it did not threaten his own. The social milieux and the human types they each wrote about were quite different. For James, Wells's description of lower-middle-class life – of the social dynamics of the draper's shop, for example – was a revelation, and what is interesting about his letter is the emphasis he gives to the book's effect of truthfulness to life, and the contrast he draws between Wells and his Victorian precursors in this respect. I think James exaggerates this contrast – there is in fact plenty of authorial 'interference' in *Kipps* – but he does draw our attention to an important aspect of the novel: the almost documentary realism of its descriptions of architecture, decor, possessions, clothes, manners and speech. I remarked earlier on Wells's debt to Dickens, which Wells himself more than once acknowledged; but James is right to point out that there is nothing of Dickens's fantastic and grotesque imagination in *Kipps*. In Dickens the familiar world is constantly transformed by metaphor and simile:

human beings behave like things, while objects are invested with an eerie and sinister life. When Dickens describes the interior of a room it is made to express its occupants through metaphorical suggestion. In a corresponding passage by Wells every detail is observed with literal exactness, and the objects function as metonyms of the taste, class, habits and prejudices of those who accumulated them. Take, for example, the description of Coote's study, which contains not a single figurative expression to relieve the remorseless inventory of his idea of culture:

You must figure Coote's study, a little bedroom put to studious uses, and over the mantel an array of things he had been led to believe indicative of culture and refinement – an autotype of Rossetti's 'Annunciation', an autotype of Watts' 'Minotaur,' a Swiss carved pipe with many joints, and a photograph of Amiens Cathedral (these two the spoils of travel), a phrenological bust, and some broken fossils from the Warren. A rotating bookshelf carried the *Encyclopaedia Britannica* (tenth edition) and on the top of it a large, official-looking, age-grubby envelope, bearing the mystic words, 'On His Majesty's Service,' a number or so of the *Bookman*, and a box of cigarettes were lying. A table under the window bore a little microscope, some dust in a saucer, some grimy glass slips, and broken cover glasses, for Coote had 'gone in for' biology a little. The longer side of the room was given over to bookshelves, neatly edged with pinked American cloth, and with an array of books – no worse an array of books than you find in any public library; an almost haphazard accumulation of obsolete classics, contemporary successes, the Hundred Best Books (including Samuel Warren's *Ten Thousand A Year*), old school-books, directories, the *Times* Atlas, Ruskin in bulk, Tennyson complete in one volume, Longfellow, Charles Kingsley, Smiles, a guide-book or so, several medical pamphlets, odd magazine numbers, and much indescribable rubbish – in fact, a compendium of the contemporary British mind.

What had happened to the novel between Dickens and Wells was the development of a new kind of realism, and its mutation into naturalism, in the work of French writers such as Flaubert, the Goncourts, Maupassant and Zola, who influenced younger British novelists like George Gissing, Arnold Bennett, George Moore – and H. G. Wells. James's commendation of Wells for handling the vulgarity of lower-middle-class life 'in so *scientific* and historic a spirit' (my emphasis) seems to make this connection, for some of the French novelists, notably Zola, consciously emulated the empirical methods of scientific research. The example of Flaubert, however, seems more relevant to *Kipps* than Zola. Its subtitle *The Story of a Simple Soul* echoes the title of Flaubert's tale, *Un Coeur Simple*, in *Trois Contes* (1877), which describes the life of Félicité, a housemaid in a bourgeois household. Her intelligence is so limited that she barely understands anything outside the humdrum domestic tasks which she performs so dutifully, and her frustrated capacity for love is finally displaced onto a stuffed parrot. Flaubert's last, unfinished work, *Bouvard et Pécuchet* (1881), is about two humble clerks who, like Wells's hero, are released from wage-slavery by a legacy, which they apply with disastrous incompetence to ambitious schemes of self-improvement, scientific, commercial and cultural. Wells's characters often seem to be speaking from 'The Dictionary of Received Ideas' which forms an appendix to Flaubert's novel. I have found no evidence that Wells had read either of these works, but it is unlikely that he was completely un-familiar with Flaubert, and in any case literary influence can work by contagion as well as directly. Wells, to be sure, does not imitate the unsettling authorial inscrutability of Flaubert's narrative method – he is always 'interfering' to gloss his own effects (e.g. 'in fact, a compendium of the contemporary British mind') – but the link between the two writers can be illustrated by putting this description of Félicité's room next to the passage just quoted from *Kipps*:

A big wardrobe prevented the door from opening properly. Opposite the window that overlooked the garden was a little round one looking on to the courtyard. There was a table beside the bed, with a water-jug, a couple of combs, and a block of blue soap in a chipped plate. On the walls there were rosaries, holy medals, several pictures of the Virgin, and a holy-water stoup made out of a coconut. On the chest of drawers, which was draped with a cloth just like an altar, was the shell-box Victor had given her, and also a watering-can and a ball, some copy-books, the illustrated geography book, and a pair of ankle-boots. And on the nail supporting the looking-glass, fastened by its ribbons, hung the little plush hat.[16]

Henry James's treatment of the material world, especially in his later work, is in contrast impressionistic, subjective, lacking in specificity. In *The Spoils of Poynton*, for instance, a novel all about precious 'things' (i.e. antiques), hardly any of them are actually described, and then in no great detail. In James's fiction everything is filtered through the consciousness of the characters, and it is their emotional and psychological reaction to the world and to each other, rendered in exquisitely nuanced prose, that is of central importance. James, who knew Flaubert's work very well, and wrote a fine essay about it, revered him primarily for his complete dedication to his art, his tireless pursuit of the perfectly appropriate form for his subject, however unpromising it might be. To Wells the subject of a novel, and its relevance to contemporary life, was all-important. He was never much bothered about formal perfection, and in due course it became evident to both him and James that their respective concepts of the novel were incompatible. In 1914 James wrote critically about Wells's recent work in a survey of contemporary fiction in the *Times Literary Supplement*,[17] and the following year Wells retaliated with a cruel caricature of James's late style in his satire *Boon* (1915). After an exchange of letters, pained on James's part, unrepentant on Wells's, the two men severed relations, and James died in the following year. But in 1905 the friendship was still intact, and James was able to appreciate and enjoy, along with many other readers, the originality and verve of *Kipps*.

Notes

1 Norman and Jean Mackenzie, *The Time Traveller: The Life of H. G. Wells* (1973), p. 193.

2 H. G. Wells, *Experiment in Autobiography: discoveries and conclusions of a very ordinary brain (since 1866)*, two vols (1934; reissued 1966), p. 148.

3 Ibid., p. 155.

4 Ibid., p. 387.

5 H. G. Wells, *The Wealth of Mr Waddy*, edited with an introduction by Harris Wilson (1969).

6 Ibid., p. xix.

7 Mackenzie and Mackenzie, *The Time Traveller*, p. 192.

8 Quoted in J. R. Hammond, *An H. G. Wells Chronology* (1999), p. 18.

9 Lovat Dickson, *H. G. Wells: His Turbulent Life and Times* (1969), p. 145.

10 Letter to Pinker in June 1904, quoted by Wilson, ed., *The Wealth of Mr Waddy*, p. xxii.

11 Wells, *Experiment in Autobiography*, pp. 660–1.

12 Mackenzie and Mackenzie, *The Time Traveller*, p. 193 and n.

13 Dickson, *Wells*, p. 143.

14 Ibid., pp. 146–7.

15 Philip Horne, ed., *Henry James: A Life in Letters* (1999), p. 424.

16 Gustave Flaubert, *Three Tales*, translated by Robert Baldick (1961), p. 49.

17 Henry James, 'The Younger Generation', *Times Literary Supplement*, 19 March and 2 April 1914.

THE MAKING OF 'GEORGE ELIOT':

Scenes of Clerical Life

Scenes of Clerical Life is not a title likely to set the pulses of modern readers racing with anticipation, even if they misinterpret it as referring to the lives of office-workers, rather than clergymen. It is, however, well worth reading: a book of considerable intrinsic merit, and of special interest as the first work of fiction by one of England's greatest novelists. With these three tales (or novellas, as we might call them today), 'George Eliot' was born.

In 1857, when they were first published, as serial stories in *Blackwood's Magazine*, there would have been no uncertainty as to the meaning of 'clerical', and no lack of interest in the subject. The Victorians' concern with matters of religious belief and practice can only be compared with our own era's preoccupation with sexuality (a parallel amusingly reinforced by the fact that the word 'pervert' was commonly used in the nineteenth century in the religious sense of 'convert') and fiction reflected the earlier kind of interest as fully as it now does the later. 'This is an age of Religious Novels', a writer in the *Dublin Review* observed in 1846, calculating that at least a third of the novels published that year had been 'either directly religious . . . or possessed more of religious character than would have been sufficient, ten years ago, to damn any novel . . .'.[1] That, admittedly, was at the height of the controversy provoked by the Oxford Movement in the Church of England, but a decade later religious themes and ecclesiastical settings still figured prominently in current fiction. It was in 1857 that Trollope made a hit with *Barchester Towers*.

Nevertheless there is something surprising and paradoxical, on the face of it, about George Eliot's choice of subject for her fictional debut. In September 1856, when she began writing 'The Sad Fortunes of Amos Barton', Mary Anne Evans (or Marian Evans, as she preferred to be known) was in her thirty-seventh year, and had not been a Christian believer since she was twenty-two. In the intervening years she had translated two of the century's most powerful intellectual assaults on Christian orthodoxy – Strauss's *Life of Jesus* (1846) and Feuerbach's *The Essence of Christianity* (1854) – and had been both editor of and contributor to the *Westminster Review*, the principal organ of radical, progressive, free-thinking opinion in its day. The intellectual and bohemian social milieu in which Marian Evans moved was discreetly permissive in sexual morals, but even her liberal friends were startled and shocked when, in 1854, she began to live openly with a married man, George Henry Lewes, while 'respectable' society shunned her henceforth. Most members of her family, already alienated by her apostasy, reacted similarly. It is hardly surprising therefore that for some time neither her friends nor her relations guessed that she was the author of three widely admired stories about provincial clergymen published under the name of 'George Eliot', stories in which there was no overt questioning of Christian belief, and the longest of which ('Janet's Repentance') was a wholly approving account of the redemption of a woman from drink and despair through the selfless endeavours of an Evangelical clergyman – a representative, that is, of precisely the kind of Protestant Christianity against which Marian Evans had herself rebelled fourteen years before, and of which she had written a withering critique little more than a year previously, describing it as 'a Goshen of mediocrity in which a smattering of science and learning will pass for profound instruction, where platitudes will be accepted as profound wisdom, bigoted narrowness as holy zeal, unctuous egoism as God-given piety'.[2]

In fact the contradiction was more apparent than real. Not very far beneath the surface Christian orthodoxy of *Scenes*, we find the Feuerbachian 'religion of Humanity' with which George Eliot sought to replace it. The same is true of her first full-length novel, *Adam Bede* (1859), and those that followed it: religion is allowed to serve as the vehicle for humanistic values without itself being radically called into question. George Eliot never wrote the great novel of religious Doubt for which she, above all English novelists, was best equipped, and which might have been predicted from the tenor of the essays and reviews she wrote in the 1850s. (Instead the task was left to the inferior talents of Mrs Humphry Ward, in *Robert Elsmere* [1888].) Marian Evans's decision to change from writing criticism to writing fiction coincided with a significant shift in her stance towards Christianity, from scepticism to conciliation. It also coincided with a momentous change in her personal life – her union with Lewes. Virginia Woolf plausibly suggested that the achievement of this happiness, after many years of emotional suffering, frustration and rejection, released the springs of her creativity, and also, by isolating her socially, threw her back upon herself and her memories of a provincial childhood and youth.[3] In so many ways the writing of *Scenes of Clerical Life* was the hinge on which her life turned, changing Marian Evans into George Eliot, and we can recover some sense of this transformation from the note, 'How I Came to Write Fiction', which she entered in her journal in December 1857.

She begins by recalling that 'it had always been a vague dream of mine that some time or other I might write a novel' but that she never got further than writing 'an introductory chapter describing a Staffordshire village and the life of the neighbouring farm houses', until she started to live with George Lewes, who encouraged her to make another attempt. When they went to Tenby in South Wales for an extended holiday in 1856 he urged her to begin.

> One morning as I was lying in bed, thinking what should be the subject of my first story, my thoughts merged themselves into a dreamy doze, and I imagined myself writing a story of which the title was – 'The Sad Fortunes of the Reverend Amos Barton'. I was soon wide awake again, and told G. He said, 'O what a capital title!' and from that time I had settled in my mind that this should be my first story.[4]

Lewes warned her not to expect immediate success. He told her, 'You have wit, description and philosophy', but questioned whether she possessed the power of 'dramatic presentation'. She soon settled his doubts. The first chapter of her story, in which Amos Barton is introduced to the reader through the gossipy chit-chat of a provincial tea-party, demonstrated that she had a wonderful ear for ordinary speech and a talent for satirical characterisation; and when, later, she read him the scene of Milly Barton's death, 'We both cried over it, and then he came up to me and kissed me, saying, "I think your pathos is better than your fun."' Lewes sent the story to John Blackwood, Scottish publisher and editor of the famous magazine, as the work of a male friend who wished to conceal his identity under a nom de plume. Blackwood responded favourably, but asked to see more of the proposed series of 'Scenes' before committing himself. When Lewes replied that his 'friend' had been somewhat discouraged by this caution, Blackwood quickly offered to publish the story at once, and paid fifty guineas for it, with a proposal for eventual book publication of the series. The career of George Eliot had begun.

The 'Note' describes how she began writing fiction, but it does not explain why the Rev. Amos Barton, the most unpromising of fictional heroes, was the first fictional character to be summoned up by her imagination. To answer that question, and others raised by the subject matter of *Scenes of Clerical Life* – to unravel its intimate but complex connections with her own experience – it is necessary to put the tales in their historical and biographical context.

Mary Anne Evans was born on 2 November 1819, at South Farm on the estate of Arbury Hall, in the parish of Chilvers Coton, a village near Coventry and Nuneaton in Warwickshire, in the heart of England. Her father Robert Evans was agent to the owner of Arbury Hall, Francis Paget Newdigate, who had inherited it from Sir Roger Newdigate, founder of the celebrated poetry prize at Oxford University.

From 1750 till shortly before his death in 1806, Sir Roger devoted most of his time, energy and income to remodelling his house in the Gothic style, then coming into vogue. Arbury Hall, described with meticulous – perhaps too meticulous – accuracy, is the 'Cheverel Manor' of 'Mr Gilfil's Love Story', the second tale in *Scenes of Clerical Life*. Sir Christopher Cheverel and his wife are closely modelled upon Sir Roger and Lady Newdigate, and Mr Gilfil is thought to be a portrait of the Vicar of Chilvers Coton, the Rev. Bernard Gilpin Ebdell, who baptised Mary Anne Evans, though the character of Caterina, the Italian girl adopted by the Newdigates, with whom Gilfil falls in love, was George Eliot's invention.

The next significant date in Mary Anne's life was 1828, when she went as a boarder to Miss Wallington's school in Nuneaton. One of the teachers there, Maria Lewis, was to be Mary Anne's closest and most influential friend for the next twelve years. Miss Lewis was an earnest young woman who became one of many disciples of a young Evangelical clergyman called John Edmund Jones, who was appointed in that same year Perpetual Curate of the chapel-of-ease at Stockingford, on the outskirts of Nuneaton, and licensed to give a series of Sunday evening lectures at Nuneaton parish church. This innovation gave offence to the more conservative Anglicans in the town, leading to demonstrations and disturbances which provide the background to the third story in *Scenes of Clerical Life*, 'Janet's Repentance', where Jones is represented in the character of Mr Tryan. Although the Church of England is still riven with disagreements between the High (or Anglo-Catholic), Low (or Evangelical) and Broad (or liberal) parties in its communion, the issues that divide them most sharply today are sexual ethics and women priests, rather than the matters of doctrine and devotional practice to which the Victorians attached such great importance. To fully appreciate *Scenes of Clerical Life* it is necessary to have some idea of what Evangelicalism meant in those days.

Because the Church of England emerged, historically, out of a kind of compromise, attempts to reinvigorate it have usually taken the form of emphasising either its Catholic or its Protestant inheritance, and the Evangelical movement was emphatically Protestant in spirit. It arose in the late eighteenth century, largely in response to the development of Methodism, which itself began as a movement for renewal within the Church of England, but became a separate Church. The Evangelical movement had much in common, theologically, with Methodism and other independent or 'dissenting' sects whose members worshipped in chapels rather than churches. It stressed justification by faith, not works, the experience of personal 'conversion', the absolute authority of the Bible, and the priority of preaching over liturgy, and affirmed these principles within the Established Church with considerable success. Until the antithetical, Catholic-oriented Oxford Movement began in the 1830s, led by Keble and Newman, the Evangelical party was the most dynamic in the Church of England, and its influence persisted throughout the century. The qualities that we now think of as most characteristic, for better or worse, of Victorian culture and society were mostly Evangelical in inspiration: earnestness, idealism, and the kind of repressiveness that encourages hypocrisy. The abolition of slavery and much humane factory legislation were typical Evangelical achievements, but it was essentially conservative as a social force. It has been said that the Evangelical movement saved the Church of England from haemorrhaging its middle- and lower-class membership to Methodism, and it must be included in the historian Daniel Halévy's plausible thesis that Methodism saved Britain from revolution in the nineteenth century.

It is not surprising that a gifted, sensitive, middle-class girl, whose plain appearance offered no great temptations to worldliness, growing up in the English midlands at this time, should have come under the influence of Evangelicalism; or that she should have followed, with a precocious child's sharp observation and tenacious memory, the dramatic ministry of the Rev. John Edmund Jones. This clergyman's huge success as a preacher, which caused something of a religious revival in Nuneaton, also provoked envy and hostility from the more traditionalist and materialistic sections of the community, who campaigned aggressively against him under the banner of orthodoxy until his premature death from consumption in 1831. The following year Mary Anne moved to a new school, run by the Miss Franklins in Coventry, where she boarded until 1835. The Franklins being Baptists, there was nothing in the school's ethos to discourage the young girl's piety, and there is evidence that in 1834, around the time of her fifteenth birthday, Marian underwent the experience of 'conversion' – acknowledgement of one's sinfulness, combined with a conviction of one's personal salvation through the imputed merits of Christ's sacrifice – which was central to the faith of Evangelical Anglicans and Dissenters alike.

In 1836, Mary Anne's mother died, and the following year her sister Chrissie married. Mary Anne now became her father's housekeeper, reading voraciously and learning languages in her spare time. It was, as Kathryn Hughes says, 'one of the greatest self-educations of the century'.[5] The resident clergyman at Chilvers Coton at this period was a curate, the Rev. John Gwyther. He was also of the Evangelical persuasion, but lacked the charisma of the Rev. John Edmund Jones.

Indeed he was notorious for his obstinacy and tactlessness, and caused considerable resentment among his parishioners on numerous occasions (by, for instance, substituting Methodist-style hymns for the traditional singing of psalms in church services) and gave some scandal by his association with a newcomer to the parish who styled herself as a 'Countess' and whose alleged father was suspected by many of being her lover. In 1841 Gwyther was rather unfairly ousted from the parish to make room for a relative of the incumbent. Many years later, as a regular subscriber to *Blackwood's*, he was startled to find himself so faithfully portrayed in the story of Amos Barton that his own daughter suspected him of writing it.[6]

Mary Anne's correspondence, mainly with Maria Lewis, which has survived from this period when she was at home looking after her father, is impressive testimony to her intellectual power and industry, but gives a rather forbidding impression of the Evangelical piety, at once severe and slightly unctuous, which could produce such a comment as this, on the art in which she was later to distinguish herself:

> The Scriptural declaration, 'As face answereth to face in a glass, so the heart of man to man', will exonerate me from the charge of uncharitableness or too high an estimation of myself if I venture to believe that the same causes which exist in my own breast to render novels and romances pernicious have their counterpart in that of every fellow-creature.[7]

But not long after that was written, in 1839, there are hints in her correspondence that her sharp intellect was finding that some of the books she was reading, purporting to defend

Christian 'evidences' against rationalist and scientific criticism, raised more problems than they solved. At this period, when most Christians still believed in the literal truth of the Bible, orthodox theologians were mounting a desperate defence against the findings of geological science and the systematic textual and historical study of Scripture, both of which in different ways undermined the authority of the Bible. Evangelicals, who regarded the Bible as the sole and absolute source of religious truth, were particularly vulnerable to demonstrations of its unreliability as a factual record, which perhaps explains the abruptness of Mary Anne Evans's transition from belief to unbelief.

In 1841 she moved with her father to Coventry, where, in November of that year, she made the acquaintance of a progressive intellectual couple, Charles and Caroline Bray, and a close friendship quickly developed. The Brays were Unitarians – just about the most theologically liberal version of Christianity available at the time – but Caroline's brother, Charles Hennell, was the author of a book called *An Inquiry into the Origins of Christianity*, published in 1838, which had shaken her faith in even that diluted system of belief, and she stopped going to church. Hennell's book, as Basil Willey lucidly demonstrated,[8] was remarkable for the extent to which it anticipated or independently confirmed the essential arguments of distinguished German biblical scholars like David Strauss: that the Gospels could not be regarded as the historical depositions of eye-witnesses, but were, like the books of the Old Testament, essentially *mythical* writings, composed some time after the events they purported to report, containing only a small element of historical fact, but expressing authentic spiritual ideas in terms appropriate to the superstitious and relatively unrefined culture from which they originated. It is not entirely clear whether the Brays introduced Mary Anne to Hennell's book, or whether she was already acquainted with it. Caroline Bray later denied that she and her husband were responsible for Mary Anne's loss of faith, claiming that she was as sceptical as themselves when they met. What is certain is that discussing these matters with the Brays, and either reading or rereading Hennell's study in that context, tipped her over the edge between private doubt and public apostasy.

Only two months after meeting the Brays she announced the change in her views by refusing to go to church on the first Sunday of 1842, and was immediately embroiled in a long and painful dispute with her father and other members of the family. Various Evangelical divines were called in to persuade her out of her infidelity, but they were invariably bested in disputation with her. A respected Baptist minister retreated saying, 'That young lady must have the devil at her elbow to suggest her doubts, for there was not a book I recommended to her in support of Christian evidences that she had not read.'9 The stress of the situation naturally threw her more and more into the sympathetic company of the Brays and their circle of progressive – and permissive – friends. Both the Brays had discreet affairs with other partners, and it is possible that Marian's friendship with Charles was more than platonic. It was through them that she was commissioned to translate Strauss's *Life of Jesus*, and met John Chapman, who in due course published it. After her father's death in 1849, Marian, as she now called herself, moved to London. For a while she lodged in John Chapman's house, where the ménage included his mistress as well as his wife, and there is evidence in Chapman's diary that she had a sexual relationship with this incorrigible philanderer. Chapman was an intellectual lightweight who recognised Marian Evans's ability, and when he acquired the *Westminster Review* in 1851 he invited her to become, in effect, his managing editor. One of its contributors, and a member of the progressive, free-thinking, somewhat bohemian circle in which Marian now moved, was George Henry Lewes, a versatile man of letters who had turned his hand to journalism, drama and fiction, and would soon make his reputation with a life of Goethe and popular books on biology. He too led a very unconventional domestic life. His wife had an ongoing relationship with another man by whom she had several children whom Lewes generously adopted. By so doing he was deemed to have condoned her adultery and thus barred himself from seeking a divorce under the laws of the time. When he and Marian Evans fell in love they decided to consider themselves married, and announced the fact by making an extended trip to Germany in the summer of 1854, leaving a buzz of scandalised comment in their wake.

Marian ceased to be editor of the *Westminster Review*, but Chapman continued to publish her essays and reviews in the journal. These writings, published anonymously, as was the custom, have a special interest for the glimpses they afford of George Eliot's thinking about life and art as she prepared herself to attempt fiction. Of particular importance in this context is the concept of realism. One of the earliest recorded uses of this word in an aesthetic sense occurred in George Eliot's review of Ruskin's *Modern Painters*, Volume III, in 1856:

> The truth of infinite value that he teaches is *realism* – the doctrine that all truth and beauty are to be obtained by a

humble and faithful study of nature, and not by substituting vague forms, bred by imagination on the mists of feeling, in place of definite, substantial reality. The thorough acceptance of this doctrine would remould our life . . .[10]

It is worth noting that for George Eliot 'realism' involved not only a positive commitment to the observation of reality, but a negative attitude towards false romanticism, and that it had not merely an aesthetic justification, but a moral one too. She developed these ideas further, shortly afterwards, in a long review article entitled 'The Natural History of German Life', on the work of Wilhelm Heinrich von Riehl, a pioneer in sociology. George Eliot contrasted Riehl's exact, clear-sighted observation of the German peasantry with the false idealisation of literary pastoral: 'We want to be taught to feel, not for the heroic artisan or the sentimental peasant, but for the peasant in all his coarse apathy and the artisan in all his suspicious selfishness.' But note that we are to be taught to *feel*. That is because 'the greatest benefit we owe to the artist, whether painter, poet or novelist, is the extension of our sympathies', because 'Art is the nearest thing to life. It is a mode of amplifying experience and extending our contact with our fellowmen beyond the bounds of our personal lot.'[11] We come, here, upon an idea that persists through George Eliot's letters and novels, which has been called her 'doctrine of sympathy'.[12] It was her substitute for the faith she had lost, and the moral force behind her fiction, from *Scenes of Clerical Life* onwards.

For George Eliot, as for most thoughtful Victorians who lost their faith, the main problem was how the ethical idealism of Christianity might be retained after its supernatural sanctions had been discredited. Liberation from the doctrine of original sin, salvation and damnation was a great relief, but could righteousness survive without a system of eternal rewards and punishments? George Eliot took her stand on the power of love – most forcefully in her essay on the eighteenth-century poet of pious reflection, Edward Young, who confidently declared:

> As in the dying parent dies the child,
> Virtue with Immortality expires.

'The fact is,' George Eliot retorts, turning upon a poet she had revered in early youth, 'I do *not* love myself alone, whatever logical necessity there may be for that in your mind.' She loves her family and friends and 'through that love I sympathise with like affections in other men'.[13]

The essay on Young, begun in 1856 before the composition of 'Amos Barton', and completed after it, was George Eliot's last fling as an explicit critic of Christian orthodoxy. Its confidently secular scorn finds no echo in *Scenes*, or in the novels that followed, for reasons that George Eliot tried to explain to a Swiss friend who, having just read *Adam Bede*, published in 1859, whose heroine is a Methodist preacher, could hardly recognise in its authorial voice the bold free-thinker he had met ten years previously in Geneva:

> When I was in Geneva, I had not yet lost the attitude of antagonism which belongs to the renunciation of *any* belief – also, I was unhappy, and in a state of discord and rebellion towards my own lot. Ten years of experience have wrought great changes in that inward self: I have no longer any antagonism towards any faith in which human sorrow and human longing for purity have expressed themselves

> . . . I have not returned to dogmatic Christianity . . . but I see in it the highest expression of the religious sentiment that has yet found its place in the history of mankind . . . on many points, where I used to delight in expressing intellectual difference, I now delight in feeling an emotional agreement.[14]

In her developing philosophy of life, Christianity was something to be, not rejected, but assimilated into a nobler and more comprehensive humanist faith – a project in which she was encouraged by passages like this in Ludwig Feuerbach's *The Essence of Christianity*, which she first read in 1851, and translated in 1854:

> . . . out of the heart, out of the inward impulse to do good, to live and die for man, out of the divine instinct for benevolence which desires to make all happy, and exclude none, not even the most abandoned and abject, out of the moral duty of benevolence, in the highest sense . . . out of the human nature, therefore, as it reveals itself through the heart, has sprung what is best, what is true in Christianity.[15]

What George Eliot did in her fiction – and this is where her commitment to literary realism came in – was to test Feuerbach's rather vague and abstract assertion against the hard facts of experience, showing how love and sympathy might be cultivated in the most unpromising circumstances and in the teeth of the bitterest discouragement. She chose, for her first attempt, to take as her human material the lives of clergymen, thus making the old faith witness, despite itself, to the validity of the new; or, as Lewes more reassuringly put it when he wrote, under George Eliot's direction, to Blackwood, proposing *Scenes of Clerical Life*:

> It will consist of tales and sketches illustrative of the actual life of our country clergy about a quarter of a century ago; but solely in its *human* and *not at all* in its *theological* aspect . . . representing the clergy like any other class with the humours, sorrows and troubles of other men.[16]

The clearest indication in George Eliot's journalism at this time of what she was aiming to do, and to avoid, in her fiction, came in a long and witty review article in the *Westminster Review* entitled 'Silly Novels by Lady Novelists'. Most of the novels she was reviewing were religious in theme, and she found that:

> As a general rule, the ability of a lady novelist to describe actual life and her fellowmen, is in inverse proportion to her confident eloquence about God and the other world, and the means by which she actually chooses to conduct you to true ideas of the invisible is a totally false picture of the visible.[17]

She noted a contradiction between the spiritual pretensions of the lady novelists and their fascination with the glamour and wealth of the aristocracy – a feature that was particularly incongruous in novels written from an Evangelical point of view. 'The real drama of Evangelicalism – and it has abundance of fine drama for anyone who has genius enough to discern and reproduce it – lies among the middle and lower classes', she declared, blowing a trumpet, under cover of journalistic anonymity, to herald her own fictional endeavours.[18]

George Eliot finished writing 'Silly Novels' on 12 September 1856. Eleven days later she began writing 'The Sad Fortunes of Amos Barton'.

In many respects 'Amos Barton' was the most original (though not of course the greatest) work of fiction George Eliot ever wrote. In no other novel or story did she carry out so uncompromisingly her own programme of making the commonplace and unglamorous figure the centre of attention, or allow her narrative such freedom to follow its own inner logic, assuming a shape that seems given by experience rather than dictated by art or moral purpose. In 'Mr Gilfil's Love Story', 'Janet's Repentance', and still more obviously in the novels that followed, George Eliot grew in eloquence, wisdom, social vision and psychological penetration, but at the same time she tended, in the interest of thematic explicitness, to idealise her heroes and heroines, and to moralise her narratives into patterns of reward and retribution through the construction of a complex and sometimes contrived 'plot'. Her namesake, T. S. Eliot, overstated the matter when he wrote to a friend in 1918, 'George Eliot had a great talent, and wrote one great story, *Amos Barton*, and went steadily down hill afterwards.'[19] But paradoxically the longer she went on writing, the more 'Victorian' a novelist George Eliot seemed to become; while her first story has about it a naturalness, a clean economy of line, a confidence in the significance of the quotidian, which anticipate the early modern masters of the short story, like Maupassant, Chekhov, or the Joyce of *Dubliners*, and it was these qualities to which T. S. Eliot responded. It was probably because she was conscious of not producing what was generally expected of a 'story' in her day, that she called her earliest attempts in fiction at first 'Sketches', and then 'Scenes', and insisted on 'Amos Barton' appearing in *Blackwood's* under the general title of *Scenes of Clerical Life* even though the future of the series was at that point uncertain.[20]

It is true that the character of Amos's wife, Milly, is very much a Victorian 'Angel in the House', somewhat idealised by the narrator, but this is not allowed to falsify her speech or behaviour, and her death, although as an action it can be paralleled a hundred times in Victorian fiction, achieves a rare pathos by the restraint and sensitivity with which it is treated. Particularly effective is the description of the younger children's naïve, uncomprehending response. 'They cried because mamma was so ill and papa looked so unhappy; but they thought, perhaps next week things would be as they used to be again.' And at the funeral, as the officiating minister, Mr Cleves, pronounces the final prayers at the graveside, 'Dicky stood close to his father, with great rosy cheeks, and wide open blue eyes, looking first up at Mr Cleves and then down at the coffin, and thinking he and Chubby would play at that when they got home.' These touches are not put in just to wring our hearts; they show that death is more bitter and more meaningful to the adult mind which comprehends its finality, but at the same time they give a sense of life going on, lifting the oppression of the sad occasion. Unlike his children, Amos cannot express and control his grief through play. When he returns to the bleak, empty vicarage (one of those recurrent interior settings in George Eliot's fiction which Barbara Hardy has aptly categorised as 'the disenchanted daylit room')[21] he feels nothing but the sense of loss and the sense of regret:

. . . now she was gone; the broad, snow-reflected daylight
was in all the rooms; the Vicarage again seemed part of the
common working-day world, and Amos, for the first time,
felt that he was alone . . . she was gone from him; and he
could never show her his love any more, never make up for
omissions in the past by filling future days with tenderness.

'Perhaps I am doing a bold thing to bespeak your sympathy on behalf of a man who was so very far from remarkable,' says the narrator early in the tale, 'a man who was . . .
palpably and unmistakably commonplace.' Amos Barton is
indeed a man hard to like, and easy to ridicule. Like the Fat
Lady in J. D. Salinger's *Franny and Zooey*, he is the acid test of
love. 'It is only the largest souls who will be able to appreciate and pity him – who will discern and love sincerity of
purpose amid all the bungling feebleness of achievement.' The
only such soul in the world of the story is the liberal-minded
clergyman Mr Cleves. The other members of the community,
in varying degrees, mock, despise, slander and exploit Amos,
until his suffering shocks them into fellowship and sympathy,
a process that is likely also to be enacted in the reader's
response. Thus the story's structure – vignettes of Amos's life,
alternating with the choric comments of his parishioners and
other acquaintance – and the gradual modulation of its tone
from ironic humour to pathos, are perfectly adjusted to its
theme.

Every new writer, however 'original', is inevitably influenced
by his or her precursors, and George Eliot was no exception.
In her first story we can discern an indebtedness to the two,
very different, novelists she loved best: Jane Austen and Walter
Scott. From Jane Austen she surely learned the art of exposing, without explicit emphasis, the selfishness and insincerity

of a character like the Countess Czerlaski, who battens on the
indigent Bartons, and the ability to hit off a minor character
with a few well-chosen words – the old widow Mrs Patten, for
instance, who:

> . . . used to adore her husband, and now she adores her
> money, cherishing a quiet blood-relation's hatred for her
> niece Janet Gibbs, who, she knows, expects a large legacy,
> and whom she is determined to disappoint.

From Scott, George Eliot probably derived the technique of
playing off various social strata against one another, contrasting earthy dialect speech with the language of the gentry and
professional classes, and also the tone of her authorial voice,
genial, reminiscent and a little ponderous. If the narrator's
knowing high-cultural allusions, and efforts to wring humour
out of elaborate circumlocution, seem at times excessive, it
must be remembered that George Eliot was consciously affecting a male persona – and very successfully: Blackwood, and
most of her other early readers, were completely taken in.

Just as Scott, adopting the stance of an enlightened modern
looking back upon a picturesque but fanatical past, achieved
an objectivity which he could scarcely have brought to bear
on the political issues of his own day, so George Eliot used
the reminiscent narrator as a means of taking the theological heat out of her treatment of Evangelicalism. 'Amos Barton'
begins with an evocation of Shepperton as it was well before
that zealous but tactless pastor appeared on the scene, and
the narrator seeks to draw his audience into a wistful nostalgia for the good old days when religion was a social bond
rather than the cause of controversy and dissension. In this
way George Eliot establishes a position within the story from

which she can distinguish between Amos's doctrines and his ministry, gently satirise the former without appearing to discredit religion itself, and convey to a largely Christian audience an essentially humanist set of values. It is very subtly done, and one scarcely notices that the bereaved clergyman is never observed to pray or to derive any consolation from his belief in an afterlife. 'No outward solace could counteract the bitterness of [his] inward woe. But outward solace came', says the narrator, neatly sidestepping the possibility of inward solace. 'Cold faces looked kind again, and parishioners turned over in their minds what they could best do to help their pastor.'

At the heart of the story is a paradox, passed off as a joke in Chapter 5, at the time of Milly's first illness: 'as matters stood in Shepperton, the parishioners were more likely to have a strong sense that the clergyman needed their material aid, than that they needed his spiritual aid.' The primary source of Barton's troubles is economic: his stipend of eighty pounds a year is simply not enough to support his wife and family. The size of the family – six children, of whom the oldest is nine – is of course also a factor. Frequent childbearing, combined with the stress of trying to run a household with inadequate means, is what breaks Milly's health. George Eliot makes the point through Mrs Hackit's prophetic remark, when Milly becomes pregnant again, 'That poor thing's dreadful weak and delicate; she won't stan' havin' many more children.' We know that George Eliot and Lewes, having made a decision not to have children, used some form of birth-control,[22] but that was something neither the Bartons nor the readers of Blackwood's could have contemplated. So the overt cause of Amos's sad fortunes is his genteel poverty, which is exacerbated when the Countess becomes his uninvited guest. Not only does she add to the expenses of the household without contributing to them, but the scandal she creates further alienates the parishioners from their pastor. Only when the Countess is sent packing through the intervention of the household's loyal maid-of-all-work, and Milly herself becomes fatally ill, does the community rally round the stricken family with material and practical help. A more typical Victorian tale would end on this upbeat note, of good coming out of evil in the new solidarity between pastor and people, but George Eliot avoids this easy resolution by having poor Amos unfairly removed from the parish just as he is beginning to recover from his bereavement, and obliged to accept a curacy in a grim-sounding distant industrial town. 'It was another blow inflicted on the bruised man.' The prophet Amos gave his name to one of the books of the Old Testament. George Eliot's Amos, as the title of her story suggests, is more like Job, but a modern, demythologised Job, denied the biblical patriarch's sublime patience and divine reward. Blackwood said, 'the conclusion is the lamest part of the story'.[23] He was wrong. It was the boldest and most original part of the story.

Blackwood published the first part of 'Amos Barton' in the January 1857 number of his magazine, and George Eliot was able to supply him with instalments of the other two stories promptly enough to maintain unbroken continuity throughout the year. The publisher did not know the identity of his new author during this period, or her sex. He was obliged to communicate with her via Lewes, who pretended the writer of the Scenes was a rather shy male friend who wished to hide behind a nom de plume. As Kathryn Hughes observes, there were several motives for the adoption of a pseudonym. *Blackwood's* was a family magazine of conservative values, and Lewes knew that the publisher would hesitate to run the work of a woman notorious in metropolitan circles for living openly with a married man. (Indeed there is evidence that Blackwood, after correctly guessing the identity of 'George Eliot', preferred to be kept officially in ignorance for this reason, and played along with the deception.) Another reason was that if George Eliot failed as a writer of fiction, Marian Evans's reputation as a journalist and writer of serious non-fiction would not be damaged. Several women writers – most famously the Brontë sisters – had adopted male pen names in the hope of getting a more respectful reception, but it is unlikely that this consideration weighed strongly in the case of George Eliot. A masculine pseudonym made a better disguise than a female one, and it had a functional appropriateness to the subject matter of *Scenes*. She explained late in life that the name was chosen because 'George was Mr Lewes's Christian name, and Eliot was a good, mouth-filling word'.[34]

John Blackwood, the son of the original founder of the magazine, was a shrewd and efficient editor, with an intuitive feeling for literary quality tempered by a businessman's caution and a certain conventionality of taste. His mild criticisms of the work George Eliot submitted to him elicited some characteristic and revealing defences of her artistic aims and methods, which Blackwood invariably accepted with good grace. In the first episode of 'Mr Gilfil's Love Story', the heir to Cheverel Manor, Wybrow, is shown trifling with the affections of Caterina, the young Italian girl adopted by Sir Christopher and Lady Cheverel, and loved by the young clergyman Mr Gilfil. Blackwood commented:

> It is not a pleasant picture to see a good fellow loving on
> when the lady's heart is *openly* devoted to a Jackanapes . . .
> I think the objection would be readily met by making
> Caterina a little less openly devoted to Wybrow and giving
> a little more dignity to her character.

George Eliot sternly replied:

> My artistic bent is directed not at all to the presentation
> of eminently respectable characters, but to the presentation
> of mixed human beings in such a way as to call forth toler-
> ant judgment, pity and sympathy. And I cannot stir a step
> aside from what I feel to be *true* in character.[25]

Blackwood's suggestion that it would be more decorous if, at
the climax of the story, Caterina dreamed of stabbing Wybrow
instead of actually intending to do so, met with the sharp and
absolutely typical retort, 'it would be the death of my story
to substitute a dream for the real scene. Dreams usually play
an important part in fiction, but rarely, I think, in actual life.'[26]

Even without Blackwood's suggested emendations, 'Mr
Gilfil's Love Story' seems a little insipid after its predecessor.
The opening evocation of Mr Gilfil in his later years, as a
crusty old clergyman whom none of his parishioners would
suspect of having had a tragic romantic experience in early
life, is well done in the style of 'Amos Barton', but the focus
of the retrospective narrative that follows is not on Mr Gilfil
at all, but on Caterina, a character who all too obviously
derives from 'fiction' rather than 'actual life'. This is evident
from the narrator's over-anxious appeals to the reader to
appreciate the intensity of the heroine's emotions:

> See how she rushes noiselessly, like a pale meteor, along the passages and up the gallery stairs! Those gleaming eyes, those bloodless lips, that swift silent tread, make her look like the incarnation of a fierce purpose, rather than a woman.

Altogether 'Mr Gilfil's Love Story', though it has considerable charm as a period piece, was a regression from 'Amos Barton' in terms of fictional technique. Thought is often represented in long, rather theatrical soliloquies, and there is an over-reliance on the pathetic fallacy in descriptions of the weather. An elaborate strand of animal imagery applied to Caterina foreshadows George Eliot's later and more subtle use of metaphorical symbolism in the depiction of character. Sir Christopher's pet-names for her – 'singing-bird' and 'little monkey' – are frequently repeated and taken up by the other characters and by the narrator, and she is on occasion compared to a marmoset, a kitten, a frog, a stock-dove, a puppy, a linnet, a Blenheim spaniel, a grasshopper and a mouse, expressing a wide range of attitudes towards the girl: that she is appealing, vulnerable, attractive in an unconventional way, somewhat wild and untamed, slightly odd and out of place, foreign, of low birth. These images make her into an object, something less than human, a pet. Wybrow, trying to allay his fiancée's jealous suspicions, makes this explicit. 'She has always been the pet of the house,' he says; and a little later, 'One thinks of her as a little girl to be petted and played with' – a telling betrayal of his essentially narcissistic and exploitative character. Sir Christopher, too, is guilty in a lesser degree, as he himself finally acknowledges, of stereotyping her as a kind of pet, and failing to perceive the intensity of her emotional life. Unfortunately the moral implications of this imagistic pattern are blurred by the fact that the nominal hero, Mr Gilfil, is himself associated with it. We are told that he became fond of Caterina in childhood because he 'was an affectionate lad, who retained a propensity to white rabbits, pet squirrels, and guinea-pigs, perhaps a little beyond the age at which young gentlemen usually look down on such pleasures as puerile'. Possibly George Eliot had not fully worked out her own attitude to her pretty but rather empty-headed heroine, a type for which she never had much real sympathy.

The eponymous heroine of 'Janet's Repentance' is more rooted in observed reality than Caterina, but the strengths of this story, which contains some of the finest writing in *Scenes*, are again in the framing and general composition of the picture rather than in the treatment of its central subject. Janet is the abused wife of the bullying, hard-drinking lawyer Dempster, leading opponent of the charismatic Evangelical clergyman Mr Tryan in the town of Milby. She seeks escape from her miserable existence in drink, which causes her to be shunned in the community; but in the depths of despair she turns for help to the target of her husband's hatred, and Tryan, by sharing with her his own personal experience of sin and redemption, restores her faith in religion and herself. There is a suggestion of romantic attraction between the two, but although Dempster's accidental death sets Janet free, Tryan dies not long afterwards from consumption, leaving her to seek fulfilment, like him, in serving others. George Eliot's gifts are most evident in her evocation of the social background against which the drama of Janet's repentance is played out. The first three chapters of the tale are superb: the bar-room bluster of Dempster and his cronies at the Red Lion in the first, contrasted with the more genteel but competitive chat of the gathering of ladies, all admirers and disciples of Tryan, who are assembling a library of religious books in the third, separated by the narrator's subtly ironic but scrupu- lously realistic account of Milby and its inhabitants (closely based on Nuneaton) in the second chapter. As Lewes observed in a letter to Blackwood, 'One feels the want of a larger canvas so as to bring out these admirable characters, Old Mr Jerome, – the Linnets – and the rest',[27] and one can indeed see that George Eliot was now poised on the brink of her career as a novelist. Perhaps she was rationalising an instinctive eager- ness to tackle the expansive form of the full-length Victorian novel when she said she would write no more 'Scenes' because she was disappointed by Blackwood's want of sympathy for the first two parts of 'Janet's Repentance'.

Blackwood was certainly disconcerted by the uninviting setting of the story, nervous about the treatment of the reli- gious parties there, and not too happy at having an alcoholic as a heroine. George Eliot made a few revisions of her text in response, but defended herself in characteristic style:

> There is nothing to be done with the story, but either to let Dempster and Janet and the rest be as *I* see them, or to renounce it as too painful . . . Art must be either real and concrete, or ideal and eclectic. Both are good and true in their way, but my stories are of the former kind. I under- take to exhibit nothing as it should be; I only try to exhibit some things as they have been or are, seen through such a medium as my own nature gives me. The moral effect of the stories of course depends on my power of seeing truly and feeling justly . . .[28]

As U. C. Knoepflmacher has observed,[29] there is a certain ambiguity at the heart of George Eliot's aesthetic, as to whether her power of seeing truly and feeling justly was enough to guarantee the moral effect of her stories without the help of an element of idealisation. Her reply to Blackwood's first letter about this story is revealing:

> Everything is softened from the fact, so far as art is permitted to soften and yet remain essentially true. The real town was more vicious than my Milby; the real Dempster was more disgusting than mine; the real Janet, alas! had a far sadder end than mine, who will melt away from the reader's sight in purity, happiness and beauty.[30]

In the same letter George Eliot emphasised that she was not taking up a partisan stance on the religious issue: 'The collision in the drama is not at all between "bigoted churchmanship" and evangelicalism, but between irreligion and religion. Religion in this case happens to be represented by evangelicalism.'[31] And religion, one might add, is deeply coloured by George Eliot's own 'doctrine of sympathy'. Tryan understands that 'the first thing Janet needed was to be assured of sympathy . . . The tale of the Divine Pity was never yet to be believed from lips that were not felt to be moved by human pity.' Without going as far as Feuerbach, who advocated translating the entire language of Christianity into secular, humanist terms, George Eliot manages to suggest that Mr Tryan's Evangelical doctrine is accidental to the real value and efficacy of his ministry, showing us that he is admired by characters like Mrs Raynor and Old Mr Jerome, whose Christianity is simple, tolerant and pragmatic. Nevertheless 'Janet's Repentance' is closer in spirit to Evangelical Christianity than anything George Eliot had written since the trauma of her loss of faith, and in it she finally made peace with the religion of her childhood and youth. She even compromised with her disbelief in personal immortality to the extent of allowing her hero and heroine a 'sacred kiss of promise' on his deathbed.

George Eliot's contemporaries immediately recognised the distinction and originality of *Scenes of Clerical Life*. Blackwood knew he was on to a good thing, and sent back to his new author encouraging reports of reader reactions. 'I could not explain the exact symptoms of popularity,' he wrote to her about the reception of 'Amos Barton', 'but to me they are literally unmistakeable.' Thackeray was reported to be impressed, Mrs Gaskell was flattered to be suspected of being the author, and Dickens, to whom George Eliot sent a copy of *Scenes* when it was published as a book in 1858, wrote to her.

> I have been so strongly affected by the first two tales in the book you have had the kindness to send me through Messrs Blackwood that I hope you will excuse my writing to you to express my admiration of their extraordinary merit. The exquisite truth and delicacy, both of the humour and the pathos of these stories, I have never seen the like of; and they have impressed me in a manner that I should find very difficult to describe to you, if I had the impertinence to try.[32]

No writer of the period could have asked for a more encouraging response to her first book.

There was inevitably keen speculation in the literary world

as to the identity of 'George Eliot'. Dickens shrewdly guessed that the writer was a woman, though Jane Carlyle supposed that George Eliot must have 'a wife from whom he has got those beautiful *feminine* touches in his book'.[33] Lewes and Marian revealed to John Blackwood the truth which he had long suspected in February 1858, shortly after *Scenes* was published as a book, and gave him the first thirteen chapters of her next work of fiction, *Adam Bede*. He scanned the first page of the manuscript, said with a smile, 'This will do,' and read as much as he could on the train back to Edinburgh, reporting that he felt 'very savage when the waning light stopped me as we neared the Scottish border'.[34] He was anxious, for the same reasons as before, that George Eliot's identity should not become public knowledge and jeopardise the reception of *Adam Bede*, but soon after that novel was published in February 1859 events compelled her to admit her authorship.

Not surprisingly, speculation about the author of *Scenes of Clerical Life* had been particularly intense in and around Nuneaton, since the tales were so closely based on real persons and places. As a beginner in the art of fiction, Marian Evans did not perhaps appreciate the advisability of disguising her source material, or perhaps she thought the fact that she was writing about events twenty-five years or more in the past made it unnecessary to do so – in which case she reckoned without the retentiveness of local memory. The story of 'Janet's Repentance' in particular was read as a *roman-à-clef*, though not intended as such, and 'keys' to the story began to circulate in Nuneaton shortly after it was serialised. It was obvious that the author must be of local origin, and in May 1858, a candidate was named publicly: a down-at-heel Nuneaton resident called Joseph Liggins, a baker's son who had been educated at Cambridge University and was subsequently disappointed in his hopes of a career in the Church. It is not clear whether Liggins instigated this rumour, or merely failed to deny it for his own advantage. At first the report gave more amusement than concern to George Eliot and her publisher, who saw it as a useful distraction of public attention from the truth. But a year later, when 'George Eliot' had become famous as the author of the hugely successful *Adam Bede*, the Liggins affair took a more serious turn. In April 1859 a group of Warwickshire gentlemen set up a subscription for Liggins, maintaining that he had been defrauded of his rightful earnings. George Eliot wrote an indignant letter to *The Times* under her pen name denouncing Liggins as an imposter, but the campaign, or hoax, persisted. In May work by George Eliot written out in Liggins's hand was circulating in Warwickshire, and soon a London gossip columnist, who obviously knew who the novelist was, accused her of encouraging the Liggins story for her own purposes. In July she agreed with Blackwood that she would no longer conceal the identity of George Eliot. But she retained the pen name for the rest of her career: it pleased her to preserve a distinction between her public persona as a novelist and her private life.

It was *Adam Bede*, originally conceived as another 'Scene', which made George Eliot's fame and fortune, selling well over ten thousand copies in the first year of publication, compared to the thousand copies sold of its predecessor, and being translated into many languages. In the opinion of her biographer, Gordon Haight, 'No book had made such an impression since *Uncle Tom's Cabin* swept the world', and he quotes the magisterial judgement of the reviewer in *The Times*: 'It is a first-rate novel, and its author takes rank at once among the masters of the art.'[35] But that author could not have achieved such a triumph without the apprenticeship of writing *Scenes of Clerical Life*, and George Eliot herself always had a special fondness for her first attempt at fiction. In 1860, with the enormous success of *Adam Bede* behind her, and *The Mill on the Floss* approaching completion, she wrote to Blackwood, urging that *Scenes* should be kept in print and

> have every chance of impressing the public with its existence, first because I think it of importance to the estimate of me as a writer that 'Adam Bede' should not be counted as my only book; and secondly, because there are ideas presented in these stories about which I care a good deal, and I am not sure that I can ever embody again.[36]

Notes

1 *Dublin Review*, 21 (1846), p. 261.

2 'Evangelical Teaching: Dr Cumming', *Westminster Review*, 64 (1855), p. 464. Goshen was the area of Egypt allocated to the exiled Israelites by the Pharaoh, as recorded in Genesis.

3 Virginia Woolf, 'George Eliot', in *The Common Reader* (1925).

4 *The George Eliot Letters*, ed. Gordon S. Haight (1954–6), Vol. II, p. 407.

5 Kathryn Hughes, *George Eliot: The Last Victorian* (1998), p. 44.

6 Gordon S. Haight, *George Eliot: A Biography* (1968), pp. 285–6; Hughes, *George Eliot*, pp. 252–3.

7 *The George Eliot Letters*, ed. Haight, Vol. I, p. 22.

8 Basil Willey, *Nineteenth Century Studies* (1949), Chapter 8.

9 Hughes, *George Eliot*, p. 75.

10 Quoted by Haight, *George Eliot*, pp. 183–4.

11 *Essays of George Eliot*, ed. Thomas Pinney (1968), pp. 170–1.

12 Thomas A. Noble, *George Eliot's 'Scenes of Clerical Life'* (1965), pp. 55ff.

13 *Essays of George Eliot*, ed. Pinney, pp. 373–4.

14 *Letters*, ed. Haight, Vol. II, pp. 230–1.

15 Quoted by Derek and Sybil Oldfield in *Critical Essays on George Eliot*, ed. Barbara Hardy (1970), p. 3.

16 *Letters*, ed. Haight, Vol. II, p. 269.

17 *Essays*, ed. Pinney, p. 311.

18 Ibid., p. 318.

19 *The Letters of T. S. Eliot*, ed. Valerie Eliot (1988), p. 227.

20 *Letters*, Vol. II, p. 277.

21 Barbara Hardy, *The Novels of George Eliot* (1964), p. 190.

22 Haight, *George Eliot*, p. 205.

23 Hughes, *George Eliot*, p. 257.

24 Ibid., p. 262.

25 *Letters*, Vol. II, pp. 297–9.

26 Ibid., pp. 308–9.

27 Ibid., p. 378.

28 Ibid., pp. 348 and 362.

29 U. C. Knoepflmacher, *George Eliot's Early Novels: The Limits of Realism* (1968), p. 24ff.

30 *Letters*, Vol. II, p. 347.

31 Ibid.

32 Ibid., p. 423.

33 Hughes, *George Eliot*, p. 267.

34 Ibid., p. 273.

35 Haight, *George Eliot*, p. 279.

36 *Letters*, Vol. II, p. 240.

GRAHAM GREENE AND THE ANXIETY OF INFLUENCE

It is of course impossible to write anything without being influenced. Nobody ever wrote a novel or a poem or an essay without having read at least one and more probably hundreds of such works by others. Most creative writers were voracious readers in their childhood and youth, and most began themselves by imitating and emulating, consciously or unconsciously, the writers they admired. Literary influence is therefore inevitable. But attitudes to this phenomenon changed significantly over the last two or three centuries. In earlier times writers felt no hesitation or uneasiness about borrowing stories and rhetorical devices from their predecessors. Classical and medieval literature endlessly recycled well-known myths and legends. In neo-classical literature the explicit 'imitation' of precursors, adapting an ancient model to contemporary themes, was seen as not merely an apprentice exercise but as a prestigious and genuinely creative kind of writing. But in the modern era there is a new emphasis on 'originality' as an absolute value in literature. The privileging of individual consciousness in post-Renaissance culture, which can already be seen in the soliloquies of Shakespeare's plays and was further developed in the rise of the novel in the eighteenth century, combined with the Romantic view of writing as essentially *self*-expression, caused literary influence to be seen as something potentially threatening as well as inspiring – something you must struggle against when it threatens your claim to originality. The American critic Harold Bloom coined the phrase 'the anxiety of influence', in a book of that title published in 1973, to signify this ambivalent attitude of the modern writer towards his precursors. He observes that the use of the word 'influence' as a literary critical term actually begins in the nineteenth century.[1] Influence was so taken for granted as a component of writing in previous ages that they didn't need a word for it.

Harold Bloom is a brilliant but somewhat idiosyncratic critic, who employs an esoteric jargon of his own, and makes few concessions to his readers by way of explanation. I am not going to discuss his theory in detail, but rather to take from it some hints and ideas which seem to throw light on Graham Greene's development as a writer, and his use of precursor writers. Bloom is almost exclusively concerned with poets and poetry, especially with what he calls 'strong' poets – in other words, major poets who make, or aspire to make, a fundamentally original contribution to the poetic tradition. There are relatively few such poets at any one time; they tend to know who they are themselves, and to be recognised fairly quickly by their peers. Bloom sees poetry in the modern period being carried forward by the struggle of such poets to absorb and assimilate the achievement of their great predecessors, while themselves producing something that is different but equally great, and according to Bloom this involves a *misreading* of their strong precursors. Here is a crucial passage in his book:

> Poetic influence – when it involves two strong, authentic poets – always proceeds by a misreading of the prior poet, an act of creative correction that is actually and necessarily a misinterpretation. The history of fruitful poetic influence, which is to say the main tradition of Western poetry since the Renaissance, is a history of anxiety and self-saving caricature, of distortion, of perverse, wilful revisionism, without which modern poetry as such could not exist.[2]

Another closely related Bloomian jargon term is 'misprision'. He doesn't explain what he means by it, but the dictionary offers two definitions: (1) contempt (archaic) and (2) failure to appreciate the value of something. In other words, creative misreading often involves depreciation of the precursor. An example of such poetic revisionism – though Bloom doesn't I think mention it in his book, which has no index – would be T. S. Eliot's reading of Milton and post-Miltonic English poetry as flawed by 'a dissociation of sensibility' which it was the mission of modern poets like himself to repair.[3] Poetic revisionism doesn't always find such explicit articulation – indeed, it is more often a private inner struggle of the poet, manifested publicly only in his work – but when the writer is also a critic it is easier to trace the anxiety of influence. Graham Greene wrote criticism, if more occasionally and less systematically than Eliot, and he left some valuable clues to his literary influences, and the way he assimilated them, in his essays, especially those first collected under the title *The Lost Childhood* (1951).

The modern novelist is in a way even more vulnerable to the anxiety of influence than the modern poet. Most modern poetry is lyric, the expression of the poet's own thoughts and experiences; and since every individual is unique, with a unique personal history, the poet can be confident of achieving a measure of originality through self-expression. But the novelist works in narrative; he undertakes to tell a story involving more than one person, and a story that is new every time. The novelist character Helen Reed in my novel *Thinks...* reflects on the effort this entails:

> Before the rise of the novel there wasn't the same obligation on the storyteller – you could relate the old familiar tales over and over, the matter of Troy, the matter of Rome, the matter of Britain . . . giving them a new spin as times and manners changed. But for the last three centuries writers have been required to make up a new story *every time*. Not absolutely new, of course – it's been pointed out often enough that at a certain level there are only a finite number of plots – but the plot must be fleshed out each time with a new set of characters, and worked out in a new set of circumstances.[4]

Furthermore the novel was a totally new kind of writing in the history of literature – an anti-generic genre. Unlike the classical genres of epic, tragedy, comedy, pastoral, etc., the novel has no rules except those that it chooses to borrow eclectically from those traditional forms. The novel evolved and continues to evolve by perpetually breaking its own rules and deviating from its own conventions – *Tristram Shandy*, written very early in the novel's history, is in that sense an exemplary text. Popular fiction, of course, is shamelessly formulaic and imitative, but for novelists of any literary ambition the pressure to be original in form and content is intense – hence their anxiety of, or about, influence.

But not all influences arouse anxiety. A writer will acknowledge some kinds of influence quite happily when no real competition with the precursor is involved – for example, the effect of books encountered in childhood and adolescence. Graham Greene was particularly interested in this kind of influence, which he believed was important for everybody, not just for future writers. He says in *A Sort of Life*: 'The influence of early books is profound. So much of the future lies on the shelves: early reading has more influence on conduct than any religious teaching.'[5] The title essay of *The Lost Childhood*, which he wrote in 1947, is all about his own early reading of adventure fiction: authors like Rider Haggard, Percy Westerman, Stanley Weyman, Anthony Hope. Elsewhere he recalls the time when he devoured the imperialistic and historical yarns of Henty, of which there was a whole shelf-full in the nursery at home. He was also drawn to the tales of his distinguished cousin, Robert Louis Stevenson. As a schoolboy he was a great fan of John Buchan, and as an undergraduate at Oxford rather cheekily invited the famous writer to contribute to *Oxford Outlook* when he became editor of that magazine. The relevance to Greene's mature work of all this saturation in adventure fiction at an impressionable age is obvious. What he did in his novels was to combine the structures and conventions of adventure fiction

– for example, the story of a pursuit or quest, often in an exotic setting, involving situations of constant jeopardy for the protagonist – with a focus on adult moral and spiritual conflicts and dilemmas not usually associated with such fiction. He also inverted the stereotypical hero of the adventure novels – the chivalrous, courageous, resourceful, clean-cut, upper-class Englishman, like Haggard's Allan Quatermain and Henry Curtis in *King Solomon's Mines*, or Hope's Rudolf Rassendyll in *The Prisoner of Zenda* – putting at the centre of his stories characters who were weak, sinful, guilt-ridden, and self-loathing: the hit-man Raven in *A Gun For Sale*, Pinkie in *Brighton Rock*, the whisky priest in *The Power and the Glory*, Scobie in *The Heart of the Matter*.

In his essay 'The Lost Childhood' Greene attributes his first realisation that he wanted to become a writer to the experience of reading, when he was about fourteen, Marjorie Bowen's *The Viper of Milan* (1906), a novel set in the late medieval period in Italy. It appealed to him because Bowen turned the conventions of the historical adventure story in the direction of a much darker and more pessimistic vision of life than usual, one that answered to his own unhappiness and despair at the time, a schoolboy who was persecuted and distrusted by his peers as the headmaster's son:

> It was no good in that real world to dream that one would ever be a Sir Henry Curtis, but della Scala who at last turned from an honesty that never paid and betrayed his friends and died dishonoured and a failure even at treachery – it was easier for a child to escape behind his mask. As for Visconti, with his beauty, his patience, and his genius for evil, I had

watched him pass by many a time in his black Sunday suit
smelling of mothballs. His name was Carter . . . Goodness
has only once found a perfect incarnation in a human body
and never will again, but evil can always find a home there.
Human nature is not black and white but black and grey. I
read all that in *The Viper of Milan* and I saw that it was so.

It was the thrill of reading this novel, Greene says, that started
him on his vocation as a writer, filling exercise books with
imitations 'marked with enormous brutality and a despairing
romanticism'. In adult life he never attempted to write a novel
set in the same period (he went no further back in time than
the early nineteenth century, in two early novels), but one can
see how *The Viper of Milan* formed a kind of bridge in his
literary formation between the ripping yarns of Henty,
Haggard and Hope, and the moral or metaphysical thrillers
with contemporary settings which he went on to write
himself. The diabolical Visconti is, like Greene's later anti-
heroes, a negative image of the endlessly resourceful hero of
adventure stories who survives all the perils he encounters –
with this important difference: that Greene solicits sympathy
for his characters because they are failures, whereas Visconti
is flawlessly evil. He frequently seems about to be defeated in
the course of the story, but always manages to wriggle out
of a tight corner by committing some new act of infamy. Only
on the penultimate page does he get the quittance he deserves,
and it is described in a brief, almost throwaway fashion, when
the hero of the tale is already dead, 'dishonoured and a failure even at treachery', as Greene says. Actually that is not
quite accurate: della Scala is a failure at revenge rather than
treachery. Della Scala betrays his cause in order to ransom his
beloved wife, a forgivable motive which Greene does not

mention. Visconti cheats on the deal by sending back the Duchess dead from poison, and the enraged Duke just fails to kill Visconti in revenge. Greene misrepresents *The Viper of Milan*, reading back into his memories of Marjorie Bowen's novel his own obsession as a novelist with the theme of betrayal, which derived from traumatic experiences at school.

There are formal features of *The Viper of Milan* which may have influenced Greene's fictional technique. For instance, Marjorie Bowen cuts from scene to scene in an almost cinematic fashion, briefly summarising the events which connect them, and the scenes are usually dramatic rather than performative – that is, they present the characters discussing their hopes, fears and dilemmas, or confronting each other over some issue of strategy or honour. The fights and battles which are described in great detail in conventional adventure stories like Haggard's *She* or Hope's *The Prisoner of Zenda*, and which were the main source of interest and excitement for their readers, are just briefly reported or alluded to in *The Viper of Milan*. This displacement of emphasis from action to motive in stories of adventure was also characteristic of the novels and tales of Joseph Conrad, who later exerted considerable influence on Greene – but one that, unlike Marjorie Bowen's, created considerable anxiety in him, because, in Bloomian language, Conrad was a 'strong' novelist of the preceding generation against whom the young Greene had to measure himself.

The essays in *The Lost Childhood* are not arranged in chronological order, but they are dated, and the earlier ones, written in the 1930s, reveal a writer very conscious of where he is situated in the history of the English literary novel, struggling to assimilate the lessons of his admired precursors without being excessively influenced by them. Harold Bloom has a word for the generalised anxiety most young writers experience: 'belatedness', the feeling that it is impossible to surpass or improve on the achievements of one's great predecessors. Greene's generation felt belated in life as well as literature: they were born just too late to fight in the Great War, and although that war seemed more and more, in historical perspective, a shocking and futile waste of human life which they had been fortunate to escape, nevertheless they felt a kind of guilt, an obscure sense of failure, at having missed the great test of manhood, a feeling perhaps engendered at an almost unconscious level by the imperialist ethos of the juvenile fiction they read in childhood, and often reinforced by a public school education. It was a feeling which many of them, including Greene, sought to expiate or dispel by adventurous travel and exploration in adulthood. In literary terms these writers were very conscious of coming immediately after a period, extending roughly from 1890 to 1930, of great innovation and experiment in fiction and poetry, to which we now usually give the name of Modernism. This was what Greene, in a 1939 essay on Ford Madox Ford, called 'the heroic age of English fiction'. James, Conrad, Joyce, Lawrence, Virginia Woolf, and Ford himself – how was a young writer to compete with them? The answer, of course, was not to try to excel in the same kind of fiction, and Greene's generation, which included writers like Evelyn Waugh, Anthony Powell, Christopher Isherwood and George Orwell, accordingly followed a quite different path from the great modernists, eschewing formal experiment, mythological allusion, poetic symbolism, the stream of consciousness, and emphasising story, dialogue, and the comic or realistic evocation of the contemporary public world, often with a political slant. But they never entirely escaped the sense of belatedness. Evelyn Waugh, for instance, in his transparently autobiographical *The Ordeal of Gilbert Pinfold* (1957), introduces his alter ego thus:

> It may happen in the next hundred years that the English novelists of the present day will come to be valued as we now value the artists and craftsmen of the late eighteenth century. The originators, the exuberant men, are extinct and in their place subsists and modestly flourishes a generation notable for elegance and variety of contrivance . . . Among these novelists Mr Gilbert Pinfold stood quite high.

Graham Greene said something rather similar to Yvonne Cloetta, as she recalls in her memoirs, when he read an article in which he was described as a 'genius': 'I am not a genius. I am a craftsman who writes books at the cost of long and painful labour.'[6] Greene's 'geniuses', we might deduce, would be the same writers that Waugh refers to as 'the originators, the exuberant men', the giants of Modernism.

Although there are some respectful references to Lawrence in Greene's early essays, there is no detailed discussion of Lawrence's work, and this is not surprising: these two writers were very different in temperament, background, beliefs and interests. Nor does Greene seem very interested in or impressed by James Joyce, for he seldom alludes to him. He was better acquainted with Virginia Woolf, but his published remarks about her are rather prejudicial, for reasons I shall suggest in a moment. Although he experimented occasionally with passages in the stream-of-consciousness style in the early novels, *It's a Battlefield* (1934) and *England Made Me* (1935), Greene soon abandoned the technique. Of the novelists of the Heroic Age, the two that Greene most admired, and on whom his 'anxiety of influence' was therefore most intensely focused, were Henry James and Joseph Conrad. They are in many ways an odd couple, as Greene himself implied in the essay 'Remembering Mr Jones', remarking on 'the strange fate which brought these two to settle within a few miles of each other [in East Sussex] and produce from material gained at such odd extremes of life two of the great English novels of the last fifty years: *The Spoils of Poynton* and *Victory*'.

At first glance, it is easier to understand the appeal of Conrad, for his work seems to have much more in common with Greene's than does James's, and more continuity with the fiction on which Greene's imagination was nourished in childhood and adolescence. The 'despairing romanticism' which Greene discovered in *The Viper of Milan*, and tried to imitate in his juvenilia, is a quality to be found in many of Conrad's tales, and he obviously showed Greene how the form of the adventure novel might be applied to the exploration of moral, psychological and spiritual themes in literary fiction. In *A Sort of Life* (1971) Greene himself describes his second attempt at writing a novel shortly after coming down from Oxford, in these terms: 'Conrad was the influence now, and in particular the most dangerous of all his books, *The Arrow of Gold*.' It was dangerous because it was by Conrad's standards rather a bad book, but Greene didn't at the time appear to perceive just how and in what ways it was bad. The background of the plot is the anti-republican Carlist movement in nineteenth-century Spain, and it concerns a group of Spanish Carlist exiles and other expatriate sympathisers in the South of France. The narrator, an Englishman, engages in gunrunning for them mainly because, like most of the other characters, he is hopelessly in love with a woman at the centre of the Carlist movement called Doña Rita. There is actually very little action in the novel: only the faintest ghost of the traditional adventure novel is perceptible in the slow-moving and overwritten narrative. Most of the gun-running takes place offstage or is briefly summarised, while the effort to build up the character of Doña Rita into an irresistible *femme fatale* becomes increasingly absurd, e.g.:

> She listened to me, unreadable, unmoved, narrowed eyes, closed lips, slightly flushed face, as if carved six thousand years ago in order to fix for ever that something secret and obscure which is in all women. Not the gross immobility of a Sphinx proposing roadside riddles but the finer immobility, almost sacred, of a fateful figure seated at the very source of the passions that have moved men from the dawn of ages.[7]

After transcribing those words I looked up Jocelyn Baines's biography of Conrad to see what he has to say about *The Arrow of Gold* and found that he quotes the same passage to make the same point. He also says that Conrad dictated the first draft of the novel and added such purple passages later.[8] Perhaps that was what Greene meant when he observes, in *A Sort of Life*, that *The Arrow of Gold* was written 'under the tutelage of Henry James', because James also dictated his later novels, with an effect on his style that many readers have deplored.

The influence of the late, romantic Conrad, with its strong element of sentimental 'love interest' generally absent from the early work, and its self-indulgent, portentous rhetoric, is perceptible in Greene's first three published novels, *The Man Within* (1929), *The Name of Action* (1930), and *Rumour at*

Nightfall (1931). The last of these is actually about the same Carlist Wars in Spain that provided the background of *Arrow of Gold*. In *A Sort of Life* Greene describes how he deliberately stopped reading Conrad's fiction in 1932 because he felt it had become an excessive and negative influence on his own work. That was at a crisis point in Greene's career. The success of his first novel, *The Man Within*, had encouraged him to resign his sub-editing job on *The Times* and to become a freelance writer, but the next two books were critical and commercial failures, and his publisher told him he would get no more advances until he had earned out those already given to him. With his mind wonderfully concentrated by this ultimatum he wrote *Stamboul Train*, a slick, exciting contemporary thriller, which rescued him from financial anxiety, at least for a while, through the sale of the film rights, but he blamed Conrad, especially the Conrad of *The Arrow of Gold*, for the faults of his previous novels, the second and third of which he did not allow to be reprinted:

> Never again, I swore, would I read a novel of Conrad's – a vow I kept for more than a quarter of a century until I found myself with *Heart of Darkness* in a small paddle boat travelling up a Congo tributary in 1959.

That of course was the journey which produced *A Burnt-out Case* (1961). According to Norman Sherry, however, Greene read, or reread, one more Conrad novel in the year of 1932 before renouncing him, an earlier, better and very different novel from *Arrow of Gold*: *The Secret Agent* (1907).[9] And Greene's next novel, *It's a Battlefield* (1934), is in some respects an *hommage* to Conrad's. It centres on a case of murder with political implications, as Conrad's centres on a botched act of terrorism, and cross-cuts between a variety of characters who are closely or tangentially connected to this event and its consequences. Several of these characters – for instance, the Assistant Commissioner of Police and a minister's private secretary – correspond closely to equivalent figures in *The Secret Agent*. The hero, if he can be so called, of Greene's novel, is named Conrad, after a Polish sea-captain who once lodged with his parents. These intertextual allusions are, however, in some ways misleading. *It's a Battlefield* is really a very different novel from *A Secret Agent*: in its multiplicity of characters and cinematic cutting from short scene to short scene it is more like Greene's own *Stamboul Train*, while in style and overall structure, as Cedric Watts has observed, it sometimes surprisingly resembles Virginia Woolf's *Mrs Dalloway*. In both novels, the characters' paths and fortunes intersect by chance as they move around London; in both a car passes through the streets carrying royalty or some head of state, drawing crowds, causing traffic jams, exciting speculation and a variety of thoughts and emotions in those who observe it. The overt nods to Conrad in the text may be in part designed to disguise an influence that Greene was less ready to acknowledge because Virginia Woolf was closer to Greene himself than Conrad in age, and still writing.

Greene unlearned the bad lessons he had acquired from Conrad, but in one respect the older novelist left a permanent mark on his work of which Greene himself may not have been conscious. The narrator of Conrad's *Under Western Eyes* speaks of the necessity of finding 'some key-word . . . a word that could stand at the back of all the words covering the pages, a word which, if not truth itself, may perchance hold truth enough to help the moral discovery which should be the object of every tale'.[10] In *Under Western Eyes* that word is 'cynicism', but other works of Conrad have different keywords – 'dark' and 'darkness' in *Heart of Darkness*, for instance, or 'material interests' in *Nostromo*. As I pointed out in my first published criticism about Graham Greene,[11] his novels also have their thematic keywords: *trust* and *distrust* in *The Confidential Agent*, for instance, *good* and *evil*, *right* and *wrong* in *Brighton Rock*, *pity* in *The Heart of the Matter* and *love* and *hate* in *The End of the Affair*. The insistent recurrence of these abstract nouns in dialogue and description is one of the signatures of Greene's style.

Greene's decision to stop reading Conrad in 1932 was a drastic expression of the anxiety of influence, a kind of Oedipal violence committed against a literary father-figure. His way of dealing with the influence of Henry James was more subtle and complex. It may seem surprising that there was ever a problem for him in this respect, because there is no very obvious similarity between Greene's fiction and James's. The adventure story element so crucial to nearly all Greene's fiction is absent from James's, as is dogmatic religious belief; and the social milieux they dealt with were entirely different. Temperamentally there could hardly be two more different men: the fastidious, celibate James, and Greene with his very active sex life and fascination with 'seediness'. Nevertheless there is no question that for Greene as a young aspiring novelist Henry James was the Master whom he both learned from and emulated. There are more essays about Henry James in *The Lost Childhood*, and more references and allusions to him throughout the book than to any other writer. He praises James in the highest terms: 'He is as solitary in the history of the novel as Shakespeare in the history of poetry.' We might infer from his own novels that what Greene valued and emulated in James was his technical and stylistic virtuosity, his grasp of the fundamental importance of point of view in fiction, and his ability to convey the subjectivity of human experience without sacrificing the discipline of the well-made plot and the well-formed sentence, and there are hints and asides in the essays which imply as much. But these are not the aspects of James's work which Greene emphasises in arguing for his greatness. He concludes the 1936 essay, 'Henry James: the Private Universe', by saying: 'it is in the final justice of his pity, the completeness of an analysis which enabled him to pity the most shabby, the most corrupt, of his human actors, that he ranks with the greatest creative writers.'

To anyone who knows Henry James's work well this is surely a rather surprising, even eccentric comment. In fact it seems far more applicable to Greene's own work, to what he had written by 1936 and what he aspired to write and would write in the future. At the beginning of the same essay he attributes to James a 'sense of evil religious in its intensity'. In another essay written a few years earlier, but placed after the 'Private Universe' essay in The Lost Childhood, called 'Henry James: the Religious Aspect', Greene argued against the view of Desmond MacCarthy that the religious sense was 'singularly absent from [James's] work', again emphasising James's examination of evil in human behaviour:

> The novels are only saved from the deepest cynicism by the religious sense; the struggle between the beautiful and the treacherous is lent . . . the importance of the supernatural. Human nature is not despicable in Osmond or Densher, for they are both capable of damnation.

And he goes on to quote a passage from T. S. Eliot's essay on Baudelaire, 'the glory of man is his capacity for salvation; it is also true that his glory is his capacity for damnation' – a passage that several critics, including myself, have applied to Greene's heroes, or anti-heroes. There is a certain amount of truth in these observations on James, but it is exaggerated and distorted. Osmond in *The Portrait of a Lady* is certainly a nasty piece of work, but Merton Densher in *The Wings of the Dove* is weak and confused rather than evil, and full of remorse after Milly's death for his and Kate Croy's exploitation of her. In his essay on *Portrait of a Lady* Greene says of James: 'what deeply interested him, what indeed was his ruling passion, was the idea of treachery, the "Judas complex".' This phrase, the 'Judas complex', is put inside quotation marks, but is not attributed to anybody, and I wonder if Greene himself didn't in fact make it up. It certainly seems much more applicable to Greene's interest in treachery and betrayal than to James's. He says we may never know 'what it was at the very start of life that so deeply impressed on the young James this sense of treachery' – but he knew, and *we* know now from Norman Sherry's biography, what it was in his own case. He felt he had betrayed the schoolboy ethic when he ran away from home, which led to the unmasking of the bullying from which he had suffered and his persecutor's removal from the school.[12] His first novel, *The Man Within*, has a hero full of self-loathing and guilt on account of having betrayed his friends, the chief of whom describes the hero as 'a sort of Judas'. The essay 'The Lost Childhood' ends with lines from A.E.'s poem, 'Germinal':

> *In the lost boyhood of Judas*
> *Christ was betrayed.*

In short, Greene is misreading James, in Bloom's sense of the word, for his own creative purposes – making him seem like the kind of novelist he himself was, or hoped to become, so that he could present himself as carrying on the great tradition represented by James, but in a new key.

In later essays Greene became less reverential towards the Master. A pivotal text in this respect was his 1945 essay on François Mauriac. This was one of the most tendentious pieces of literary criticism Greene ever wrote, and it was a kind of personal manifesto. It begins:

> After the death of Henry James a disaster overtook the English novel; indeed long before his death one can picture that quiet, impressive, rather complacent figure, like the last survivor on a raft, gazing out over a sea scattered with wreckage . . . For with the death of James the religious sense was lost to the English novel, and with the religious sense went the sense of the importance of the human act. It was as if the world of fiction had lost a dimension: the characters of such distinguished writers as Mrs Virginia Woolf and Mr E. M. Forster wandered like cardboard symbols through a world that was paper-thin.

This is palpably unfair to Forster and Woolf, and makes the characterisation of Henry James as an essentially religious novelist seem odder than ever. Forster and Woolf in fact had far more in common with James's essentially humanist philosophy of life than did Greene. As the essay proceeds it becomes clear that Greene's real target is the narrative impersonality of modernist fiction, its refusal to judge or comment morally and metaphysically on the actions of its characters, as the classic nineteenth-century novelists did.

M. Mauriac's first importance to an English reader, therefore, is that he belongs to the company of the great traditional novelists: he is a writer for whom the visible world
has not ceased to exist, whose characters have the solidity
and importance of men with souls to save or to lose, and
a writer who claims the traditional and essential right of a
novelist, to comment, to express his views. For how tired
we have become of the dogmatically 'pure' novel, the tradition founded by Flaubert and reaching its magnificent
tortuous climax in England in the works of Henry James
. . . I am not denying the greatness of either Flaubert or
James. The novel was ceasing to be an aesthetic form and
they recalled it to the artistic conscience. It was the later
writers who by accepting the technical dogma blindly made
the novel the dull devitalised form . . . it has become. The
exclusion of the author can go too far. Even the author,
poor devil, has a right to exist, and M. Mauriac reaffirms
that right.

This was not the first or the last attack on the modernist
novel – it has much in common with polemics by the novelists of the 1930s, like Edward Upward, and of the 1950s, like
C. P. Snow and Kingsley Amis, arguing against aesthetic experiment and for the return of social realism in fiction. But in
praising Mauriac, whom he had been reading with admiration since 1932, Greene was covertly making the case for his
own kind of fiction, especially the novels from *Brighton Rock*
onwards, in which the characters and the action are put in
an explicitly Catholic theological perspective by the narrative
voice. At the time Greene wrote the essay he must have been
thinking about his own next novel, *The Heart of the Matter*,
and he was publishing Mauriac as a director of Eyre &

Spottiswoode. He had two motives for promoting the Catholic Novel.

Although Henry James is exculpated from blame for the godlessness of the modernist novel he acquires a certain guilt by association with it in this essay. A few years later, in an essay about the *Collected Plays* of Henry James, just published by Leon Edel, Greene seems much less reverent towards him than ever before. It begins: 'There has always been – let us face it – a suspicion of vulgarity about the Old Master.' He lists a number of features of Henry James's work which nourish this suspicion, but focuses particularly on Henry James's yearning for popular commercial success, which he thought he could obtain as a playwright without compromising the aesthetic purity of his novels. 'Until Mr Edel published this huge volume . . . we had no idea how completely James had failed', says Greene. He is particularly scathing about *Guy Domville*, the play whose first night, when James was booed by the gallery, brought his five-year campaign on the London stage to a disastrous end. 'To us today the story of *Guy Domville* seems singularly unconvincing, one more example of the not always fortunate fascination exercised on James by the Christian faith and by Catholicism in particular.' Greene has travelled some distance from that early essay on 'Henry James: the Religious Aspect' which at times came near to making him an honorary Catholic. In 1950, when he wrote the later essay, his own career was in the ascendant, and his originality as a novelist universally acknowledged. He no longer felt the anxiety of influence in relation to James, or the need to 'misread' James in order to indicate how he wished his own novels to be read. It cannot be coincidental that at the time he wrote this essay he was thinking about writing a play himself. Greene told journalists in Boston early in 1950, after an unsuccessful production of a stage adaptation by other hands of *The Heart of the Matter*, that the idea of writing an original play of his own 'was actively in his mind'.[13] That turned out to be *The Living Room*, which he began writing in 1951 and completed early in 1952. It was his first play to be professionally produced, and a very Catholic one in subject matter. Graham Greene must have been conscious that in turning in mid-career as a novelist to the theatre he was risking the same fate as Henry James, and by disparaging Henry James's dramatic efforts he was privately raising the stakes for his own success or failure. In the event he was justified by the reception of *The Living Room*. At the first night of the London production, at Wyndham's Theatre in April 1953, there were multiple curtain calls, and cries of 'Author! Author!' which, unlike those that lured Henry James on to the stage at the St James's Theatre in January 1895, expressed only sincere admiration. Greene took his bow, but warded off hubris in a characteristic speech. 'Do not call me a success,' he said. 'I have never known a successful man. Have you? A man who is a success to himself? Success is the point of self-deception. Failure is the point of self-knowledge.'[14] Well, perhaps so; but only writers who are ambitious for artistic success are subject to the anxiety of influence.

Notes

1 Harold Bloom, *The Anxiety of Influence: a Theory of Poetry* (1973), p. 27.

2 Ibid., p. 30.

3 'The Metaphysical Poets', in *Selected Essays* (1951), p. 288.

4 *Thinks...* (2001), p. 83.

5 *A Sort of Life* (1971), pp. 52–3.

6 Yvonne Cloetta, *In Search of a Beginning: My Life with Graham Greene* (2004), p. 68.

7 *The Arrow of Gold* (Uniform Edn., 1924), pp. 145–6.

8 Jocelyn Baines, *Joseph Conrad* (Penguin edn., 1971), pp. 492–4.

9 Norman Sherry, *The Life of Graham Greene, Volume I: 1904–1939*, (1989), p. 457.

10 Joseph Conrad, *Under Western Eyes* (Uniform Edn., 1924), p. 67.

11 *Graham Greene* (1966), Columbia Essays on Modern Writers, no. 17.

12 Sherry, *The Life of Graham Greene, Volume I, 1904–1939*, pp. 65–91.

13 Ibid., Vol. II, pp. 450–1.

14 Quoted by Sherry from a report in the *Daily Express*, ibid., p. 456.

VLADIMIR
NABOKOV:
Pnin

Vladimir Nabokov was a literary genius. There is no other word with which to describe a writer who in mid-life became a stylistic virtuoso in a language that was not his mother tongue. Circumstances – which is to say, the convulsions of twentieth-century European politics – impelled him to achieve this feat, exchanging Russian for English as the medium of his art (as well as acquiring an enviable fluency in French and German along the way). He was born, in 1899, into a patrician Russian family who were driven into exile by the Bolshevik revolution of 1917. After studying at Cambridge University in England, he scraped a living as a writer in Berlin, and later in Paris, publishing novels in Russian (some of which were translated variously into English, German and French) without making any great impression on the literary world. He came to America in 1940, with his Jewish wife, Véra, and their son, Dimitri, as virtually penniless refugees from Nazi-occupied France. In spite of lacking conventional academic credentials, Nabokov was able to find employment as a university teacher of Russian and comparative literature, first at Wellesley College, Massachusetts, and from 1948 at Cornell University in upstate New York. Over the same period he began to rebuild his career as a writer of fiction. His first novel in English, *The Real Life of Sebastian Knight* (1941), had the misfortune to appear only days after the attack on Pearl Harbor, and was barely noticed. But his essays and stories attracted the attention and admiration of editors and fellow writers, and in 1944 *The New Yorker*, which at this time enjoyed a uniquely prestigious position in the American literary world, acquired the right to first consideration of his work. His second novel in English was, however, only a little more successful than its predecessor. This was *Bend Sinister* (1947), a dark fable about an imaginary (but obviously European) state under brutal totalitarian rule.

Over the next few years Nabokov, in the intervals allowed by his teaching duties and other literary and scholarly projects, began to work on a novel set for the first time in America, based on a story about a man sexually attracted to prepubescent girls which he had written in Russian in 1939 but left unpublished. *Lolita* grew in scale and complexity and caused him much labour and anxiety. In the summer of 1953, when (on sabbatical leave from Cornell) he was at last drawing towards the end of this novel, Nabokov wrote a short story called 'Pnin', about the comical misadventures of an expatriate Russian professor on his way to deliver a lecture to a women's club in a small American town. He created the new character partly as a relief from the dark obsessive world of Humbert Humbert – in his own words (in a letter to a friend) as a 'brief sunny escape from [*Lolita's*] intolerable spell'.[1] But it is clear that the new project was also a kind of insurance against the difficulties that he expected to encounter in trying to publish a novel in which a middle-aged man describes in lavish and eloquent detail his infatuation with and seduction of a twelve-year-old girl. From an early stage in the development of the character of Pnin he planned to write a series of stories about him which could be published independently in *The New Yorker*, and later strung together to make a book, thus ensuring some continuity of publication and income while he tried to find a publisher for *Lolita*. This proved to be a shrewd professional strategy. It also partly explains the unusual form of *Pnin*.

Is it a novel or a collection of short stories? Critics have disagreed about the answer to this question, and some have grumbled that it is neither one thing nor the other – arguing that the chapters are too slight either to satisfy as individual stories or to add up to a proper novel. In fact the stories are artfully well formed, and reward close and careful reading. What seems like a random detail often turns out to be a narrative clue, the full significance of which only becomes evident later. The repetition of motifs also gives the stories a satisfying symmetry, individually and collectively. Chapter Two, for instance, begins with the sound of the bells of Waindell College, and ends with a picture of the bells on a magazine cover. Chapter Four begins and ends with descriptions of rain falling while the characters sleep, or fail to sleep. Squirrels pop up in one form or another in nearly every story, as do reflections in windows, puddles and mirrors. In spite of the temporal gaps between them, the stories describe a continuous narrative arc, poignantly tracing Pnin's quest, which is ultimately frustrated, to find a home, or to make himself 'at home' in alien Waindell. To point out these formal features, however, does not quite meet the challenge of defining exactly what kind of fictional work *Pnin* is.

If we need a generic provenance for *Pnin*, we might trace it back to the character-sketches of representative 'types' written by the classical Greek author Theophrastus and his later imitators. Although the narrator assures us that 'Pnin . . . was anything but the type of that good natured German platitude of last century, *der zerstreute Professor*', there *is* something of the stock 'absent-minded professor' in his character. That 'Pnin' is the only genuine name in the Russian language consisting of just one syllable, however, emphasises the character's rich individuality rather than his typicality. In the text his name takes on a linguistic life of its own, becoming an adjective (he is in a 'Pninian quandary' in the first story), a verb (he 'Pninises' his office by his choice of furniture and fittings) and an incitement to word-play both intentional ('Ping-pong, Pnin?') and unintentional, as when the chairwoman of his lecture at Cremona introduces him as 'Professor Pun-neen'. Considered as a novel, *Pnin* is certainly a prime example of what the Chicago Aristotelian critics called 'the novel of character' (as distinct from the novel of plot or the novel of ideas). The very title indicates that its aim is to evoke a person rather than to tell a story – or to evoke a person by telling a series of anecdotes about him. When Nabokov was looking for a publisher for the completed book he stressed the element of character:

> In Pnin I have created an entirely new character, the like of which has never appeared in any other book. A man of great moral courage, a pure man, a scholar and a staunch friend, serenely wise, faithful to a single love, he never descends from a high plane of life characterised by authenticity and

integrity. But handicapped and hemmed in by his incap-
ability to learn a language, he seems a figure of fun to many
an average intellectual . . .[2]

Nabokov was not always so admiring of his creation.
Sending the first story, entitled 'Pnin', to his editor at *The New
Yorker*, Katharine White, he wrote in a covering letter, 'he is
not a very nice person but he is fun'.[3] The stance of author
to character implied in the work itself comes somewhere
between these two extremes, and is complicated by the
ambiguous relationship (to be discussed later) between the
narrator and Vladimir Nabokov. The Pnin that emerges from
the whole sequence of stories is certainly an engaging
character, in whose fortunes (mainly misfortunes) we take a
sympathetic interest. We approve of the characters who
befriend him and disapprove of those who exploit him. But
he is an essentially comic character – pathetic at times, to be
sure, but not a tragic hero. His physical appearance – the
impressive combination of head, shoulders and torso that
tapers off disappointingly in 'a pair of spindly legs . . . and
frail-looking, almost feminine feet' – is an anatomical anti-
climax, an emblem of the kind of situation he is constantly
getting himself into by some error of understanding or judgement. Pnin inhabits a Pninian world, but unfortunately
nobody else does, and he is constantly bumping into uncomfortable or embarrassing evidence of this fact. Bathos is also
a recurrent rhetorical trope in the stylistic surface of the book.

Where did this character come from? There have been
several suggestions for real-life models, the most plausible
being the historian Marc Szeftel, an émigré Russian historian
who was a colleague of Nabokov's at Cornell (which is recognisable as 'Waindell College' in *Pnin*, according to those who

229

THE YEAR OF HENRY JAMES

know both the actual and the fictional campus). Galya Diment
has collected and displayed the evidence for this identification
in her *Pniniad: Vladimir Nabokov and Marc Szeftel* (1997). By
collating the *New Yorker* texts of the Pnin stories with their
eventual form in the published book, she shows that Nabokov
revised some of the biographical facts of Pnin's life, making
them correspond more closely to Szeftel's curriculum vitae,
and suggests that this process was connected with a perceptible warming of the author's attitude to his character as the
book progressed (for which there is some warrant in the two
contrasting descriptions by Nabokov quoted above). Diment
believes that 'the "humanized" Pnin is, in many ways, the
"Szeftelized" Pnin'. It is certainly significant that Szeftel was
Jewish, because it is Pnin's association with his Jewish sweetheart Mira, and his anguish at her tragic fate (revealed in
Chapter Five), that dignifies his character more than any other
single trait. But there were other things Pnin apparently had
in common with Szeftel, such as his imperfect English, which
would have seemed less flattering to the putative model.

It is fairly obvious that Pnin was not an instantly recognisable portrait or caricature of Szeftel, for this would have been
impossibly embarrassing for both men, who were not only
colleagues, but also collaborators on a scholarly project (a
study of a medieval Russian epic, *The Song of Igor's Campaign*)
and met socially in private life. There is evidence, however,
that Szeftel suspected the character of Pnin was partially based
on himself, and somewhat resented the resemblance, without
ever explicitly complaining about it. Szeftel was both fascinated by and jealous of Nabokov's meteoric success with *Lolita*
shortly after the publication of *Pnin*. He wrote an article entitled '*Lolita* at Cornell' for the *Cornell Alumni News*, long after
both men had left the institution, and meditated a book-length

study of the novel which never materialised. Relations between the two men became increasingly cool, but while they were colleagues they seem to have made a tacit mutual agreement not to bring out into the open the extent to which Nabokov had borrowed traits from Szeftel to create the character of Pnin (a not unusual accommodation, in fact, between novelists and their friends and relatives).

In the *New Yorker* text, Pnin is said to have come to Waindell College in 1948, the same year that Nabokov himself joined the faculty at Cornell; but in the book version the date of Pnin's arrival is put back to 1945, when Szeftel was appointed at Cornell. Very few readers of either version would have seen anything significant in these dates – except members of the Cornell faculty. This suggests to me that Nabokov may have used Szeftel as a model partly to distance *himself* from the character of Pnin in the eyes of those who knew him, because the author did have some things in common with his fictional character. Nabokov's lecturing style, for instance – reading from a carefully written text and making little or no eye contact with his audience – was similar to Pnin's. Nabokov too was capable of absent-mindedness, and on one famous occasion began lecturing obliviously to the wrong class until rescued by a student who had seen him entering the wrong lecture-room. (He dealt with the mistake more suavely than Pnin would have managed, however, saying before he left the room: 'You have just seen the "Coming Attraction" for Literature 325. If you are interested, you may register next fall.'[4]) Pnin also shares, in a milder form, several of his creator's intellectual prejudices – against Freud and psychotherapy, for instance. But what links Nabokov to Pnin most strongly is that they are both exiles with painfully nostalgic memories of pre-revolutionary Russia and an inveterate hatred of and contempt for the communist regime that deprived them of their birthright. The ache of loss throbs not far below the comic surface of these tales and occasionally grips Pnin with the intensity of a heart-attack. It may have been to keep this powerful current of emotion under control that Nabokov made Pnin a more comical and absurd character than himself, borrowing traits from other émigré professors such as Szeftel. Pnin is Nabokov as he might have been in American exile if he had not possessed a mastery of the English language, a supportive and cherished wife, and the resource of literary creativity: a quaint, eccentric, rather sad figure, doomed never to fully understand the society in which he finds himself. Pnin, in short, is a composite of observation, introspection and invention, like most fictional characters.

To consider the possible sources of *Pnin* in Nabokov's experiences at Cornell is to be reminded that the book was a very early example of the 'campus novel', a subgenre which is very familiar to us now, but was only just beginning to manifest itself in the early 1950s. Mary McCarthy's *The Groves of Academe* (1952) has some claim to be the first in the field, and Nabokov would certainly have been familiar with it, since he knew both McCarthy and her husband, Edmund Wilson, who was one of his closest literary friends at this time (they fell out later). Randall Jarrell's *Pictures from an Institution* (1954), which was for those in the know a riposte to Mary McCarthy's book, gave a further impetus to the new genre, though Nabokov was already embarked upon the Pnin stories when it appeared. What the three books have in common is a pastoral campus setting, a 'small world' removed from the hustle and bustle of modern urban life, in which social and political behaviour can be amusingly observed in the interaction of characters whose high intellectual pretensions are often let down by their very human frailties. The campus novel was from its beginnings, and in the hands of later exponents like Alison Lurie and Malcolm Bradbury, an essentially comic subgenre, in which serious moral issues are treated in a 'light and bright and sparkling' manner (to borrow the phrase applied to *Pride and Prejudice* by Jane Austen, who would certainly have written a campus novel or two if she had lived in our era). Chapter Six of *Pnin* is a kind of campus novel in miniature:

> The 1954 Fall Term had begun. Again the marble neck of a homely Venus in the vestibule of Humanities Hall received the vermilion imprint, in applied lipstick, of a mimicked kiss. Again the *Waindell Recorder* discussed the Parking Problem. Again in the margins of library books earnest freshmen inscribed such helpful glosses as 'Description of nature,' or 'Irony'; and in a pretty edition of Mallarmé's poems an especially able scholiast had already underlined in violet ink the difficult word *oiseaux* and scrawled above it 'birds.'

Aficionados of the campus novel (there are some austere readers of course who consider it a trivial and introverted subgenre) will hug themselves with glee at this beginning. Academic institutions are in a sense always the same. That is why, like the country house of classic murder mysteries, they make cosily reassuring settings for a tale, but why, also, we appreciate witty variations on the familiar themes and types. The earnest freshman's marginal gloss, 'Irony', in this passage is itself a deliciously appropriate comment on the sentence in which it appears. We may note too the irresistibly funny bathos of the last word, 'birds', which gets something of its effect by echoing the American slang expression, 'strictly for the birds'.

The two principal sources of motivation in the campus novel, which generate conflict between the characters and move the plot, are sex (usually illicit) and power (often involving a struggle over promotion or tenure). The first of these motives is only discreetly touched on in *Pnin* (perhaps because Nabokov felt he had enough sexual transgression on his hands in *Lolita*), but the efforts of Dr Hagen to secure Pnin's appointment in Chapter Six is a good example of the second. It is typical that for most of the duration of the story Pnin is unaware that his job is in jeopardy. He is only concerned that his 'house-heating party' should be a success, while the reader is privy to the machinations of academic politicians which threaten his expulsion from Waindell. In fact Pnin is also unaware of the circumstance that most threatens the success of his party – the fact that he has confused the identities of two colleagues and invited the anthropologist Professor Tristram W. Thomas under the impression that he is the ornithologist Thomas Wynn. The two plot strands are very neatly intertwined in the extended treatment of this social event, which forms the climax to the story. Parties are a staple feature of campus novels because they conveniently bring the characters together in large groups, and loosen their tongues and reduce their inhibitions with alcohol, thus provoking amusing, indecorous or impolitic revelations. Throughout this party sequence we are kept in comic suspense as to whether Pnin will betray his mistake and suffer acute embarrassment in consequence. In the event he narrowly escapes exposing himself. The party is a great success (in his own eyes anyway) and he bids his guests goodbye feeling well pleased with himself. Then Dr Hagen, the head of the German department, under whose umbrella Pnin teaches at Waindell, learns from another departing guest that Pnin is planning to buy the house he has just rented, and Hagen feels obliged to return and tell him (in a well-meaning but clumsy way) that because of his own imminent departure and the intransigence of his colleagues (the Professor of French Literature Leonard Blorenge 'who disliked literature and . . . had no French' being the chief villain) Pnin's appointment will soon be terminated. Pnin's euphoria is shattered by this news. Sadly washing the soiled dishes and glasses afterwards he accidentally drops a pair of nutcrackers into the soapy suds containing the beautiful crystal bowl given to him by his son Victor and hears a sickening muffled noise of cracking glass. The reader winces in sympathy with Pnin as he suffers this cruel, additional blow of Fate.

Pnin hurled the towel into a corner and, turning away, stood for a moment staring at the blackness beyond the threshold of the open back door . . . Then with a moan of anguished anticipation he went back to the sink and, bracing himself, dipped his hand deep into the foam. A jagger of glass stung him. Gently he removed a broken goblet. The beautiful bowl was intact. He took a fresh dish towel and went on with his household work.

It is a brilliantly executed reversal of expectation, which relieves the reader almost as much as Pnin himself, and ensures that the essentially comic tone of the book is preserved even at the lowest point in Pnin's fortunes.

As well as being a pioneer of campus fiction, Nabokov was one of the first writers to whom the epithet 'postmodern' may be usefully applied: that is to say, he had absorbed the lessons and achievements of modernism (in prose fiction represented supremely for him by Joyce and Proust) without feeling the need to reject the social realism of the nineteenth-century novel (he was devoted to Tolstoy and Jane Austen, for instance), but he developed an innovative form of fiction that was distinctively different from both of these traditions. Many of his novels take the basic narrative material of popular fiction about crime and detection, and play ingenious variations on the formulaic models – making the criminal an eloquent apologist for his actions (as in *Lolita*, for example), or a complete incompetent (e.g. *Despair*), or one and the same person as the detective (e.g. *The Eye*). *Pnin* is not a book of this kind. There are no crimes or even misdemeanours in the action. It has been pointed out that it is the only full-length work of fiction by Nabokov which does not describe a violent death (the death of Mira in the camps is recalled retrospectively, and is all the more harrowing for Pnin because its details are unknown, inviting his imagination to conjure up innumerable horrors). Its narrative model seems to be the kind of modern literary short story classically exemplified by James Joyce in his *Dubliners*, and (in a somewhat blander form) favoured by *The New Yorker* in the 1940s and '50s, where the emphasis is on ordinary, mundane, even trivial, experience, which is made to shimmer with meaning and implication by the writer's stylistic virtuosity and given aesthetic form by repeated motifs and symbols as much as by narrative structure. This kind of short story does not usually end with a dramatic twist of the plot, but with what Joyce called an 'epiphany', when the central character grasps the nature of existence, of his or her fate, in a moment of piercing insight, or such a revelation is vouchsafed to the reader in a passage of lyrical symbolism. Chapter Two of *Pnin* ends with an epiphany of loss, when his hopes of a reconciliation with his ex-wife are dashed:

> 'Doesn't she want to come back?' asked Joan softly.
> Pnin, his head on his arm, started to beat the table with his loosely clenched fist.
> 'I haf nofing,' wailed Pnin between loud, damp sniffs. 'I haf nofing left, nofing, nofing.'

That Pnin's mispronunciation of 'nothing' echoes the final consonant in his first name, 'Timofey', lends an extra pathos to this complaint. Chapter Five also ends on a note of romantic-erotic deprivation for Pnin, as painful memories of his separation from Mira are evoked, rendered more poignant by the final vivid image of a courting couple on the summit of a distant hill at sunset. But at the last moment the serenity of this purely aesthetic resolution is undermined:

> . . . two dark figures in profile were silhouetted against the ember-red sky. They stood there closely, facing each other. One could not make out from the road whether it was the Poroshin girl and her beau, or Nina Bolotov and young Poroshin, or merely an emblematic couple placed with easy art on the last page of Pnin's fading day.

The metafictional aside, *'placed with easy art on the last page'*, is a typical postmodernist move, breaking the storyteller's spell to call attention to the irreducible gap between even the most eloquent literary language and real human pain.

There is another group of novels by Nabokov with which *Pnin* has more in common than with his novels of crime and detection, namely those which experiment with the form of memoir or biography (such as *The Defence* and *The Real Life of Sebastian Knight*), and it is the memoirist character and function of the narrator in *Pnin* that most obviously distinguishes it as a postmodernist work. This feature of the book becomes more and more obvious and obtrusive the deeper we get into it. Initially it is suggested only by a certain idiosyncrasy of phrasing in the discourse:

> The elderly passenger sitting on the north-window side of that inexorably moving railway coach, next to an empty seat and facing two empty ones, was none other than Professor Timofey Pnin.

This opening sentence of 'Pnin' in *The New Yorker* was the first mention of Pnin in print; but the phrase 'none other than' is normally used to introduce a figure well-known to the addressee at least by name. The demonstrative 'that' applied to 'coach' also produces an unsettling effect on the reader, as if one had just missed the proper beginning of the story. The narrator adopts the tone of the traditional 'omniscient' author: 'Now a secret must be imparted. Professor Pnin was on the wrong train. He was unaware of it, and so was the conductor, already threading his way through the train to Pnin's coach.' But before the conductor has apprised Pnin of his plight, the narrator mentions that Pnin's wallet contains, among other things, 'the newspaper clipping of a letter he had written, with *my* help, to the New York Times in 1945 anent the Yalta conference . . .' [emphasis mine]. Suddenly the authorial voice has become a character on the same plane as Pnin. A question arises, and periodically recurs: how can he therefore know so much about the minutiae of Pnin's experience and his private thoughts?

Further self-references to the narrator as 'I' and to his acquaintance with Pnin are sprinkled through the book, and in the last three stories they begin to cohere into a kind of sub-plot. It is revealed in the last chapter that the narrator knew Pnin's wife Lisa in Paris before the war and had a brief affair with her when Pnin was courting her, provoking her to attempt suicide (there is a veiled reference to this connection in Chapter Two which only a very percipient first-time reader would pick up). Lisa in fact married Pnin because of her rejection by the narrator and subsequently confessed the affair to Pnin. This explains why, in Chapter Six, when Hagen tells Pnin that the English Department has just appointed a man who might become his new protector and patron at Waindell – 'one of your most brilliant compatriots, a really fascinating lecturer . . . I think he's an old friend of yours' – Pnin replies: 'Yes, I know him thirty years or more. We are friends, but there is one thing perfectly certain. I will never work under him.' This brilliant compatriot is obviously Nabokov himself. He is never fully and explicitly named, though he is clearly the amateur lepidopterist 'Vladimir Vladimirovich' whose absence from the house-party is mentioned in Chapter Five. The basic facts of his exile from Russia, his expatriate life in Europe, and successful career as writer and academic in America, correspond exactly to Nabokov's own life.

This creates a puzzle for the reader, and an effect, not uncommon in postmodernist fiction, to which deconstructionist critics give the name 'aporia' – a Greek word meaning, literally, 'a pathless path', used in philosophy to refer to a group of statements which are individually plausible but mutually inconsistent or contradictory. How can the omniscient authorial narrator of *Pnin*, and the 'I' who reports his encounters with Pnin, and the real, historic individual Vladimir Nabokov, be one and the same person? If 'I' is a fictional character he cannot claim omniscience (which is a literary convention restricted to authors). If 'I' is *not* a fictional character, then neither is Pnin – Pnin must be as real as Nabokov. But in that case 'the real Nabokov' cannot claim omniscient knowledge of him (and indeed Pnin accuses the 'I' narrator of telling lies and making up stories about him). Nabokov teases us with this insoluble conundrum, bringing himself closer and closer in the last chapter to a confrontation with Pnin without ever quite clinching it.

There is an interesting note of authorial unease in this section of the book, as if Nabokov felt almost guilty at having created a character so much less happy and successful than himself, and subjecting him to a series of embarrassing and humiliating experiences. This theme is worked out through the character of Jack Cockerell, the head of the English Department, whose expert mimicry of Pnin is a sour, second-order version of the author's original creation of the character. Cockerell's imitation of Pnin is his party piece, his hobby, his occupation, and increasingly his obsession. When the narrator (let us call him 'N.') arrives in Waindell to give a public lecture prior to taking up his appointment, Jack Cockerell puts him up for the night and treats him to the whole repertoire of his Pnin imitations, a performance which amuses N. at first but becomes increasingly wearisome and leaves him finally 'with the mental counterpart of a bad taste in the mouth'. Very early the next morning N. goes out and glimpses Pnin driving out of Waindell for the last time, in his old blue sedan packed with possessions, accompanied by a dog that has never been mentioned before (a final hint, perhaps, of the limitations of N.'s knowledge of Pnin), but fails to attract his attention. Returning to Cockerell's house, N. is trapped by his host and led, like a prisoner to punishment, to 'a British breakfast of depressing kidneys and fish'.

> 'And now,' he said, 'I am going to tell you the story of Pnin rising to address the Cremona Women's Club and discovering he had brought the wrong lecture.'

This, the last sentence in the book, takes us back to the end of the first story, but gives it a new twist. Chapter One ends with Pnin having survived all the various disasters which threatened the successful delivery of his lecture. Confident that he has the text safely stowed in the pocket of his jacket, he listens to the chairwoman's bathetic introduction (a masterpiece of mimicry, this, by the way) without being in the least bothered by it. He is rapt in reverie, triggered by a memory of reciting a poem by Pushkin as a boy in the presence of his proud parents. It is a poignant yet sweet epiphany of the world he has lost: 'Murdered, forgotten, unrevenged, incorrupt, immortal, many old friends were scattered through the dim hall among more recent people.' Are we to suppose that, after this moving experience, another characteristic pratfall awaited the unfortunate Pnin? There is of course no way of deciding with certainty whether Cockerell is right or wrong in claiming that Pnin had after all contrived to bring the wrong lecture: the relation between the two versions of the episode is another example of aporia. There are hints in Chapter Seven that some of Cockerell's Pnin anecdotes are unreliable, the product of mischievous invention rather than accurate reporting, and we may choose to place this one in that category. But this merely underlines the way in which Cockerell's storytelling casts a cold light on N.'s (or Nabokov's) own storytelling and perhaps on the whole process by which writers turn life into art.

Novel of character, *roman-à-clef*, campus novel, epiphanic short story, postmodernist metafiction – *Pnin* contains elements of all these fictional subgenres, but ultimately it is *sui generis*, uniquely and quintessentially Nabokovian, having a family resemblance to his other works without being exactly like any of them. For those who know their Nabokov well it is full of allusions to and foreshadowings of those other works (especially *Pale Fire*, where Pnin reappears, happily ensconced in a tenured professorship at Wordsmith College), authorial in-jokes and hobby horses, and coded meanings concealed in proper names. A formidable body of commentary and exegesis has by now accumulated around this slim volume. But even first-time readers cannot fail to appreciate Nabokov's marvellous and distinctive way with words. The apparently effortless fertility of his metaphorical imagination is never employed ostentatiously for its own sake, but always to give us an enhanced awareness of reality. For example, Pnin's habit of breaking off from the prepared text of his lectures to interpolate some personal reminiscence is described as 'those unforgettable digressions of his, when he would remove his glasses to beam at the past while massaging the lenses of the present' – a brilliant fusion of the literal and the metaphorical, of the physical and the emotional. Or take the more elaborated account of Pnin's reaction to the extraction of his teeth:

> It surprised him to realize how fond he had been of his teeth. His tongue, a fat, sleek seal, used to flop and slide so happily

among the familiar rocks, checking the contours of a battered but still secure kingdom, plunging from cave to cove, climbing this jag, nuzzling that notch, finding a shred of sweet seaweed in the same old cleft; but now not a landmark remained, and all there existed was a great dark wound, a terra incognita of gums which dread and disgust forbade one to investigate.

Were the effects of this banal but unpleasant operation ever described so vividly, sympathetically and humorously?

Nabokov, however, does not simply aim at a perfect match between his language and his imagined world. There are always in his work reminders that reality is larger, denser and more various than any work of art can encompass – moments when the discourse suddenly seems to take off on its own and break through the formal limits of the story into the world outside the story, where the author and the reader exist, sometimes sadly – e.g.:

During the eight years Pnin had taught at Waindell College he had changed his lodgings . . . about every semester. The accumulation of consecutive rooms in his memory now resembled those displays of grouped elbow chairs on show, and beds, and lamps, and inglenooks which, ignoring all space-time distinctions, commingle in the soft light of a furniture store beyond which it snows, and the dusk deepens, and nobody loves anybody.

The reference in Chapter Seven to Pnin's conference paper 'Homer's and Gogol's use of the Rambling Comparison' acknowledges precedents for this trope, but Nabokov uses it in a wholly original way. And it is not only in figurative language that he is constantly reminding us of how much of reality the economy of art excludes. That is surely the point of the extraordinary plethora of proper names in this short text – over three hundred of them. Some are fictional, some historical; some are mentioned only once, and others reappear unexpectedly in the story. Most trail with them some anecdotal fragment of a whole life, which if reported in its entirety, would expand the book to epic proportions. This sentence, for example, wonderfully defies comprehension by sheer overload of disparate information, so that by the time you get to the end of it you have forgotten how it began:

> Should one trace Victor's passion for pigments back to Hans Andersen (no relation to the bedside Dane), who had been a stained-glass artist in Lübeck before losing his mind (and believing himself to be a cathedral) soon after his beloved daughter married a gray-haired Hamburg jeweler, author of a monograph on sapphires and Eric's maternal grandfather?

When Nabokov submitted the complete *Pnin* to his American publishers, Viking, in the fall of 1955, they rejected it on the grounds that it was 'too short', which was probably a euphemistic way of saying that they thought it was too unconventional in form for the fiction market. Harper, whom Nabokov tried next, also passed. Finally, in August 1956 Doubleday undertook to publish the book, and it appeared in March of the following year. Over the same period Nabokov had experienced mixed fortunes with *Lolita*. Despairing of publishing it in America, he had agreed to its publication in 1955 by Maurice Girodias, a Paris-based publisher of works in English too sexually explicit to be tolerated in Britain and

America. When Graham Greene picked *Lolita* as one of his 'Books of the Year' he drew international attention to it, and provoked a controversy about the morality of Nabokov's novel which still continues. For a time the book was banned in France, but contraband copies circulated among the literati in England and America. In consequence, when *Pnin* was published Nabokov already enjoyed a kind of celebrity in America as the author of a highly controversial but generally unobtainable novel, variously described as a masterpiece and a piece of pornography. This ensured extensive review coverage for *Pnin*, which was also largely favourable. Though some critics complained that it was a collection of sketches rather than a novel, the book indubitably demonstrated that Nabokov was no pornographer but a literary artist of rare ability. *Pnin* was reprinted twice within two weeks of publication. Nabokov had never known such success before, but it was nothing to what awaited him. When *Lolita* was at last published in America in the following year, 1958, it went on to sell in millions, world-wide, and completely eclipsed *Pnin* in public consciousness. *Lolita* is the book for which Nabokov will always be best known, but it was *Pnin* which first established his reputation as a writer of distinction and originality in the medium of English, and as an American rather than an émigré author, representing the manners and speech and landscape of his adopted country as vividly as the Russia from which he was exiled.

Notes

1 Galya Diment, *Pniniad: Vladimir Nabokov and Marc Szeftel* (1997), p. 44.

2 Brian Boyd, *Vladimir Nabokov: The American Years* (1991), pp. 292–3.

3 Ibid., p. 225.

4 Ibid., p. 259.

UMBERTO ECO:
The Name of the Rose

In the middle of June 1979, when I was still a full-time professor at the University of Birmingham, I attended a conference in Israel on 'Narrative Theory and Poetics of Fiction' organised by the Porter Institute for Poetics and Semiotics at Tel-Aviv University. Some fifty scholars from all over the world assembled in a hotel in Tel-Aviv to deliver and debate papers on subjects like 'Fictionality and the Role of Conventions in Aesthetic Communication' and 'Isotopic Organisation and Narrative Grammar'. One evening we were all bussed into the university for an official reception, followed by two public lectures. I had been asked to give one of them, and the other was to be given by Professor Umberto Eco of the University of Bologna, whom I had not previously met: a barrel-chested, bearded, genial man, who spoke fluent English accompanied by all the expressive body language one expects of Italians. To be invited to lecture was a kind of honour, but it was one both of us would gladly have relinquished. The weather was extremely hot, and the lecture theatre was not air-conditioned (I think the system had broken down). Our *colleagues from the conference, who had already listened to five papers that day, were understandably resentful at being required to sit through two more lectures delivered end to end in conditions of stifling heat, and even the 'public' members of the audience looked somewhat listless. The chairman begged us to abbreviate our lectures from the customary fifty-five minutes to forty-five, and, making cuts on our feet, we managed to get through the session in just under an hour and a half. At the end Umberto Eco, his shirt soaked with perspiration from his animated performance, turned to me and said with a smile, 'Well, we did it!'*

I spoke on problematical endings in English fiction;[1] he on 'What is Semiotics?' The short answer to that question is: 'the systematic study of signs'. Umberto Eco was well qualified to give a fuller answer, being the author of A Theory of Semiotics *(1976) and numerous other publications highly regarded by specialists in literary and linguistic theory. At that time, outside Italy where he was also well known as a critic and journalist, his readers were almost exclusively academics like those attending the conference in Tel Aviv. What we did not know, in June 1979, was that he was writing a novel, which must have been well on the way to completion by then, and would be published in Italy the following year under the title,* Il Nome della Rosa. *What even Umberto Eco did not know was that over the next three or four years he would in consequence become one of the most famous writers in the world.*

It is impossible to write about *The Name of the Rose* without considering its extraordinary global success with both critics and the reading public at large. It is an example of that rare publishing phenomenon, the literary mega-bestseller which transcends linguistic boundaries. By 'mega' I denote sales calculated in millions, not thousands, and by 'literary' I mean

a novel with the kind of artistic ambition and stylistic individuality that usually deters a mass audience: a category which
includes, say, *Midnight's Children* but not *The Da Vinci Code*.
The difference, as Umberto Eco himself has said, is between
the kind of book that gives readers what they want and the
kind of book that makes its readers realise that unconsciously
they have always wanted it.[2] Only a very few novels of the
latter kind in recent times have become major bestsellers not
only in their own countries, but in translation as well, and it
is a particularly difficult feat for books translated into English
from other languages to achieve, since Anglophone readers
are already well supplied with high-quality literary fiction and
tend to be lazily incurious about new work from other
cultures. You can almost count on the fingers of one hand
books of real distinction which have overcome this resistance:
Dr Zhivago, *The Leopard*, *The Tin Drum*, *One Hundred Years of
Solitude*, *The Name of the Rose* . . . There may be a few other
candidates, but not many. And of those examples, the global
success of *The Name of the Rose* was in many ways the most
surprising and unpredictable. To be sure, it is a kind of murder
mystery, a universally popular narrative form; but bookshop
shelves are stacked with murder mysteries that attract only
modest audiences, and the special features of this one include
a formidable amount of non-narrative discourse about philosophy, theology, and a particularly complicated chapter of
medieval European history, all of which the reader must nego-
tiate in order to discover whodunnit. The book also contains
numerous passages in Latin which are not translated into the
vernacular. Given Eco's reputation in Italy, *The Name of the
Rose* was sure to do fairly well there, and his Italian publisher
Bompiani ordered a first print run of 15,000 copies, hoping
for an eventual sale of about 30,000. But its prospects in the

international market must have seemed slim before publication. To date it has sold some nine million copies – the majority of them in translation.[3]

The Name of the Rose was enthusiastically received in Italy on its publication in 1980, soon sold 500,000 copies there and was awarded three literary prizes the following year. It was quickly translated into German and French, and became a bestseller in both countries, winning the Prix Medici Etranger in France in 1982. The English-language edition was slower to appear, being published in Britain and America in 1983. It so happens that the English publishers of *The Name of the Rose*, Secker & Warburg, are also the publishers of my own novels, and the managing director of the firm at that time, Tom Rosenthal, is a personal friend. I asked him how he came to acquire the rights in Eco's novel, and his account was interestingly revealing about the book's fortunes in the marketplace and the processes of modern publishing. Bompiani had acquired world rights in the novel, and after its successful publication in Italy sent out copies to leading literary publishers all round the world – to more than one in each country – inviting offers. It was a kind of auction, but not one on which Tom was inclined to risk a great deal of money. Publishing wisdom decreed that literary novels in translation do not sell. This one was extremely long (thus expensive to translate and produce), and even to the casual non-Italian eye seemed full of dense and difficult material. It was the first novel of a writer known in England (if at all) as the author of scholarly books of limited appeal. Tom Rosenthal prudently sought the co-operation of an American publisher, Helen Wolff, of Harcourt Brace, and suggested that if they got good reports on the novel they should share the cost of translation. Helen Wolff agreed,

Secker obtained a favourable report from Isabel Quigley (very well qualified for the task, being fluent in Italian, a regular reviewer of fiction and a Catholic), and Tom made his offer to Bompiani: an advance against royalties of £1,000. (This implied a cautious projected sale of between 1,500 and 2,000 copies.) Tom recalls that 'Bompiani kept phoning to say, "Can't you offer more?"' from which he deduced that no other British publisher had made a better offer – indeed he suspected that no one had made any offer at all. Had he been given first refusal of the English rights he might have gone up to £3,000 to secure them, but in the circumstances there was no incentive to improve his offer, and so the deal was done.

While the book was being translated (superbly, by William Weaver, probably the best translator from Italian into English in the world), *The Name of the Rose* became a critically acclaimed bestseller in Germany and France, but Secker & Warburg were by no means confident this success would be replicated in Britain. Their initial print order from Harcourt Brace (it was at that time cheaper to import finished copies from the USA than to produce them in England) was only 2,250. Tom Rosenthal recalls an editorial sales meeting early in 1983 at which he announced that the main item on the agenda was:

'What the hell do we do about *The Name of the Rose?*' Everyone looked very blank. I said, 'It's become for me a matter of national pride. We just can't be the illiterate, insular Brits yet again. I've got the sales figures from Italy, Germany, France. I can't face my colleagues at Frankfurt if we make a flop of it. I want some ideas.'

The main idea that emerged was to send six or seven hundred of the finished copies imported from Harcourt Brace to literary 'opinion-formers' in the UK (of whom I was one) instead of the drably bound uncorrected proofs usually circulated in advance of publication, in the hope that this handsome gift would demonstrate the publishers' faith in the book and ensure that it was read. The strategy seemed to be successful inasmuch as *The Name of the Rose* received ecstatic reviews and reached the number one position in the *Sunday Times* bestseller list. It sold about 60,000 copies in hardback, and Picador, who paid just £2,000 advance for the paperback rights, had sold 850,000 copies of their edition by 1992 and the novel was still selling 70,000 copies a year.[4]

In America, with its larger market, the book's success was even more spectacular, something Secker were able to exploit in their advertising. It had been turned down by nearly every major American publisher, sometimes more than once, before Harcourt Brace took it for a modest advance of $4,000. It was published in June 1983. Within two weeks it was in the *New York Sunday Times* bestseller list, by the beginning of August it was at number one position (just ahead of *The Return of the Jedi*) and it stayed on the list for twenty-three weeks. By the end of September it had sold more than 200,000 copies, and the paperback rights had been sold for a record sum for a translated novel. A rival publisher commented: 'It's not marketing, so it must be something in the book.'[5] Indeed. Something like: a gripping mystery, vivid characterisation, an atmospheric setting, fascinating period detail, sly humour, dramatic confrontations, stunning set pieces, and a supple, eloquent prose that can shift its register to encompass the experience of faith, doubt, horror, erotic ecstasy, and despair. 'A delight for an elite, yet giving pleasure to all', was one journalistic description of *The Name of the Rose*.[6] Or as Nicholas Shrimpton wittily observed when reviewing the novel, 'Whether you're into Sherlock Holmes, *Montaillou*, Borges, the *nouvelle critique*, the Rule of St Benedict, metaphysics, library design or *The Thing from the Crypt*, you'll love it. Who can that miss out?'[7]

Readers of the novel are fortunate to have the author's own account of its genesis and composition: a little book entitled *Reflections on 'The Name of the Rose'*, published a few years later.[8] Being a sophisticated literary theorist, Eco is well aware of the status and limitations of such revelations. 'The author must not interpret. But he may tell why and how he wrote his book.' A writer must not deliver an 'authorised' interpretation of his book because that would compromise the potential of a genuinely literary text to generate different meanings from different readings, without ever being completely exhausted; but telling why and how he wrote his book may throw a uniquely valuable light on the creative process, information which the reader can freely apply to his reading of the work. In short, the *Reflections* are themselves open to interpretation. Eco tells us, 'I began writing in March of 1978, prodded by a seminal idea: I felt like poisoning a monk.' But he does not tell us why he felt like poisoning a monk. From what follows, and from the novel itself, we might deduce that there were two possible reasons, not mutually exclusive. One is that as a critic and semiotician fascinated by the productions of popular culture, and the structural principles and conventions that underlie them, and as a long-standing fan of the classic detective story exemplified by the Sherlock Holmes stories of Sir Arthur Conan Doyle, Eco had a 'yen' (his, or his translator's, word) to try his hand at such a story, and thought that a monastic community would provide a novel setting for one. His working title for some time was *The Abbey of the Murder*, suggesting a piquant variation on a familiar formula. But we might speculate that there was a deeper, personal and psychological motivation for wanting to murder a monk (or, as it turned out, several monks) if only in make-believe.

Originally he intended to set the story in contemporary Italy, but he soon shifted it to the late Middle Ages, adding more and more levels of meaning through intertextual references and correspondences between medieval and modern times, drawing on a great store of knowledge which he had accumulated early in life, but hardly used in his career as a critic and semiotician ('I was a medievalist in hibernation', he observes). As a student at Turin University, Umberto Eco switched from studying law (his father's recommendation) to medieval literature and philosophy, writing a thesis on the aesthetics of St Thomas Aquinas which was his first published book. *The Name of the Rose* is manifestly the work of a man who knows the Catholic religion and its underlying meta physic with the intimate, detailed understanding of someone who was once a believer. He was brought up as a Catholic, and was once 'a militant Catholic activist', but at some stage of his adult life Umberto Eco ceased to believe, and described himself in 1983 as 'a *cane sciolto*, a stray dog, who eschews rigid affiliation with any movement, religious or political'.[9] The element of transgression inherent in murder, which makes it such a perennial source of literary interest, acquires an extra *frisson* when placed in a monastic context – when both the victims and the suspects are members of a religious community. It is possible therefore that this narrative idea attracted Eco and excited his imagination partly because it dramatised his own ambivalent attitude to the faith of his childhood, a mixture of respect and repulsion, nostalgia and rejection. The detective-hero of *The Name of the Rose*, William of Baskerville, is a Franciscan friar who has many intellectual traits that belong to the modern secular world, is highly critical of the institutional Church, and in the eyes of his devoutly orthodox acolyte, Adso, the narrator of the tale, comes perilously close to questioning the philosophical foundations of the Christian faith.

As Eco makes beautifully clear in *Reflections*, the composition of a novel entails making choices or decisions which are governed by certain constraints, comparable to, but quite different from, the constraints of metre and rhyme which govern the choice of words in the composition of verse. 'I discovered . . . that a novel has nothing to do with words in the first instance. Writing a novel is a cosmological matter, like the story told by Genesis.' That is to say, in order to tell a story you must construct a world which has a logical and consistent relation to the real world, and the challenge for the novelist is to explore and develop his narrative idea or ideas within those constraints. The relation between the fictional world and the real world need not be that of realistic imitation (allegory, for instance, may have a logical and consistent but non-realistic relation to the real world) but in the case of *The Name of the Rose* it is. Although the labyrinthine library which is the centre of the story is Eco's invention, its architecture is entirely coherent, and the layout of the monastery in which it is situated corresponds closely to Benedictine monasteries of the period. The plan provided in the endpapers of the book allows the reader to trace the characters' movements precisely, and these are completely credible in terms of temporal sequence and duration. In short, the laws of time and space in the real world are scrupulously observed in the fictional one.

The same applies to the historical and cultural background to the story. Eco tells us he would have found it much easier to set his story in the twelfth or thirteenth centuries, a period he knew well; but the intertextual device of making his detective a medieval precursor of Sherlock Holmes was already central to the project, and this compelled him to set his story in the fourteenth century, about which he was initially much less well informed, because William's empirical investigative approach to the crime, anticipating modern scientific method, could only have been adopted by a Franciscan friar influenced by the philosophical teachings of fellow Franciscans Roger Bacon and William of Occam, the second of whom lived in the first half of the fourteenth century. (The fact that very few of Eco's readers would be equally well informed is immaterial: once a novelist 'cheats' by disregarding his own knowledge about an important matter he risks losing faith in his own imaginary world.) Having placed the action of the novel early in the fourteenth century, and after doing some research into this period, Eco quickly realised that a prominent Franciscan at that time would inevitably have been involved in the debate about 'poverty' which was then dividing the Order, and critically affecting relations between it and the papacy, and between the papacy and the Holy Roman Empire. This then became the political context of his story, and the source of many intriguing parallels between medieval and modern times. The process demonstrates an interesting aspect of the composition of fiction, namely, that the acceptance of a constraint which may seem frustrating and bothersome at first often leads to the discovery of new ideas and story-stuff.

The history of the poverty debate is complicated, and not even Eco's medieval narrator, Adso, is able fully to grasp all its ramifications, but at the heart of it was the question: does perfect obedience to Christ's teaching entail the renunciation of all worldly goods and power? St Francis founded his Order on the principle that it did: his friars were forbidden to own property or money and required to live by the work of their hands or by begging. In due course the rigour of this rule was relaxed for practical reasons, leading to the breakaway of groups known as the 'Spirituals' or Fraticelli, who insisted on an extreme interpretation of 'poverty' and were denounced as heretics or schismatics by the official Church. While distancing themselves from these extremists, the Franciscans still tried to defend a moderate version of the ideal of poverty, and they were supported in this by the Holy Roman Emperor who, for his own political motives, wished to restrict the power of the Pope to jurisdiction over spiritual matters, while Pope John XXII, at that time in exile from Rome and based in Avignon, viewed the Franciscans with disfavour for opposite reasons. In 1321 the head of the Franciscan Order, Michael of Cesena, was invited to Avignon to discuss these issues, but hesitated, fearing, with some reason, that it might be a trap. This is the context of Eco's fictional story: William of Baskerville comes to a Benedictine monastery in the mountains of northern Italy in November 1321 to attend a meeting of the Emperor's and the Pope's theologians which will prepare the ground for a settlement of the dispute in the presence of the Pope himself in Avignon, but his visit coincides with a series of shocking murders in the abbey which then become the focus of narrative attention. Why in November? Because Michael of Cesena actually went to Avignon in December 1321. And why is the monastery in the mountains? Because the plot required a murder victim to be found head down in a vat of pig's blood, and pigs were customarily slaughtered in cold temperatures, which in Italy in November would be most plausible at high altitude. And why did a victim have to be dunked in pig's blood? Because the different methods employed by the murderer must seem to correspond to the prophecies of the seven angels of the Apocalypse, or Book of Revelation, announcing the end of the world, the second of which says that part of the sea will turn into blood.

These logical links are the nuts and bolts which hold the structure of the narrative together in the mind of the novelist; they are hardly perceived as such by the reader, who experiences the book in a quite different way, as a flow of information in which many different strands are interwoven, at times confusingly. For instance, it is not until well over a hundred pages into the book that the precise nature of William's mission is explained, though there are oblique allusions to it.* Nor are these the only challenges to the reader's patience and pertinacity. First he must pass through the portals of the spoof scholarly apparatus which explains how Adso's story came into the possession of the 'editor'; then he must assimilate the rules, routines and protocol of monastic life, learn the temporal division of the day into the canonical hours of Matins, Lauds, etc., attend to Adso's exhaustive and

---

* This perhaps accounts for the inaccuracy of some descriptions of the novel. The blurb on the jacket of the first Secker edition begins: 'Franciscans in a wealthy Italian abbey are suspected of heresy, and Brother William of Baskerville arrives to investigate.' This misrepresentation derived from the American printing of the jacket and was corrected in subsequent editions. But the catalogue entry for the most recent English edition of the novel on the Amazon UK website states: 'One after another, half a dozen monks are found murdered in the most bizarre of ways. A learned Franciscan *who is sent to solve the mysteries* finds himself involved in the frightening events' [my emphasis].

exhausting description of the carving on the door of the church in which the medieval world picture is lavishly illustrated, and grapple with all manner of recondite theological and scriptural allusions. Eco reveals that friends and editors who read his novel in manuscript recommended that he abbreviate the first hundred pages, which they found 'very difficult and demanding'. He refused on the grounds that these pages were like a 'penance or initiation'. Those who could not get through them would never finish the book anyway; those who did would have learned how to read it, and would not be able to stop. This remarkable demonstration of faith in his own work was in the event fully justified, but he tested his readers' application and attentiveness to the very last lines of the novel, which contain a cryptic Latin clue to the meaning of its title. (I shall return to this later.)

Umberto Eco wrote what was in effect his own 'blurb' on the dust jacket of the first Italian edition of *The Name of the Rose*, in which he predicted that it would be read in three different ways:

Difficult to define (Gothic novel, medieval chronicle, detective story, ideological narrative *à clef*, allegory) this novel . . . may perhaps be read in three ways. The first category of readers will be taken by the plot and the *coups de scène*, and will accept even the long bookish discussions and the philosophical dialogues, because it will sense that the signs, the traces and the revelatory symptoms are nesting precisely in those inattentive pages. The second category will be impassioned by the debate of ideas, and will attempt to establish connections (which the author refuses to authorise) with the

> present. The third will realise that this text is a textile of other
> texts, a 'whodunnit' of quotations, a book built of books.[10]

Michael Caesar plausibly suggests that there is an implied hierarchy in the listing of these kinds of reading, the most
approved being the last.[11] A fully appreciative reading of the
novel must, however, combine all three.

The first kind of reading responds to the novel primarily
as a story of crime and detection, in which the chief narrative question is 'Whodunnit?' A crime is committed, or a
series of linked crimes, and the reader is involved in the quest
to find the culprit, perhaps pitting his own wits against those
of the detective in the interpretation of clues. This undoubt-
edly is the prime source of interest for many readers of *The
Name of the Rose*, the lure which more than any other factor
impels them to go on turning the pages. But such a reader
could hardly fail to notice that the medieval Franciscan detective is a literary reincarnation (or historically a pre-incarna-
tion) of Sherlock Holmes. William's place of origin alludes
to one of the most famous Sherlock Holmes stories, 'The
Hound of the Baskervilles', and William's companion Adso
has many of the character traits, and the same narrator-
function, as Holmes's faithful sidekick, Dr Watson. In the
very first chapter William demonstrates his powers of deduc-
tion to the admiring Adso, extrapolating from a few hoof-
prints in the snow a circumstantially accurate account of how
a particular horse has escaped from the abbey, an almost parodic reprise of many similar scenes in the Sherlock Holmes
stories. The abbey is often swathed in fog at crucial moments,
a favourite meteorological device of Conan Doyle's to
heighten mystery and suspense; and when William finally
confronts the villain of the story there is the same mutual

respect between them as between Holmes and Moriarty. In short, it is hardly possible to be a reader in Eco's first category without enjoying some of the intertextual pleasures that are relished by his third category.

The Name of the Rose conforms in several respects to the structure of the classic detective story as elegantly analysed by the narratologist Tzvetan Todorov.[12] He points out that it actually consists of two stories: the story of the crime, which the detective is trying to reconstruct from the available evidence, working from effect to cause, and the story of the investigation itself, which proceeds from cause to effect (the ultimate effect being the unmasking of the culprit). The second story is often reported by a friend of the detective (e.g. Watson) who acknowledges that he is writing it, while the story of the crime never admits its literariness. The Name of the Rose conforms to this pattern. Many modern detective stories take place in an enclosed setting – for instance, a country house – which limits the number of possible suspects and creates interesting relationships between them; Eco's abbey and its community provide a perfect medieval equivalent. The form tends towards a 'geometric structure' – Todorov cites the example of Agatha Christie's Murder on the Orient Express, which contains, between a prologue and epilogue, twelve chapters, twelve suspects and twelve interrogations. The action of The Name of the Rose is divided into seven days, like God's creation of the world in Genesis, on each of which a murder occurs. In the classic whodunnit, Todorov observes, even one in which a serial murderer is at large, 'a rule of the genre postulates the detective's immunity'. This is true of The Name of the Rose: William and Adso never seem to fear for their own lives as the corpses pile up, and what most disturbs the former is the threat that he may be banished from the abbey before he has completed his investigative task. Although the murderer makes a cunning attempt to kill William in the denouement it is foiled before we know it has been attempted.

In spite of all these correspondences, however, *The Name of the Rose* deviates from the formula of the Sherlock Holmes stories and their successors in several crucial respects. The classic detective story affirms the victory of good over evil, reason over passion, law and order over anarchy; a state of harmony and civility which was ruptured by a violent act is healed and restored to normality by the skill and dedication of the detective-hero. *The Name of the Rose* has no such consoling conclusion. Although William unmasks the man behind the deaths, the old blind monk Jorge, the latter is not surprised, but sets up their final confrontation in a way that enables him to escape arrest. Furthermore William's intervention brings about the destruction of one of the greatest libraries in Christendom, including a unique work of Aristotle's long assumed to have been lost, a catastrophe that causes the scholarly William to weep. And when Adso tries to console him by saying that he has defeated Jorge 'because you exposed his plot', William replies, 'There was no plot . . . and I discovered it by mistake.' He had supposed there was one murderer, when in fact each crime was committed by a different person, albeit manipulated by Jorge; he had formed the theory that the murderer was consciously imitating the prophecies of the Last Days in the Apocalypse, whereas Jorge actually derived this idea from William himself and then used it to justify his own actions. 'Where is all my wisdom, then?' asks William. 'I behaved stubbornly, pursuing a semblance of order, when I should have known well that there is no order in the universe.' This is a conclusion that is as heretical in the world of the detective story as it would have been in a medieval monastery.

The second kind of reader described by Eco in his jacket note is 'impassioned by the debate of ideas, and will attempt to establish connections . . . with the present'. True to this prediction, when the novel first appeared it was seen, especially in his native Italy, as referring obliquely to the troubled political and ideological climate of the 1960s and '70s. The mixture of utopianism, anarchism and violence in the behaviour of the groups who broke away from the Franciscan Order in the Middle Ages to form their own communities, sometimes practising a kind of primitive communism which included sexual promiscuity, foreshadowed the development of extreme Protestant sects during the Reformation; but these communities also offer parallels to the activities of various revolutionary cells in modern Europe like the Baader–Meinhof gang or the Italian Red Brigades, and countless radical guerrilla-style movements in North and South America; while the ruthless and cruel methods of the medieval Inquisition which sought to stamp out any threat to the Church's authority can be compared to the actions of repressive governments and secret neo-fascist groups to stamp out radical dissent in the late twentieth century. This dimension of the novel becomes most evident in the trial of Remigio the cellarer, when the conflict between William and the Inquisitor Bernard Gui comes to a head. It transpires that before he joined the Benedictine community of the abbey, Remigio was a member of the schismatic Franciscan sect led by Fra Dolcino, who under the banner of 'poverty' lived a semi-bandit-like existence, defying all the laws of Church and state. Remigio admits to having been a Dolcinian, and his confession evokes the attitudes of modern ideologically inspired terrorists:

> '. . . we burned and looted because we had proclaimed poverty the universal law, and we had the right to appropriate the illegitimate riches of others, and we wanted to strike at the heart of the network of greed that extended from parish to parish, but we never looted in order to possess, or killed in order to loot. We killed in order to punish, to purify the impure through blood. Perhaps we were driven by an overweening desire for justice: a man can sin through overweening love of God, through superabundance of perfection. We were the true spiritual congregation sent by the Lord and destined for the glory of the last days: we sought our reward in paradise, hastening the time of your destruction.'

In his journalistic articles in the '70s Eco drew comparisons between medieval millennial sects and modern far left groups, and in the course of researching his novel he discovered that Dolcino came from Trento, as did Renato Curcio, founder of the Red Brigades, and that Italian anarchists still made an annual pilgrimage to the site of Dolcino's fortified camp.[13] The experience of living through a violent period in Italian political history, in which colleagues and students of his died, obviously provided some of the imaginative energy that fuelled *The Name of the Rose*. But in the quarter of a century since it was published the novel has acquired a new topicality. There are uncanny echoes in Remigio's words of threats from Islamist groups like Al-Qaeda and the pronouncements of their counterparts in fundamentalist Christian sects: the note of arrogant intolerance, and callous indifference to the lives of those who do not share your world-view.

Remigio admits to complicity in the excesses of the Dolcinians, but swears he is innocent of the murders in the abbey. Bernard, however, is eager to pin the crimes on Remigio, in order to demonstrate that the Franciscan cult of 'poverty' leads eventually and inevitably to heresy and abomination. Taking advantage of some circumstantial evidence, he threatens to extort a confession from Remigio by means of torture, upon which the wretched man capitulates and says he will confess to any and all of the murders as well as heresy, preferring to go straight to the stake and die from suffocation than to be tortured. This travesty of justice, which has numerous parallels in twentieth-century history, gains an element of pathos (for Remigio himself is not a very endearing character) from the circumstance that the girl with whom Adso has experienced the ecstasy of erotic and romantic love is unluckily implicated and condemned as a witch.

In old age Asdo believes that 'inquisitors create heretics'. His mentor, William, was once an Inquisitor too, but resigned his position because he came to the conclusion that torture violates a person's free will, which is an essential component of being human. William, anachronistically, represents the modern liberal humanist mind, and he speaks, one feels, for the author himself. He perceives that Bernard's obsessive persecution of alleged heretics is motivated less by religious zeal than by a determination to defend the authority and temporal power of the official Church against any kind of individualism. The mind behind the murders, the mind of the blind old monk Jorge of Burgos, however, is more theologically motivated, and the story ends with an extended argument, a kind of philosophical duel, between him and William. This debate has already been foreshadowed in several conversations earlier in the book, and in Jorge's sermon after the death of Severinus. It centres, perhaps surprisingly, on the place of laughter in human civilisation. Here the second kind of reading of *The Name of the Rose*, the ideological, segues into the third, the intertextual.

The very name Jorge of Burgos, especially occurring in connection with an immense monastic library of labyrinthine but geometrical construction, will suggest to alert readers the name of Jorge Luis Borges, the great Argentine poet and fabulist who for many years was director of the National Library of Argentina, whose work has been anthologised in a widely read book entitled, in English, *Labyrinths*, which contains a story called 'The Library of Babel', beginning: 'The universe (which others call the Library) is composed of an indefinite and perhaps infinite number of hexagonal galleries . . .'[14] An early hint of this strain of allusion is to be found in the pseudo-editorial apparatus to *The Name of the Rose* – itself an *hommage* to Borges's witty inventions of fictitious works of arcane scholarship – where the author states that he first discovered some quotations from the narrative of Adso of Melk in a copy of 'the Castilian version of a little work by Milo Temesvar, *On the Use of Mirrors in the Game of Chess*', which he came across in a bookshop on the Avenue Corrientes in Buenos Aires. The same bookshop is mentioned in the first story in *Labyrinths*, 'Tlön, Uqbar, Orbis Tertius', which begins, 'I owe the discovery of Uqbar to the conjunction of a mirror and an encyclopaedia.' At the climax of *The Name of the Rose* the criminal waits for the detective to find him, hidden behind a mirror in a library. That Eco gave Borges's name to his villain implies no disrespect for the Argentine writer – quite the contrary – but, along with the old monk's blindness, it may have been designed to put the reader off the scent on the whodunnit level of the story.

The monastery's library is at the very heart of this story, and so is the idea of the library as labyrinth. A library is itself intertextuality in material form, as Adso learns from William: 'I had thought each book spoke of the things, human or divine, that lie outside books. Now I realised that not infrequently books speak of books: it is as if they spoke among themselves.' But the labyrinthine construction of this building denies a library's true function, because it is designed to prevent the spread of knowledge rather than to facilitate it. 'The library defends itself, immeasurable as the truth it houses, deceitful as the falsehood it preserves,' the Abbot declares complacently to William. 'A spiritual labyrinth, it is also a terrestrial labyrinth. You might enter and you might not emerge.' Adso later wonders aloud: 'And is a library, then, an instrument not for distributing the truth but for delaying its appearance?' and his master answers, 'In this case it is.' Later William is more explicitly condemnatory:

> 'The good of a book lies in its being read. A book is made up of signs that speak of other signs, which in their turn speak of things. Without an eye to read them, a book . . . is dumb. This library was perhaps born to save the books it houses, but now it lives to bury them. That is why it becomes a sink of iniquity.'

The murders in the abbey are all connected with the library and with one book in particular, hidden in its labyrinthine stacks, a 'forbidden book' – forbidden, that is, by its authoritarian custodians, who fear the ideas it contains.

This book turns out to be Aristotle's lost treatise on Comedy – a brilliant stroke on Eco's part, though one that perhaps only fellow scholars will relish to the full. Aristotle's *Poetics* (probably a version of his lecture notes) is one of the foundation stones of literary criticism – nothing much of value was added to the theory of narrative until the twentieth century AD – but it is incomplete. The *Poetics* deals mainly with the genre of tragedy, and refers to a complementary Aristotelian study of comedy which did not survive. The consequences of this loss were immense, because it biased literary criticism in favour of 'serious' literature, and narrative forms that obeyed generic rules and observed stylistic decorum: tragedy and epic. Comedy was relegated to an inferior cultural status, and when the novel emerged as a distinctive literary form in the modern era, it for a long time suffered a similar fate because it could not be fitted into the available generic categories. The theorist who did more than any other single writer to restore the balance of general poetics was the Russian Mikhail Bakhtin (1895–1975), and his texts are among the most important of those woven into the 'textile' of *The Name of the Rose*.

What is distinctive about the novel as a form, according to Bakhtin, is that it is not written in a single style, like classical tragedy and epic, but in a medley of many styles, or voices – literary, colloquial, regional, technical, sublime, crude, parodic, and so on – which are combined in a 'polyphonic' discourse that imitates the dialogic character of ordinary speech, where every utterance implicitly or explicitly answers or echoes a previous utterance and anticipates another response. This makes the novel a literary medium that tends to question and subvert all 'totalising' ideologies which try to impose a single world-view. Bakhtin traces the genealogy of the novel back to the tradition of classical comedy, and the parodying-travestying tradition of carnival which preserved a spirit of demotic irreverence and liberty of thought through the Middle Ages. It was Rabelais, the subject of Bahktin's best-known work, *Rabelais and His World* (1986), who pre-eminently demonstrates the link between this carnivalesque tradition and the evolution of the modern novel. When William, in his final confrontation with Jorge, offers a speculative summary of Aristotle's argument in the treatise on Comedy, he (which is to say Eco) is essentially summarising Bakhtin:

'Comedy does not tell of famous and powerful men, but of base and ridiculous creatures, though not wicked; and it does not end with the death of the protagonists. It achieves the effect of the ridiculous by showing the defects and vices of ordinary men. Here Aristotle sees the tendency to laughter as a force for good, which can also have instructive value: through witty riddles and unexpected metaphors, though it tells us things differently from the way they are, as if it were lying, it actually obliges us to examine them more closely, and makes us say: Ah, this is just how things are, and I didn't know it. Truth is reached by depicting men and the world as worse than they are, or than we believe them to be, worse in any case than the epics, the tragedies, lives of the saints have shown them to us. Is that it?'

'Fairly close,' Jorge concedes.

Not till we reach this point in *The Name of the Rose* do we realise why there has been so much discussion between William and the monks of the abbey previously about the question of whether Christ laughed (he is never described as doing so in the New Testament), or why Jorge so vehemently insists that he did not. In the denouement William asks Jorge why he is so fearful of laughter, and of Aristotle's treatise, and Jorge replies that it is because the latter might convert carnival's temporary reversal of hierarchical order into a permanent state of radical libertarianism:

'. . . this book could teach learned men the clever . . . artifices that could legitimise the reversal. Then what in the villein [i.e., peasant] is still, fortunately, an operation of the belly would be transformed into an operation of the brain. That laughter is proper to man is a sign of our limitation, sinners that we are . . . Laughter, for a few moments, distracts the villein from fear. But the law is imposed by fear, whose true name is fear of God. This book could strike the Luciferine spark that would set a new fire to the world, and laughter would be defined as the new art, unknown to Prometheus, for cancelling fear.'

In his powerful sermon Jorge cites an Oriental caliph who burned a famous library on the grounds that the books it contained were either repeating what the Koran said and were therefore redundant, or contradicting it in which case they were harmful. Jorge says the Christian practice, in contrast, is to preserve useful commentary on Scripture and also heretical and infidel literature, so that the latter can be contradicted 'in the ways and times that the Lord chooses'. In practice, however, no one is allowed to read texts in the monastery library deemed to be subversive (many of which owe their survival to Arab scholars). Jorge describes the sin of pride which tempts the scholar-monk as 'that of seeking some information not yet vouchsafed mankind, as if the last word had not already resounded in the words of the last angel who speaks in the last book of Scripture'.

In the debate between Jorge and William, therefore, immutable dogma is opposed to open-minded enquiry, and fear to laughter. To prevent William, and posterity, from reading Aristotle's dangerous treatise on comedy, Jorge first attempts to eat it, then to burn it, and this action sets fire to the library, and eventually destroys the whole monastery. In a sense this is a punishment for the arrogance of the institution, personified by Jorge – 'the arrogance of the spirit, faith without smile, truth that is never seized by doubt', as William says; but the destruction of so many priceless books is also a catastrophe for William and Adso. At the end all is ashes and disillusionment. William derives no satisfaction from solving the mystery of the murders, and in opposing the tyranny of prescriptive orthodoxy he finds himself questioning the existence of order in the universe, and therefore of God. Along with his anticipation of modern liberal values he encounters the philosophical downside of modernity – the possibility that there are no solid foundations for any belief. Paradoxically *The Name of the Rose* is an essentially tragic novel, even though it contains a good deal of incidental humour and at its climax affirms the central place of comedy in human culture.

Adso, coming to the end of his story in his old age, on the threshold of death, cannot decide whether it 'contains some hidden meaning, or more than one, or many, or none at all . . . I leave this manuscript, I do not know for whom; I no longer know what it is about: stat rosa pristine nomine, nomina nuda tememus'. At the beginning of *Reflections*, Umberto Eco reveals that many readers of *The Name of the Rose* wrote to him wanting to know the meaning of this Latin hexameter and why it gives the novel its title. Their curiosity and puzzlement are not surprising, since there is no previous significant mention of a rose in the story. Eco explains that it is a line from a poem, *De contemptu mundi*, by Bernard of Morlay, a twelfth-century Benedictine, a meditation on the inevitable transitoriness of worldly things:

> But to the usual topos (the great of yesteryear, the once-famous cities, the lovely princesses: everything disappears into the void), Bernard adds that all these departed things leave (only, or at least) pure names behind them . . . The idea of calling my book *The Name of the Rose* came to me virtually by chance, and I liked it because the rose is a symbolic figure so rich in meanings that by now it hardly has any meaning left . . . The title rightly disoriented the reader, who was unable to choose just one interpretation; and even if he were able to catch the possible nominalist readings of the concluding verse, he would come to them only at the end, having made God knows what other choices. A title must muddle the reader's ideas, not regiment them.

Tantalisingly, Eco does not supply a translation of Bernard's line. *The Key to 'The Name of the Rose'*, a useful reference book written by three enthusiasts, containing translations of all the non-English passages in the English text, offers: 'Yesterday's rose endures in its name. We hold empty names.'[15] This is elegant but takes a certain poetic licence in rendering 'pristine' as 'yesterday' and 'nuda' as 'empty'. A more literal translation would be: 'the pre-existing rose exists through its name, we have [only] bare names'. In scholastic philosophy 'nominalism' was the argument (espoused by William of Occam among others) that universals are mere names, and have no existence apart from being thought (as opposed to 'realism' which held that they had substantial existence); but Eco's commentary gives nominalism a modern, deconstructionist spin, embracing the proliferation of meanings which the poetic use of language inevitably brings into play. Signs can only be interpreted with other signs. It has since been suggested that 'rosa' in Bernard's line might be a scribe's misreading of 'Roma', which would fit better as the conclusion to a series of verses dedicated to famous Romans and would be more appropriate to the theme of transitoriness. If, as is almost certain, Umberto Eco is acquainted with this scholarly hypothesis he must be highly delighted at the possibility that a monk's mistranscription provided him with his polysemous title.

Notes

1 Published as 'Ambiguously Ever After: Problematical Endings in English Fiction', in *Working with Structuralism* (1981).

2 Umberto Eco, *Reflections on 'The Name of the Rose'* (1985), pp. 48–9.

3 These sales figures are cited in a profile of Umberto Eco in the London *Times*, 29 September 1983, and the Porto Ludovico website, http://www.themodernworld.com

4 *Bookseller*, 7 August 1992.

5 *Wall Street Journal*, 23 September 1983.

6 *The Times*, 29 September 1983.

7 *Sunday Times*, 2 October 1983.

8 See note 2, above. The first Italian edition was published in 1983.

9 *Time*, 12 December 1983.

10 Quoted and translated by Walter E. Stephens, 'Ec(h)o in Fabula', *Diacritics*, 13, 2 (1983), p. 51.

11 M. P. Caesar, 'Secrets: a Reading of Umberto Eco', Inaugural Lecture, University of Birmingham, Department of Italian Studies (1996), p. 5.

12 Tzvetan Todorov, 'The Typology of Detective Fiction', in *The Poetics of Prose*, translated by Richard Howard (1971), pp. 42–52.

13 Interview with Umberto Eco by Malcolm Imrie, *City Limits*, 14–20 October 1983.

14 *Labyrinths*, Penguin edn (1970), p. 78.

15 Adele J. Haft, Jane G. White, and Robert J. White, *The Key to 'The Name of the Rose'* (1999), p. 176.

THE BEST OF
YOUNG AMERICAN
NOVELISTS,
1996

This is a lightly revised and corrected version of a review, first published in The New York Review of Books, *of the Summer 1996 edition of the magazine* Granta, *edited by Ian Jack, devoted to samples of the work of twenty young American writers who had been chosen as* 'The Best of Young American Novelists'. *Both the edition of* Granta *and the review were attempts to take the measure of American prose fiction by young writers at a particular moment in time, and both inevitably provoke different or further reflections when reread ten years later. I have not, however, attempted to revise my piece in the wisdom of hindsight, and any afterthoughts are accommodated in footnotes, along with information for which there was no room in the original review. The implicit time base of the essay is therefore 1996.*

First, a little cultural archaeology; for the story behind this publication is almost as interesting as its contents. It begins in England in the late 1970s, when a young American expat called Bill Buford purchased the title of a languishing Cambridge University magazine, *Granta*,* and relaunched it as a literary periodical of extramural ambition and scope. Buford was a man with a mission. He thought British fiction was moribund – 'critically and aesthetically negligible' – and he aimed to revivify it by introducing the Brits to the work of their American contemporaries, 'some of the most challenging, diversified and adventurous writing today . . . a literary renaissance'. These quotations are taken from Buford's feisty introduction to his first issue, Spring 1979. In it, and the next one, he published the work of, among others, John Hawkes, Joyce Carol Oates, Susan Sontag, James Purdy, Ronald Sukenick, Donald Barthelme, Stanley Elkin, Leonard Michaels, William Gass, Walter Abish and Robert Coover.

As it happened, British fiction, invigorated partly by new immigrant cultural influences, was on the threshold of a renaissance of its own, and Buford was quick to recognise and encourage the new wave. In his third issue he showcased a long extract from the forthcoming second novel of a writer whose first attempt had sunk without trace – *Midnight's Children* by Salman Rushdie. Beside it he printed a piece by Angela Carter, who, though better known than Rushdie, was a long way from being what she eventually became (posthumously, alas), the modern author most widely studied in British universities and colleges. *Granta* soon acquired a reputation as the place to look for up-and-coming literary talent.

* *Granta* was founded in 1889, as a magazine produced by and for students, and was a stepping stone for many aspiring professional writers in its time, mainly in the area of 'light literature'. A. A. Milne, who edited it when he was an undergraduate, said later that he wanted 'He was a Granta man' engraved on his gravestone. (Ian Jack, 'Twenty-five going on 120', *Guardian*, 1 October 2004.)

It prospered, and deserved to. It grew thicker and glossier, resembling a paperback book rather than a magazine, with themed contents, and in due course was taken under Penguin's prestigious wing for distribution purposes.

There were two other developments in publishing in the early 1980s with which the fortunes of *Granta* became entwined. The Booker Prize, which had been trundling along for a decade without making much impact on the reading public, suddenly became the focus of intense media interest, and a powerful engine for generating book sales. Before 1980 the shortlist was announced and the winner secretly chosen at the same time. Under new rules, the meeting to decide the winner was held some weeks after the shortlist meeting, on the very day of the banquet at which the result was announced. This meant that bookmakers would accept bets on the outcome, and turned the banquet into an occasion of high drama and genuine suspense, a kind of literary Oscar night, broadcast live on network television. In 1980 the competition between two of England's most distinguished novelists who were on the shortlist, Anthony Burgess and William Golding (the eventual winner), caught the public's imagination. In 1981 the prize went to Rushdie for *Midnight's Children*, making him famous and confirming Buford's skill as a talent-spotter.

At around the same time a body called the British Book Marketing Council was formed. It was, as Buford recalled later, a typically '80s phenomenon, an application of 'enterprise culture' methods to a notoriously stuffy and conservative sector of retail trade. Under the direction of Desmond Clarke, the council instigated a series of promotional campaigns for literary fiction, children's books, travel writing, etc., under the general heading, *'Best of . . .'*. Participating publishers and booksellers mounted special window displays and organised signing sessions. How the books were selected, and by whom, was not disclosed; but whoever chose *The Best of Young British Novelists* in 1983 had excellent taste. Perhaps Buford was involved, because he published specimen work by the twenty writers, all under forty, in the seventh issue of *Granta*. They were: Martin Amis, Pat Barker, Julian Barnes, Ursula Bentley, William Boyd, Buchi Emecheta, Maggie Gee, Kazuo Ishiguro, Alan Judd, Adam Mars-Jones, Ian McEwan, Shiva Naipaul, Philip Norman, Christopher Priest, Salman Rushdie, Lisa St Auban de Teran, Clive Sinclair, Graham Swift, Rose Tremain and A. N. Wilson. Few of these writers failed to fulfil their early promise, and several have become very well known indeed.

Ten years later, in 1993, with the Book Marketing Council no longer in existence, Buford organised a new round of *The Best of Young British Novelists* under the aegis of *Granta*, and published extracts from their work in his forty-third issue, with an introduction that (for the first time) named the judges. They were: Salman Rushdie, A. S. Byatt, John Mitchinson (marketing director of the Waterstone's book-shop chain) and Buford himself. The writers chosen were: Iain Banks, Louis de Bernières, Anne Bilson, Tibor Fischer, Esther Freud, Alan Hollinghurst, Kazuo Ishiguro, A. L. Kennedy, Philip Kerr, Hanif Kureishi, Adam Lively, Adam Mars-Jones, Candia McWilliam, Lawrence Norfolk, Ben Okri, Caryl Phillips, Will Self, Nicholas Shakespeare, Helen Simpson and Jeanette Winterson. The publication of this list provoked a considerable amount of controversy in the British press. The chief complaint was not that the judges had over-looked deserving young writers, but that the new list compared so unfavourably with the class of '83 as to discredit the whole exercise. The implication was that whereas the earlier list drew attention to genuine talent, the new one was merely hyping mediocre or immature young writers. The judges retorted with some justice that, at the time, most of the writers on the 1983 list had yet to prove themselves. Certainly the 1993 list already looks more impressive than it did three years ago.* And it would be absurd to pretend that the 1983 list had some kind of canonical status, uncontaminated by commercial considerations. But what had begun as a mere marketing strategy, its promotions forgotten as soon as the special window displays were dismantled, had become, partly as a result of *Granta*'s involvement, something like a literary prize shared between twenty people: the right to put '*Selected as one of the Best of Young British Novelists*' on one's dust jacket. In an overcrowded marketplace, where too many authors and titles clamour for review space and the reading public's attention, such distinctions matter, and the controversy generated by competitions is grist to the media mill. In short, the '*Best of . . .*' story illustrates one of the most striking features of recent cultural history, the collaboration – some would call it an unholy alliance – of big business, the mass media, and high art, to their mutual material advantage.

In 1995 Bill Buford gave up the editorship of *Granta*, and returned to America to edit the literary pages of *The New Yorker*. Perhaps he felt he had done what he could for British fiction; or perhaps he felt that American fiction now needed his attentions more urgently. At any rate, he handed over his editorial seat to Ian Jack, a highly respected journalist and

* And even more so ten years later.

former editor of the *Independent on Sunday*, who had evidently had enough of the circulation war of attrition waged between British quality newspapers in recent years. Jack seems to have inherited, rather than instigated, an American version of 'The Best of Young British Novelists', the fruits of which are displayed in the Summer 1996 issue of *Granta*. The rules are the same – eligible writers must be under forty and have published at least one work of fiction – but the process of selection has become much more open, democratic and (one is bound to say) bureaucratic, in deference to American notions of fair play. Nominations were invited from many different constituencies, and several hundred titles were submitted. These were distributed among five regional judging panels, who forwarded their recommendations, fifty-two in all, to the final judges: Ian Jack, Robert Stone, Tobias Wolff, and Anne Tyler. There was a fifth appointed judge, Henry Louis 'Skip' Gates, professor of Afro-American studies at Harvard, who dropped out in contentious circumstances.*

Many judges of literary competitions embark on their task with pleasurable anticipation of publicly exercising their judgement and bestowing patronage, and then panic as they become aware of what is entailed: the grief and rage of disappointed writers, publishers and agents; the derision and disgust of critics who disagree with the judges' verdicts; the possible humiliation stored up for years to come if the chosen writers fail to live up to expectations. It is clear from Ian Jack's

---

* Ian Jack wrote in his editorial introduction to *Granta*, 'Professor Gates, unfortunately, could not be traced by fax or phone during the judging, and has spoken to no judge since'. Gates wrote a letter to the *New York Review* (17 October 1966, p. 62) explaining that, a late substitute for another judge who had resigned, he found he was unable to participate in the judging because of other commitments, and had telephoned Robert Stone after the final meeting to say he would accept the verdict of the other judges.

introduction that he and his colleagues suffered all these misgivings. Indeed, *The Best of Young American Novelists* is prefaced by so many apologies, caveats, rhetorical shrugs and handwringings, as almost to undermine the whole enterprise. The regional judges, says Jack, 'got [the writers] wrong, as judges tend to do . . . We wondered for a time if we might not override previous decisions and call in one or two glaring omissions [but] we decided to let the shortlist stay as it was; emendations would need to be wholesale . . . In other words, we would have picked another bunch of wrong writers.'

In fact the exercise was by no means as futile as that remark implies. Everybody knows that 'best' in this context is not an absolute and authoritative judgement, but it is not a totally arbitrary one either. A selection arrived at through such careful sifting of so many writers by such well-qualified judges must have *some* sort of representative value, must tell us *something* useful about the younger generation of American literary novelists and short-story writers. It can be used as an illustrated reading-list of young writers to look out for – on this level, it is the differences between them that matter. Or it can be used to try and identify the dominant characteristics of contemporary American prose fiction, in style, narrative technique, and subject matter – on this level it is the similarities between them that are interesting. I may say that I approached the selection with an open mind and very limited acquaintance with the work of young American writers. I recognised the names of only three or four of the chosen twenty and had previously read the work of only one, Lorrie Moore.

Perhaps for that reason, I find it hard to think of Lorrie Moore as a young writer, in the same category as the others. She needs no introduction, as the saying goes. She is already a master (or mistress) of her art, represented here by a characteristically accomplished story, wry but compassionate, called (with faint connotations of martyrdom) 'Agnes of Iowa', about a woman struggling with the fate of being plain and uncharismatic. Only once in her life does Agnes glimpse the possibility of passion and romance, when a South African poet visits the college where she teaches night-classes, but nothing comes of it, except that for some weeks after his departure the departmental secretary's memos come written on the back of scrap paper salvaged from surplus posters for the poet's reading.

> She would get a simple phone message – 'Your husband called. Please call him at the office' – and on the back would be the ripped centre of Beyerbach's nose, one minty eye, an elbowish chin. Eventually there were no more, and the scrap paper moved on to old contest announcements, grant deadlines, Easter concert notices.

What are the other best young American novelists writing about? Well, there are two novels-in-progress about Haiti. One is a historical novel by Madison Smartt Bell about the slave revolution of the early nineteenth century which reads, in the extract printed here, like a literary Western, as it describes the heroic endurance of an escaped slave searching in a pitiless landscape for the legendary General Toussaint Louverture; the other, by the gloriously named Edwige Danticat, herself born in Port-au-Prince, is about the massacre of Haitian refugees on the border between Haiti and the Dominican Republic in 1937, told from the point of view of a Haitian servant in a bourgeois Dominican family.

There are two novels about librarians. One is Alan

Kurzweil's hero and narrator, uneasily married to a French artist called Nicole, whose fractured English ('You are the apple of my eyeballs') charms him, but whose chaotic methods of storing things around the house offend his occupational devotion to order. As the man Nicole calls his 'shrimp' tells him: 'my impulse to catalog functioned as a kind of "belief system," one I maintained "with an ardor others reserve for their gods."'

The heroine of Elizabeth McCracken's first novel, *The Giant's House*, librarian of a small town on Cape Cod fifty years ago, also broods on such stereotyping:

> Librarians are supposed to be bitter spinsters, grudging, lonely. And above all stingy: we love collecting fines on overdue books, our silence.
>
> I did not love collecting fines; I forgave much more than I collected. I did not shush people unless they yelled. And though I was, technically, a spinster, I was only bitter insofar as people made me. It isn't that bitter people become librarians; it's that being a librarian may turn the most generous person bitter.

There is a touch of the bizarre (rare in the volume as a whole) in this story, inasmuch as the narrator is infatuated with a pubescent boy suffering from abnormal growth, but its strength is the revelation of her passionate character through, and in spite of, her dry, ironic, declarative prose style.

There are extracts from novels about young men from provincial backgrounds negotiating the puzzles and pitfalls of new social territory. Ethan Canin tells a Fitzgerald-like story of a freshman from the Midwest at Columbia, who comes under the spell of a charming fellow student and his cultured, eccentric family, whose male members are gifted, or cursed, with photographic memories. The hero of Jonathan Franzen's novel-in-progress is a compulsive liar whom we meet successfully defeating a polygraph test to obtain full security clearance as a federal employee.* Tom Drury's hero Paul, from rural Rhode Island, is working his way through college, and takes a night job punching felony statistics into an ageing computer under the supervision of a dour and disapproving criminologist with a passion for old cars called Leonard Draco. When Draco dies suddenly, Paul attends his funeral.

> Some of Leonard's friends got up to talk about his life. They said he liked the art of the Southwest, that he was a gifted mimic and that he had a well-hidden generous side. No one mentioned cars. Paul imagined a speech he could give: 'I did not know Leonard Draco well and yet I say to you that he loved cars and car parts.' Then the priest and his helpers gave communion. Paul knelt at the rail eating the bread and drinking the wine. He did not believe in God, but he believed in communion.

The story of his subsequent seduction by the widow is told in the same droll, deadpan style. One wonders if the hero is named in homage to Evelyn Waugh's Paul Pennyfeather.

There are four pieces about crime and/or prison. The one that made the deepest impression on me was an extract from Robert O'Connor's non-fiction novel-in-progress, based on his experiences of teaching composition to

---

* As far as I am aware, this work-in-progress was never published as a completed novel. I must admit that I failed to recognise in the extract the promise that would be richly fulfilled in Franzen's fine novel, *The Corrections* (2001), though on rereading it seems obvious enough.

convicts in a high-security penitentiary. The narrative manages to convey both the brutality and terror of prison life (generated by conflicts between prisoners rather than between prisoners and warders) and the comedy of the total incompatibility of the author's liberal humanist values with the macho ethics of his students. In one episode O'Connor sets an assignment in which the students have to tell a story and then draw a moral from it. A convict who answers to the name AKA Diaz tells the story of two men who are drinking together. Fred takes a quarter from the counter that belongs to Bill and they begin to quarrel about it:

> . . . whereupon Bill pulled out his piece which he happened to have handy, shot Fred to death and received a sentence of twenty-five to life. It was, Diaz mentioned, a true story, Bill being a pseudonym for his brother-in-law, now serving time at another state prison.
>
> Now came the moral. The moral of the story, Diaz wrote, was 'You shouldn't take what isn't yours.'
>
> 'Don't you think this is an unusual moral?' I asked.
>
> AKA Diaz looked at his paper. 'I think this pretty well covers it.'
>
> 'You might also conclude that Bill traded twenty-five years for twenty-five cents.'
>
> Diaz shook his head, as if disappointed at my obtuseness. 'Fred took his money,' he said. 'No way Bill could let him get away with that.'

After further argument, O'Connor finally understands what Diaz is saying: 'In prison . . . the thresholds were set high. Once one took the first backward step, one would never take another forward.' He gives Diaz an A.

Chris Offutt's 'Moscow, Idaho' is a story about two prisoners on some kind of parole work-scheme, unearthing coffins from a cemetery due to be covered by a new highway. They swap stories of prison life. Baker decides on impulse to steal a car and run. Tilden declines to join him.

> Tilden crossed the road and lay on his back beside the wheat. He spread his arms. Wind blew loose dirt over his body. The ground was soft, and the air was warm. In prison he had figured out that laws were made to protect the people who made the laws. He had always thought that staying out of trouble meant following those laws, but now he knew there was more. The secret was to act like the people who wanted the laws in the first place. They didn't even think about it. They just lived.

This is well done in a classic American vernacular style. Stewart O'Nan and Melanie Rae Thon use their first-person narrators in the more artful and self-conscious form of the dramatic monologue. O'Nan's unnamed speaker is a young woman convicted of murder. The crime in which she was implicated seems to have been a callous killing of some innocent strangers by drink-or-drug-crazed young people. From Death Row, on the eve of her execution, she dictates a letter to Stephen King answering his questions about her life and her crime. The premise is that Stephen King has paid her for this information, as source material for a novel, and that she is giving it to him partly to vindicate herself, partly to provide for her child, and partly because she is a King fan. Now a born-again Christian, she contemplates her imminent death with eerie calm. It is not surprising to learn from the introductory note that the novel from which this piece is extracted is currently the subject of litigation, but one hopes that it will not be suppressed.* The imaginative creation of a life, and a voice, evidently very different from the author's own is impressive.

Melanie Rae Thon's narrator and her friend Emile are teenage prostitutes working on the streets of Boston to pay for their drug habit. On a cold Christmas night they seek shelter by breaking into an unoccupied suburban home. The narrative is addressed to the hypothetical absent housewife.

> I'm your worst fear.
> But not the worst thing that can happen.
> I lived in your house half the night. I'm the broken window in your little boy's bedroom. I'm the flooded tiles in the bathroom where the water flowed and flowed.
> I'm the tattoo in the hollow of Emile's pelvis, five butterflies spreading blue wings to rise out of his scar.
> I'm dark hands slipping through all your pale woman underthings; dirty fingers fondling a strand of pearls, your throat, a white bird carved of stone. I'm the body you feel wearing your fox fur coat.

It's another creditable effort to inhabit vicariously the life of the American underclass, though the lyrical elegance of the style tends at times to work against the story's credibility.

By far the largest group in this rough-and-ready classification are the novel-extracts about childhood, growing-up, family relationships, often viewed in a nostalgic and/or pastoral

---

* It was published in 1997 as *The Speed Queen*.

perspective, evoking and celebrating a more benign and innocent America than the one reflected in the media today. '[A]
sort of Norman Rockwellization of the novel' seems to be
going on, Ian Jack observes, with a certain puzzlement.
Representative of this trend is Tony Earley's account of a
fatherless boy growing up on a farm in the corn belt. On his
tenth birthday he tries, prematurely, to enter the world of
adult work, and learns from his uncle Zeno, a stern but upright
man, that you can't play at hoeing. Uncle Zeno finds a corn
stalk that Jim accidentally severed and stuck back in the
ground.

> Uncle Zeno held the corn stalk up like a scepter, as if seeing
> it better would help Jim answer his questions. 'Jim, this was
> just a mistake until you tried to hide it,' he said. 'But when
> you tried to hide it you made it a lie.'
> Jim looked at the front of his overalls. He felt a tear start
> down his cheek and hoped that Uncle Zeno hadn't seen it.

David Guterson, who has enjoyed considerable success
with his novel *Snow Falling on Cedars* (1994), offers an extract
from a novel-in-progress set early in the century in
Washington State's apple country. 'He remembered the new,
fresh orchard country of his youth and the rows of apple
trees his father had planted on the east bank of the Columbia
River', it begins, and goes on in the same idyllic vein, evoking the childhood of the central character Ben and his brother
Aidan. Their father takes them on a hunting trip, and shoots
a buck. They kneel and thank the Lord for providing them
with meat; then the father shows his sons how to dress the
carcase.

Five minutes later, riding down the ridge, their father halted his horse. There was blood across the front of his coat and on his jaw and nose and hands.

'That's how it's done,' he said to his sons. 'That's just the way you'll want to do it when I ain't around anymore.'

One is reminded of Hemingway, of Cormac McCarthy, and occasionally, in passages of local chronicle, of Faulkner; but the tension, the possibility of evil that is always present in those writers seems quite absent here. Perhaps it will appear in later parts of the novel, when the story reaches modern times.

Mona Simpson's forthcoming novel has a similar regional setting to Guterson's. 'Jane was born in Gray Star, a settlement in remote Eastern Oregon, where her cries were lost in miles and miles of orchards stilled by a constant rain', it begins. She is the daughter of a hippyish single mother and a rich but absent father. Jane's mother teaches her ten-year-old daughter to drive a truck, with wood blocks tied to the pedals so she can reach them, and sends her off in it one night to seek her father. 'The most terrible and wondrous experience in Jane di Natale's life was over by the time she was ten, before she'd truly learned the art of riding a bicycle.'

The interest in childhood, roots and origins cuts across ethnic boundaries. The extract from Fae Myenne Ng's novel *Bone* (1993) is another affectionate memoir of childhood – in this case of attending the funeral of the narrator's grandfather in San Francisco's Chinatown. Sherman Alexie's central character is a native American Indian adopted by a white middle-class couple. The account of his problems with white middle-class girls in adolescence is somewhat predictable, but the extract begins with the hero imagining, and partly fantasising, his own birth on an Indian reservation, and being immediately snatched away by helicopter to his waiting adoptive parents. This striking sequence has the pace and immediacy of a movie and incorporates hallucinatory images of movie mayhem:

> The jumpsuit man holds John close to his chest as the heli-
> copter rises. Suddenly, as John imagines it, this is a war. The
> gunman locks and loads, strafes the reservation with explo-
> sive shells. Indians hit the ground, drive their cars off roads,
> dive under flimsy kitchen tables. A few Indians, two women
> and one man, continue their slow walk down the reserva-
> tion road, unperturbed by the gunfire. They have been
> through much worse. The what-what of the helicopter
> blades. John is hungry and cries uselessly.

Jeffrey Eugenides has a Shandean take on the story of the narrator's origins, going back to his own conception. The context is an American-Greek community in which inherited superstitions struggle against the scientific know-how of the New World. The narrator's parents want a girl, since they have two sons already. Father has been told that the best way to conceive a girl is to have intercourse twenty-four hours before ovulation, as determined by a temperature chart. Mother thinks it is a matter best left to God and the predic-tive power of grandmother Desdemona's silver spoon. Father presents Mother with a state-of-the-art thermometer and mixes them both dry Martinis to put his spouse into a recep-tive mood.

> When he brought hers over, my mother took a sip, closed
> her eyes and said, 'This is going to go straight to my head.'

She put the thermometer into the glass like a swizzle stick. She stabbed the olive with it, brought it to her mouth and ate it.

As a writer with some experience in this vein of comedy, I tip my hat to Mr Eugenides.*

There are extracts from two more novels about families. Kate Wheeler's young heroine sits at the bedside of her dying grandmother, a feisty and loquacious old lady who startlingly claims to have had an affair with an Asian Indian early in her married life. Is this senility, mischief, or true confession? The question disturbs the calm surface of the white middle-class family. David Haynes writes with a pleasantly light touch about tensions within a black family in St Louis, adopting the point of view of a woman in her late thirties, Deneen, who returns to live with her mother and young sister on the rebound from an unhappy love affair. Deneen's taste for lurid clothing and junk food offends her mother's notions of thrift and aspirations to middle-class respectability. There is an effective comic sequence involving a gadget new to me, a speaking supermarket trolley.

Viewed collectively under the aspect of fictional form and technique, this sampler confirms what Robert Stone calls, in a letter quoted by Ian Jack, 'the resurgence of realism' in American writing. The trend began in the 1980s, and Buford

---

* In the autumn of 2004 I met Mr Eugenides for the first time, at the Gothenburg Book Fair. He told me that this piece was a fragment of a project he had more or less abandoned and that my compliment had encouraged him to go on with what turned out to be the very successful *Middlesex* (2002). It's pleasing to discover that one's literary journalism can have such disproportionately beneficent effects occasionally.

was typically quick to spot it. In 1983 he dedicated a whole issue of *Granta*, the one immediately following the first *Best of Young British Novelists*, to something he called 'Dirty Realism', represented by such writers as Raymond Carver, Richard Ford, Tobias Wolff and Jayne Anne Phillips, who wrote serious literary fiction about the concerns of ordinary Americans living in dusty small towns and trailer parks, 'low-rent tragedies of people who watch day time television, read cheap romances and listen to country and western music'. Stylistically, these writers belong to the Twain–Hemingway tradition in American writing, concealing poetic and metaphysical resonances under a deceptively simple and colloquial language. It was the beginning of a reaction against the rhetorical exuberance and postmodernist experimentalism of the 1960s and '70s that now seems to be complete, if the current *Granta* is reliable evidence. Of the twenty pieces gathered together here, every one is written in the code of realism. Apart from the occasional dream or fantasy, clearly framed and controlled by a realistic context, there is no surrealism, no magic realism, no mythic subtext, little overt intertextuality, no metafictional frame-breaking,* no word-games, no abrupt switches of style or type of discourse, no parody, no radical deviation from well-formed syntax, no unconventional layout and typography. There is not a trace to be seen of the influence of John Barth, Richard Brautigan, Donald Barthelme, Thomas Pynchon, or other luminaries of the

---

* In the original review I wrote 'no intertextuality'. Mr O'Nan wrote to the *New York Review*, claiming that references to the work of Stephen King in his novel were both intertextual and metafictional. In reply, I agreed and apologised on the first count, but pointed out that I had referred specifically to 'metafictional *framebreaking* . . . a radical subversion within the text of the illusion of reality which has been created for the main narrative', which I did not find in the extract published in *Granta*. (*New York Review*, 17 October 1996, p. 62.)

'renaissance' in American writing hailed by Buford in his inaugural editorial in *Granta*.

It is also noteworthy that the contributors to *The Best of Young American Novelists* are, compared to that older generation of writers, conspicuously restrained in their use of four-letter words and descriptions of sexual behaviour. Apart from O'Connor's piece which, for obvious documentary reasons, is full of expletives, there is little here which the prudish *New Yorker* of forty years ago would have hesitated to print. This may be connected with the puzzling absence (not remarked upon by Jack) of any novel or story dealing with gay or lesbian relationships, since such fiction tends to focus on the erotic life of its characters.

A surprising reversal of the literary situation described by Buford in 1979 seems to have occurred. Young American novelists today are (to judge by these samples) less idiosyncratic, less experimental, and certainly less raunchy, than not only older American writers, but also their British contemporaries. In contemporary British fiction fabulation (represented variously by writers like Salman Rushdie, Jeanette Winterson, Ben Okri, Lawrence Norfolk, Jim Crace) flourishes alongside realism which fully earns the epithet 'dirty'. There has been a spate of novels by young writers (including women writers) in Britain recently, dealing with contemporary society in a way designed to shock, full of obscenity, scatology, violence, sexual perversion, alcoholism and drug addiction, black humour and opaque slang. Much of this fiction is crudely sensational and clumsily constructed, but it has a raw and reckless energy that is a sign of life. (Irvine Welsh's *Trainspotting* is a paradigm case.) There is no bad writing in *The Best of Young American Novelists*, but there is nothing very startling or ambitious either – nobody who, to invoke Norman Mailer in *Advertisements for Myself*, seems to be running for president in his or her head, who would 'settle for nothing less than making a revolution in the consciousness of our time'. Ian Jack

> . . . was struck by the kindness and humanity of most of these authors; their concern to be domestic and geographically specific . . . their anxiety to write open and spare prose. A lot of new British fiction is altogether wilder and stranger – less interested in clarity, less competent at storytelling. In America the influence of creative writing schools and an older generation of writers – Raymond Carver, Richard Ford, Tobias Wolff – is obvious.

If there is a certain sameness, and tameness, as well as a high standard of technical competence, in *The Best of Young American Novelists*, it is certainly tempting to look for an explanation to the influence of creative writing programmes in colleges and universities. On the evidence of the short biographical notes prefixed to each contribution, at least two thirds of the writers are graduates of master's or doctoral programmes in creative writing, and/or teach creative writing themselves, and it's a fair bet that most of the remaining third had some experience of creative writing courses as undergraduates. Creative writing as an academic subject has only recently established itself in Britain, and is virtually unknown in the rest of the world.* It is a very distinctive

---

* It is now of course an accepted part of the curriculum in many (perhaps the majority of) British universities at either the undergraduate or postgraduate level or both. An MA in creative writing is an increasingly familiar item in the CVs of young British writers, and some support their professional careers by occasional or part-time teaching in such courses. The literary cultures of Britain and America are in that respect growing more alike, but it is still too early to assess what effect, if any, this is having on new British writing.

feature of American literary culture. But by the same token it has been an influence there for a very long time. It is hard to think of more than a handful of significant postwar American writers, including the postmodernist experimentalists of the 1960s and '70s, who were not involved in some way with creative writing programmes.

So what's new? Could it be the climate of what, for lack of a less tendentious phrase, one must call political correctness, pervading the American campus these days? An intellectual environment in which it is frowned upon or expressly forbidden to say or write anything which might offend any individual's or group's values, self-esteem, sense of cultural and ethnic identity, religious beliefs, or special interests, is not one in which the budding literary imagination is likely to flourish. Important writers are often rebellious, arrogant, irreverent, even outrageous in their apprenticeship years, and some (like Norman Mailer) remain so. Political correctness encourages caution, parochialism and self-censorship. It is interesting to note how Robert O'Connor has deftly slipped the handcuffs of such inhibitions. By choosing to write in the mode of the non-fiction novel he has provided himself with an impregnable defence against anyone who might find his subject matter offensive: that's the way it is. And by making himself the narrator and central character he is able to voice the liberal pieties of tolerance, decency and fairness while exposing their total inadequacy to the facts of prison life. The irony goes deeper: venturing into the prison ostensibly to bring the hardened convicts sweetness and light, redemption through creative writing, he has stolen from them a priceless hoard of material, and carried it back to his safe suburban home to work on it as he knows, much better than they ever will, how.

The elaborate and scrupulously democratic procedure by which *The Best of Young American Novelists* were selected, designed to resist the dominance of the East Coast publishing establishment, and to open up the competition to the regional variety of new American writing, has rather surprisingly produced an anthology in which resemblances of form and content are more striking than differences, and the reader is charmed and disarmed more often than challenged. This may be an accurate reflection of the work being produced by young American writers. Or it may reflect more accurately the priorities and preferences of the regional judges, themselves perhaps sensitised by the ideological climate referred to above. The final list might have been more interesting, and conceivably more representative, if Ian Jack and his colleagues had reserved a few places on it for writers, like Nicholson Baker, David Foster Wallace, and Richard Powers, whose absence from the regional lists they noted with surprise.

After my review was published I received a number of letters from eligible writers who were not represented in the anthology generally agreeing with my comments. Some made the point that three of the four judges were themselves practitioners of realistic fiction and likely to be biased, consciously or unconsciously, in its favour. I omitted to mention in the review that the Granta *volume contained fetching photographic portraits of the selected authors by Marion Ettlinger, from which young aspiring writers might have inferred that, whatever technique you favour, to succeed in the literary marketplace you should wear black and dress up if you are a woman, but dress down, in drab grungy clothes, if you are a man – and never, ever, wear a tie. This is probably still good advice.*

J. M. COETZEE:
Elizabeth Costello

This essay is a lightly revised version of a review originally published in the New York Review of Books, *in November 2003. A few hours after I finished writing it, the award of the Nobel Prize for literature to Coetzee was announced, and reference to this was hastily inserted into the text of my article. Some subsequent related events and publications are described here in a Postscript.*

Elizabeth Costello requires, and rewards, at least two consecutive readings, but even then its import remains ambiguous, partly because of the way it mixes and transgresses generic conventions and boundaries. Its publishing history is also unusual and unsettling. The novel (as one must call it for want of a better word) consists of eight chapters and a Postscript, though the chapters are called 'Lessons' (whether they are lessons for the central character or for the reader is not made clear – perhaps both). Six of the Lessons have appeared in print before, which is not in itself remarkable, but two of them have been published previously as an independent work, which is. These were the Tanner Lectures, a series dedicated to the discussion of ethical and philosophical topics, which Coetzee gave at Princeton University in 1997–8, under the title 'The Lives of Animals'. Instead of delivering conventional lectures, he read to his audience a work of fiction, about a distinguished Australian novelist called Elizabeth Costello who is invited to Appleton College, a fictitious institution in Massachusetts, to give the annual 'Gates Lecture' and disconcerts her hosts, who expected her to choose a literary topic, by delivering a root-and-branch polemic against the treatment of animals, in zoos, scientific research and above all in the production of food. This lecture, 'The Philosophers and the Animals', and a talk Elizabeth gives to the English Department entitled 'The Poets and the Animals', are followed by debates with members of the faculty, informally over dinner, and formally in a seminar.

The effect of the fictional narrative is to generate sympathy for the main character, but it is not unambiguously clear that she is articulating the views of the author (or lecturer, as he was in this case). The whole sequence of events is seen mainly through the eyes of Elizabeth's son, John (Coetzee's own first name, it is worth noting) who happens to be a teacher of physics and astronomy at Appleton College but has previously concealed his relationship to his famous mother, and who is throughout her visit divided between filial loyalty and discomfort at the way her extreme opinions get up the noses of his colleagues and his wife. What gives most offence is the analogy she draws between the industrial production of meat and the extermination of the Jews by the Nazis. 'We are surrounded by an enterprise of degradation, cruelty and killing which rivals anything that the Third Reich was capable of, indeed dwarfs it, in that ours is an enterprise without end . . .' she asserts. A senior member of the faculty, a poet called Abraham Stern, absents himself from the dinner in protest and writes a dignified note of dissent. 'If Jews were treated like cattle, it does not follow that cattle are treated like Jews. The inversion insults the memory of the dead. It also trades on the horrors of the camps in a cheap way.'

The Tanner Lectures were published by Princeton University Press in 1999, with an introduction by a political philosopher and responses from four other distinguished members of the Princeton faculty. Not surprisingly most of the commentators felt somewhat stymied by Coetzee's meta-lectures, by the veils of fiction behind which he had concealed his own position from scrutiny. 'A lecture within a lecture; a response within a response. What is the strategy of such an appropriation?' Marjorie Garber asked, and answered her own question tartly: 'Among other things it is a strategy of *control*.' The philosopher Peter Singer complained it was hard to get a purchase on Coetzee's discourse, because 'we don't know what voice to believe', and retaliated by casting his own contribution in the form of a dialogue with his teenage daughter. In short, there was a feeling, shared by some reviewers of the book, that Coetzee was putting forward an extreme, intolerant, and accusatory argument without taking full intellectual responsibility for it.

Encountered in its new context, as Lessons 3 and 4 of *Elizabeth Costello*, 'The Lives of Animals' no longer seems vulnerable to such a criticism. The character of Elizabeth in the novel is a much more rounded figure, with a much more complex history, and is preoccupied with more than one ethical or philosophical issue. But the question of how far we are meant to identify with her and her opinions persists, partly because of the teasing similarities and differences between her and her creator. She is Australian-Irish-Catholic by birth and upbringing. Coetzee is South African, from an Afrikaaner background, but now lives in Australia; he relates in his memoir *Youth* that as a schoolboy he pretended to be a Catholic to be excused Religious Instruction classes. Elizabeth is 'a major world writer' around whom 'a small critical industry' has grown up, and the recipient of numerous prizes and awards. So is Coetzee. She 'is by no means a comforting writer'; neither is Coetzee (*Disgrace* must be one of the least comforting novels ever written). Elizabeth's most celebrated work is *The House on Eccles Street* (1969), an imaginative recension of James Joyce's *Ulysses* from Molly Bloom's point of view; Coetzee has engaged in similar intertextual games with Defoe's *Robinson Crusoe*. Like Coetzee, Elizabeth frequently travels round the world to give lectures and to attend international conferences. All the first six episodes or 'Lessons' are in fact concerned with discourses delivered and/or heard by Elizabeth on some such occasion.

The main difference between author and character, apart from gender, is that Elizabeth Costello is twelve years older than Coetzee – 'sixty-six, going on sixty-seven' in 1995, when the first episode is set. She increasingly feels her age as the novel progresses – both physically, in the weariness of flesh and bone, and metaphysically, in her troubled meditations on life and death and the art to which she has dedicated herself. Coetzee, sixty-four in the year of the novel's publication, has succeeded remarkably in creating the character of a woman undergoing the transition from middle age to old age, coming

to the end of sexuality, to the end of fulfilling personal relationships, even perhaps to the end of writing, and finding a
new urgency in the big, perennial questions: Why are we here?
What should we do? What is it all about? It is a book which
begins like a cross between a campus novel and a Platonic
dialogue, segues into introspective memoir and fanciful
musing, and ends with a Kafkaesque bad dream of the afterlife. It is progressively permeated by the language of religion,
by a dread of evil, and a desire for personal salvation. Its
keywords are 'belief' and 'soul'.

The first Lesson is called 'Realism', the topic on which
Elizabeth has chosen to speak when accepting the 'Stowe
Award' ($50,000 in cash and a gold medal) from the fictitious
Altona College in Williamsburg, Pennsylvania. Her son John
is in attendance (as he will be two years later in Massachusetts),
being on leave from Appleton College for unspecified 'reasons
of his own'. Elizabeth has flown all the way from Australia to
receive the award. That is usually a condition of getting this
kind of loot – you have to be there in person, give a speech,
submit to media interviews, meet people who are writing
scholarly books about you, field questions about your peers
('What do you think of A. S. Byatt, Ms Costello . . . what do
you think of Doris Lessing?'), sign copies of your novels, attend
receptions and formal meals – and John feels his increasingly
frail-looking mother needs his support to get her through the
exhausting routine. 'He thinks of her as a seal, an old, tired,
circus seal. One more time she must heave herself up on the
tub, one more time show she can balance the ball on her nose.'
The story of the visit is told mainly through John's eyes and
ears, with laconic metafictional interpolations by the implied

author, drawing attention to the conventions of realism that are employed, and occasionally flouted, in the narrative itself:

> The blue costume, the greasy hair [of Elizabeth], are details, signs of a moderate realism. Supply the particulars, allow the significations to emerge of themselves . . . there is a scene in the restaurant, mainly dialogue, which we will skip . . . when it needs to debate ideas, as here, realism is driven to invent situations – walks in the country, conversations – in which characters give voice to contending ideas . . . The presentation scene we skip. It is not a good idea to interrupt the narrative too often, since storytelling works by lulling the reader or listener into a dreamlike state . . .

Elizabeth's address is a kind of obsequy over, or elegy for, realism. She reminds her audience of Kafka's 'An Academic Address', in which an ape who has been captured and civilised gives a brief account of his experiences to a learned audience. The story mimics her own situation (and also anticipated Coetzee's use of the lecture as fictional discourse) but its meaning, Elizabeth says, is utterly obscure.

> There used to be a time when we knew. We used to believe that when the text said, 'On the table stood a glass of water,' there was indeed a table, and a glass of water on it, and we had only to look in the word-mirror of the text to see them. But all that has ended. The word-mirror is broken, irreparably it seems. About what is really going on in the lecture hall your guess is as good as mine.

It is not clear whether Elizabeth is referring here to the deconstructionist theory of the late twentieth century which undermined the assumption that texts have intentional, recuperable meanings – in which case Kafka is a bad example, because his texts were recognised as being radically indeterminate in meaning well before the advent of poststructuralism – or whether she is saying that Kafka was a kind of prophet of deconstruction. It is the first of several moments in the book as a whole where the reader is not quite sure whether he is intended to spot some confusion or contradiction or non-sequitur in Elizabeth's arguments.

Elizabeth's audience is not much interested in realism or its obsolescence. John senses that they are disappointed by her address, which contained nothing about feminism or postcolonialism – the isms with which she is publicly associated – and he suspects her hosts are already hoping that the Stowe Award jury will come up with a livelier recipient next time. He puts his tired mother to bed and goes down to the hotel bar where he recognises the attractive female professor, Susan Moebius, a specialist in women's writing who interviewed his mother for radio earlier that day. The attraction is mutual, and before long they are in Susan Moebius's bed together. John is aware that he is being seduced into satisfying her professional curiosity about his mother, but doesn't put up much resistance. He is both proudly admiring of Elizabeth and irritated and embarrassed by her, as the children of famous writers often are.

One of the pleasures of Coetzee's text is its wryly knowing observation of the professional lives of authors in the global village, their privileges and opportunities and compromises. Never in history, perhaps, have writers, 'serious' writers, been materially as well off as they are today – there are so many awards, fellowships, teaching posts, speaking engagements, grants and freebies available to supplement income derived directly from writing – but there is always a danger that these may become displacement activities. A typical perk is the cruise lectureship, by which a writer with a modest degree of celebrity can enjoy a free luxury vacation, and get a fee as well.

In Lesson 2, entitled 'The Novel in Africa', Elizabeth accepts a free cruise on a ship going to Antarctica in exchange for diverting the passengers with an undemanding course of lectures. She finds herself paired with an African novelist, Emmanuel Egudu, whom she met many years ago at a PEN conference in Kuala Lumpur, and then regarded as something of a *poseur*. But she is no longer confident of making such judgements. 'Which of us is what he seems to be, she seems to be?' She listens to herself giving her opening talk, on 'The Future of the Novel', and is not sure that she believes in what she is saying. Indeed 'she no longer believes very strongly in belief. Belief may be no more . . . than a battery which one clips into an idea to make it run' (a good example of Coetzee's gift for coining simple but striking metaphors). Egudu lectures with more verve on 'The Novel in Africa', but what he has to say seems to her depressing. African culture, he says, is essentially oral, and hostile to private silent reading. The African writer can draw on this oral culture to create a different kind of novel from that of the Western literary tradition, but he still won't have an African readership. He is condemned to make his professional life outside Africa, writing for foreigners. This, Elizabeth tells Egudu later, explains why there are 'so many African novelists around and yet no African novel worth speaking of'. It is the result of 'having to perform your Africanness at the same time as you write'. This is a fairly provocative assertion for a white South African

writer to put into the mouth of his white Australian heroine,
and is made even more so by the fact that Egudu's lecture
discusses the work of several real African novelists, such as
Amos Tutuola and Ben Okri, in some detail. In the fictional
scene Egudu declines to rise to the provocation, and patron-
isingly pats Elizabeth on the shoulder. '*If we were alone*, she
thinks, *I would slap him*.' As readers we are puzzled by the
violence of her reaction. She reflects scornfully that he hasn't
written a decent book in ten years, that he has become an
entertainer, working the cruise ships for money and sexual
opportunities. She is not surprised to see the Russian female
singer from the ship's band leaving his cabin early in the morning. When they meet on a shore expedition Elizabeth asks the
woman, in German, a language they have imperfectly in
common, what she sees in the African novelist. The answer
is that his voice makes her 'shudder'. Elizabeth accepts that
as a valid answer, and acknowledges her own jealousy. It transpires that she and Egudu were lovers in Kuala Lumpur.

'The oral poet,' she said to him teasingly. 'Show me what an
oral poet can do.' And he laid her out, lay upon her, put his
lips to her ears, opened them, breathed into her, showed her.

Now she feels excluded by her age from such miracles, but
the memory ends the second Lesson on a positive note. Sex,
which in Coetzee's previous books has usually been represented as phallic, compulsive, obsessive, and rather joyless (I
think particularly of *Waiting for the Barbarians* and *Disgrace*),
appears in this book as something much more polymorphous,
tender, unselfish and healing.

In Lessons 3 and 4, 'The Lives of Animals', the novel comes closest to the Platonic dialogue in form. One is quickly drawn into the debate, fascinated by the thrust and parry of argument and counter-argument, and compelled to re-examine one's own principles and assumptions – not only with reference to animal rights and vegetarianism. For these issues involve the definition of what it is to be human and where human beings stand in relation to the rest of creation, questions which have engaged the attention of several disciplines in recent years – ethology, sociobiology, anthropology, and cognitive science, as well as philosophy.

To Elizabeth our oppression of animals – keeping them in captivity, submitting them to painful or denaturing experiments, and above all breeding them in order to kill them on an industrial scale – arises from an unwarranted privileging of man and the faculty of reason. It is because we believe animals do not have the power of reasoning and the self-consciousness that comes from it – the Cartesian *cogito ergo sum* – that we claim the right to dispose of them in our own interests. She therefore attacks reason as 'a vast tautology . . . Of course reason will validate reason as the first principle of the universe – what else should it do?' The ultimate value of existence is not reason but 'fullness of being', which animals enjoy in their natural state, and compared to which 'Descartes' key state . . . has . . . the empty feel of a pea rattling round in a shell'. There is a whiff here of the antihumanist views recently expounded by the British philosopher John Gray in *Straw Dogs* (2002), where he recommends a shamanic identification with animals as a corrective to human destructiveness and discontent. Elizabeth cites the philosopher Thomas Nagel's celebrated paper, 'What Is It Like To Be a Bat?' and rejects his conclusion that the question is unanswerable. If we can imagine what it is like to be dead, if we can imagine what it is like to be a fictitious character, why should we not imagine what it is like to be a bat? (As it happens, some creative writing students in my novel, *Thinks...* [2001], are set this very exercise by their teacher.) Elizabeth has a very effective shot at imagining what it is like to be an ape subjected to a behaviourist experiment involving bananas placed out of reach:

> The bananas are there to make one think . . . One thinks: Why is he starving me? One thinks: What have I done? One thinks: Why has he stopped liking me? One thinks: Why does he not need these crates any more? But none of these is the right thought . . . The right thought to think is: How does one use the crates to reach the bananas?

Elizabeth argues her case eloquently, but she also overstates it at several points. The mediating presence of her son John, pragmatic and tolerant, allows us to see this, and to observe an element of hysteria in her state of mind. In the car on the way to the airport at the end of her visit, she admits that sometimes she thinks she must be mad to believe that the ordinary decent people around her are all 'participants in a crime of stupefying proportions . . . Yet every day I see the evidences . . . Corpses. Fragments of corpses that they have bought for money.' She turns a tearful face to him, pleading for reassurance. All he can do is stop the car, take her in his arms and murmur, 'There, there, it will soon be over.' It is not clear whether he means this gruelling trip, or her life.

At Appleton College Elizabeth startles a dinner table by saying that her vegetarianism 'comes out of a desire to save my soul'. In Lesson 5, 'The Humanities in Africa', she encounters the Christian way to salvation in a particularly uncompromising form, when she goes to a university in South Africa to attend the conferment of an honorary degree on her sister, Blanche. Blanche was trained in classics, then switched to medicine, and became a nun. She runs a hospital in Zululand dedicated to the care of AIDS victims, where native healers work along-side doctors practising modern medicine, and has achieved international celebrity as a result of a book she wrote about this enterprise. She is a kind of alter ego to Elizabeth – an equally forceful, radical, eloquent critic of modern society, but working from quite different beliefs and principles. Her address to the Faculty of Humanities has a family resemblance to Elizabeth's lectures: 'I have no message of comfort to bring to you . . . The message I bring is that you lost your way long ago.' The humanities, she says, began in the Renaissance as an effort of textual scholarship focused on the Bible. This led its practitioners to learn Greek, which caused them to be seduced by Hellenism, and to depreciate the message of Christianity; but Hellenism as a philosophy of life has failed, and the humanities with it. They have failed because they offer 'a secular vision of salvation'. Elizabeth (who severed her Catholic roots long ago) argues rather weakly against this absolutist position, handicapped by the fact that she has lost much of her own faith in the saving power of secular litera-ture. She visits her sister's hospital out of a sense of duty, admiring its care of the terminally sick, but resisting Blanche's insistence that suffering is the central, authentic human expe-rience: 'To the people who come to Marianhill I promise noth-ing except that we will help them bear their cross.' There is

308

DAVID LODGE

ancient sibling rivalry as well as ideological difference in their exchanges. Elizabeth feels that she has been lured to Africa to be chastened and chastised, and it is all the more galling to find her own critique of reason turned against her. 'If you had put your money on a different Greek you might have stood a chance,' says Blanche as they part. 'Orpheus instead of Apollo. The ecstatic instead of the rational.' Back home, in a kind of extended *esprit de l'escalier*, Elizabeth formulates a reply to her sister by recalling how as a young woman she brought comfort to an elderly neighbour dying painfully of cancer, first by posing for him bare-breasted, and later by a more intimate sexual contact, thus transcending the opposition of *eros* and *agape*, and enacting a fusion of spiritual and sensual ecstasy such as one sees in Renaissance religious paintings. But the message remains unsent – it would shock Blanche too much.

In Lesson 6, a year after her controversial visit to Appleton College, Elizabeth is once again flying long-haul, this time to Amsterdam, to contribute to a conference on 'The Problem of Evil', regretting that she has let herself in for another demand on her diminishing energy and appetite for disputation. She soon has more reason for regret. What prompted her to accept the invitation was that it arrived while she was 'under the evil spell' of a book, a novel by Paul West, *The Very Rich Hours of Count von Stauffenberg*, about the aristocratic officer who led the ill-fated July Plot of 1944 to assassinate Hitler. She was impressed by the novel at first, but horrified and disgusted by its description of the execution of the conspirators, who were hanged on Hitler's orders by the cruellest and most degrading method, and their death throes filmed for his delectation. That is a matter of record, but what particularly offended Elizabeth in the novel was the imagined behaviour of the hangman, who sadistically torments and humiliates the condemned men up to the point of death. 'Through Hitler's hangman a devil entered Paul West', and she felt the brush of his leathery wing as she read this part of the book. It is, she thinks, 'obscene' – such things should not be thought, or written, or read. That is what she has come to Amsterdam to say. The title of her paper is 'Witness, Silence and Censorship'. Paul West's book is her main exemplum.

To her consternation she discovers that Paul West is himself attending the conference. How can she deliver this attack on his book with him sitting in the audience? It is, in a way, a darkly comic situation. She tries rewriting her paper, leaving out references to him and his book, but it is impossible. She looks covertly at the men at breakfast in the conference hotel, wondering which one is Paul West. Eventually he is pointed out to her and she confronts him, and warns him of the content of the paper she is going to deliver, not apologetically, but as a courtesy. To her irritation, he listens silently, and says nothing in reply.

As some, but probably not all, of Coetzee's readers will know, Paul West is not a fictional character but a real novelist, who published *The Very Rich Hours of Count von Stauffenberg* in 1980. His CV is not unlike Coetzee's, though less brilliant: born in England, but an American citizen, he has held a number of prestigious posts as a professor of literature, and writes literary novels which have won several awards. For a writer to introduce another, living writer as a character into his fiction, in such a prejudicial light, is a very unusual, perhaps unprecedented thing to do. One might speculate that Coetzee read *The Very Rich Hours* . . . with much the same reaction as

Elizabeth's, wanted to write about that experience, and felt that inventing a fictitious novel and novelist would not serve his purpose – indeed, would involve him in the same kind of 'obscene' imagining of which Elizabeth accuses West. (Though it must be said that there are some very nasty imagined tortures in *Waiting for the Barbarians*. There may be an element of self-accusation here; alternatively Coetzee may be implying that imagining the torture of real people is more corrupting than imagining the torture of fictional creations.) When she finally accosts him, 'West, the real West, glances up from what he is reading, which seems, astonishingly, to be some kind of comic book'. In context the epithet 'real' distinguishes him from a man Elizabeth wrongly suspected of being West in the restaurant, but it also draws attention to the real existence of Paul West, and teases us with the possibility that Coetzee actually met him in circumstances not unlike these. No further reference is made to the comic book. It's the kind of detail that sticks in one's memory in real life simply because it was unexpected or incongruous, but as a signifier in the code of 'realism' its effect is to associate West with the crude exaggerations of comic books ('Supply the particulars, allow the significations to emerge of themselves . . .'). The whole episode is a startling transgression of literary protocol, and one can't help wondering what Paul West himself thinks of it. It ends in an empty corridor, without the meeting between heroine and antagonist, and the resolution of their conflict, that a well-formed story would normally require.

I have read West's novel, and agree with Elizabeth's literary judgement: it begins well, but falls off, especially towards the end, when the ghost of von Stauffenberg (who was summarily executed on the day of the abortive plot) observes and reports the horrible end of his fellow conspirators. There is a serious failure of tone in the fictional treatment of Hitler and his hangman, cranking up the horror when the known facts are horrific enough. Such subjects should certainly be handled with care – history and documentary probably being the best way – but Elizabeth surely goes too far in asserting that they should be sealed up and passed over in silence. Again there is more than a touch of hysteria in her reaction, which revives memories of an ugly sexual assault she suffered in youth and has never mentioned to anyone: the return of the repressed, perhaps.

Lessons 7 and 8 have not been previously published. 'Eros' consists of Elizabeth's whimsical musing on sexual relations between gods and humans in myth. She imagines that the gods envy us our greater orgasmic ecstasy, which is ironically linked to our mortality. This rumination is prompted by reading a poem about Cupid and Psyche by Susan Mitchell, which reminds Elizabeth of meeting and being strongly attracted to the Black Mountain poet Robert Duncan when she was a young woman. Again real writers, one living (Mitchell), are brusquely drafted into Coetzee's fiction to kick-start his heroine's thoughts, which then meander entertainingly through literature and mythology. Thinking about *Ulysses*, however, Elizabeth makes a puzzling mistake:

> *I do not like that other world*, writes Martha Clifford to her pen pal Leopold Bloom, but she lies: why would she write at all if she did not want to be swept off to another world by a demon lover?

In Joyce's novel, Leopold Bloom receives a letter from Martha Clifford, a young typist with whom he is conducting a clandestine correspondence, in which she typed 'world' when she meant to write 'word' – evidently an obscene one which Bloom had used in his previous letter. This is quite clear from the context: 'I called you naughty boy because I do not like that other world. Please tell me what is the real meaning of that word. Are you not happy in your home you poor little naughty boy?' Bloom recalls the typo later, as he leaves the churchyard in the Hades episode, finding it appropriate to his thoughts about death: 'I do not like that other world she wrote. No more do I.' It seems implausible that Elizabeth, who has rewritten *Ulysses* from Molly Bloom's point of view, would not know all this, but even more unlikely that Coetzee is unaware of it. So what is the point of making Elizabeth commit this howler (or bloomer)? It is another small enigma in a highly enigmatic book.

Lesson 8, 'At the Gate', brings the novel to its conclusion. Elizabeth, tired and hot, alights from a bus in some dusty provincial town, where there is a gate, and a gatekeeper, and a court with a panel of inquisitors who demand that she state her beliefs before she is given permission to pass through the gate. She says she has no beliefs – it is not compatible with her profession of writer. She can do an imitation of a belief if that will do. It will not. (We wonder what has happened to her passionate belief in the rights of animals.) She lugs her suitcase to a roughly constructed dormitory, and claims a wooden bunk with a greasy straw mattress, to think about revising her application. The dormitory resembles the huts of the death camps. Everything in this place reminds one of something encountered a hundred times before in books, plays, films: the Kafkaesque court, the idle customers at the café tables, the uniformed band that plays light music in the square, the stonewalling guardian of the Gate. If this is the threshold to the afterlife, Elizabeth thinks truculently, couldn't they have come up with something more original? Or is it a purgatory especially designed for writers, to torture them mercilessly with clichés? It is a brilliant piece of writing, both funny and poignant. Elizabeth goes back repeatedly to the court, and repeatedly fails to satisfy her inquisitors. If she could say, *'I believe in the irrepressible human spirit,'* she would pass, but she cannot perjure herself. She says she believes in the little frogs that, when she was a child, survived in a semi-comatose state under tons of mud in the mudflats of the Dungannon river until the rains came, but the inquisitors stare at her and snigger. They think she is 'confused'. Perhaps, then, Elizabeth is succumbing to dementia. Or perhaps she is a seer. She has a vision of a dog lying at the foot of the gate, blocking her way, 'an old dog, his lion-coloured hide scarred from innumerable manglings . . . It is her first vision in a long while, and she does not trust it, does not trust in particular the anagram GOD–DOG. *Too literary*, she thinks again. A curse on literature!'

This dog seems to have loped out of *Disgrace*, which ends with the hero dedicated to putting such unfortunate animals humanely out of their misery. Is Coetzee expressing his own loss of faith in literature here? The book's Postscript, entitled 'Letter of Elizabeth, Lady Chandos, to Francis Bacon', is an ambiguous pointer, of complex provenance. It stands in the same relation to Hugo von Hofmannsthal's 'Letter of Lord Chandos to Lord Bacon' (1902) as Elizabeth Costello's *The House on Eccles Street* does to *Ulysses*, though on a much reduced scale. In von Hofmannsthal's (entirely fictitious) text, Lord Chandos writes to Bacon, in 1603, to explain his 'complete abandonment of literary activity'. He no longer trusts the connection between language and reality and is in a state of total apathy and despondency, occasionally alleviated by astonishing, mystical visions of the Infinite through the humblest things in creation. In Coetzee's text Elizabeth Chandos, having had a sight of her husband's letter, writes to assure Bacon that her husband is not mad, but she sounds on the verge of madness herself:

> Save me, dear Sir, save my husband! Write! Tell him the time is not yet come, the time of the giants, the time of the angels. Tell him we are still in the time of fleas. Words no longer reach him, they shiver and shatter, it is as if (*as if*, I say), it is as if he is guarded by a shield of crystal. But fleas he will understand, the fleas and the beetles still creep past his shield, and the rats; and sometimes I his wife, yes, my Lord, sometimes I too creep through. *Presences of the Infinite* he calls us, and says we make him shudder; and indeed I have felt those shudders, in the throes of my raptures . . .

This makes a bit more sense when read in conjunction with von Hofmannsthal's text, but its bearing on the main story is still problematic. Elizabeth Chandos's letter seems to be simultaneously vouching for the authenticity of her husband's mystical visions and begging the empirical, rational Lord Bacon to 'save' him from his 'affliction'.

So what are we to make of the whole extraordinary book? Its first Lesson, it will be remembered, was that all texts are now open to infinite interpretation; but in spite of deconstruction we persist in trying to discern some kind of communicative intention in works of literature, for they do not come into existence by accident. The choice of a Renaissance voice to end this one is interesting. In its mixture of realistic narrative, myth, controversial polemic, Platonic dialogue, erotic interludes and gossipy allusions to fellow writers, it is more like a Renaissance prose work than the average modern novel. But Coetzee's Elizabeth Chandos is of course a modern re-creation of a Renaissance personage, expressing a modern anxiety – as indeed was von Hofmannsthal's Lord Chandos. The German writer's text reflected a creative, intellectual and psychological crisis of his own, after which his work took a different direction. Perhaps *Elizabeth Costello* will prove a similar kind of turning point, though it comes much later in Coetzee's career. Certainly one senses in the book's implied author, as well as in its heroine, a disillusionment with the value our culture attributes to literature, a strong feeling that, in Marianne Moore's words, 'there are things that are important beyond all this fiddle', and a kind of restiveness at being regarded as 'a writer of world importance'. Ironically, its publication coincides with the award of the Nobel Prize, which will cement that burdensome crown still more firmly to Coetzee's head.

Coetzee has never sought popularity or celebrity. His books are always unsettling, unexpected, and uncomforting. He seems a rather aloof figure in the contemporary literary world, who seldom gives interviews, and often declines to collect his prizes in person. But he is one of the few living writers routinely described as 'great'. He deserves the Nobel because he is exceptionally intelligent and a master of his medium. If he goes to Stockholm the acceptance speech should be memorable – but what will they serve for the main course at the banquet?

POSTSCRIPT

I don't know what was on the menu at the banquet in Stockholm, but one can safely assume that there was a vegetarian option. When I wrote the concluding paragraph of my review, I confused or conflated two separate discourses: the acceptance speech which a recipient of the Nobel Prize gives at the banquet and the lecture which he or she gives on a separate occasion, and which is usually some kind of personal credo or manifesto. Both of Coetzee's addresses (which are accessible on the Nobel website) were characteristically idiosyncratic. His very brief banquet speech began with a domestic anecdote:

> The other day, suddenly, out of the blue, while we were talking about something entirely different, my partner Dorothy burst out as follows: 'On the other hand,' she said, 'on the other hand, how proud your mother would have been! What a pity she isn't still alive!'

The assembled guests were left to speculate about the tenor of the previous discussion of the prize implied by 'On the other hand'. Coetzee made the somewhat curmudgeonly reply to Dorothy that if his mother were still alive she would be ninety-nine and a half and probably be suffering from senile dementia. But on his feet at the banquet he conceded that he had missed the point:

> For whom, anyway, do we do the things that lead to Nobel Prizes if not for our mothers?
> 'Mommy, Mommy, I won a prize!'
> 'That's wonderful, my dear. Now eat your carrots before they get cold.'

The speech concluded with a gracious thank-you to the Nobel Foundation, but its general effect was surely a gently teasing deflation of the significance of the prize.

Coetzee's Nobel lecture was equally unconventional, being in the form of a literary fiction, or metafiction, about – not Elizabeth Costello, as readers of his recent novel might have anticipated – but Daniel Defoe's Robinson Crusoe, a character whose story has long haunted Coetzee's imagination, and which he reworked in his novel Foe (1986). Entitled 'He and His Man', the 'lecture' presents Robinson Crusoe as an elderly widower, living a quiet retired life in Bristol, musing on his experiences on the desert island, while apparently receiving information from 'his man' about a host of curious and interesting subjects – the tame ducks used as decoys in the fen country, a primitive guillotine once employed in Halifax, the horror of the plague in London, and so on. We infer that 'his man' is Daniel Defoe, and that the author has been corresponding with his character. Then it is revealed that Robinson Crusoe is actually writing these reports himself:

The writing of his adventures has put him in the habit of writing . . . In the evening by candlelight he will take out his papers and sharpen his quills and write a page or two of his man . . .

Author and character have changed places; Crusoe is writing Daniel Defoe. The story, which is beautifully written, is a parable about the mysterious relationship between the author as a real human being and the author self-created and encountered in the products of his imagination. 'How are they to be figured, this man and he? As master and slave? As brothers, twin brothers? As comrades in arms? Or as enemies, foes?'

Coetzee's most recent novel, Slow Man (2005), continues this metafictional theme, and reintroduces Elizabeth Costello. The story is set in Australia and the central character is a retired, somewhat misanthropic divorcé, Paul Rayment, who in the first chapter is knocked off his bike by a car, injuring his leg so badly that it has to be amputated. The shock, pain, anger, humiliation and indignities of the accident and its aftermath are all evoked in the first third of the novel with consummate skill. The illusion of reality is complete, as Rayment argues testily with medics and friends about his handicap, and begins to have tender feelings for his down-to-earth Croatian home help. Then in Chapter Thirteen there is a ring on Rayment's doorbell and Elizabeth Costello marches into his flat and his life. She announces that he is a character in a novel she is writing, or trying to write:

> 'You came to me,' she says. 'In certain respects I am not in command of what comes to me. You came, along with the pallor and the stoop and the crutches and the flat you hold to so doggedly and the photograph collection and all the rest. Also along with Miroslav Jokic the Croatian refugee – yes, that is his name, Miroslav, his friends call him Mel – and your inchoate attachment to his wife.'
> 'It is not inchoate.'
> 'Yes it is.'

Throughout the rest of the novel Elizabeth constantly interferes in Rayment's life, criticises his actions, tells him what he should do instead, and generally gets on his nerves. One can read this narrative as an objectification, or dramatisation, of the dialogue of a writer's mind with itself, as he struggles with a recalcitrant work-in-progress. It is written with wit and ingenuity, but it risks alienating readers who resent having the enjoyable illusion of reality shattered (which was the reaction of several reviewers). Instead Slow Man offers a more specialised, even perverse pleasure, the literary equivalent of trying to force the identical poles of two magnets together, a sensation at once frustrating and fascinating. Rayment and Elizabeth belong to different planes of being between which there is an irreducible logical gap. It is therefore impossible to 'make sense' of the story. We encounter a narrative aporia, comparable to, but starker than, the one presented by Nabokov's Pnin. If Rayment is 'real' then Elizabeth is mad (as Rayment thinks at first) in claiming he is a character in her book. But her intimate knowledge of his life proves she is not mad. If we have read Elizabeth Costello we know Elizabeth is herself a fictional character, a novelist, and to some extent a surrogate for, or alter ego of, the real J. M. Coetzee. Elizabeth therefore is to Coetzee as Rayment is (she claims) to Elizabeth. This makes Rayment a doubly fictional character – yet paradoxically he seems more real, more convincing, than Elizabeth. The novel ends with Rayment giving his alleged creator her quittance:

'But what am I going to do without you?'
    She seems to be smiling, but her lips are trembling too.
    'That is up to you, Elizabeth. There are plenty of fish in the ocean, so I hear. But as for me, as for now, goodbye.'

Of course Rayment doesn't really win the struggle for autonomy. Behind him, and behind the disconsolate Elizabeth, stands the shadowy figure of J. M. Coetzee, who we know invented both of them, perhaps a little disconsolate too at being unable to bring Rayment's story to a conclusion that satisfied him. Instead, he has made his creative frustration the subject of the novel, and thus passed it to his readers, some of whom will not forgive him. But ensuring the comfort of readers has never been a feature of J. M. Coetzee's writings.

INDEX

He just wanted a decent book to read ...

Not too much to ask, is it? It was in 1935 when Allen Lane, Managing Director of Bodley Head Publishers, stood on a platform at Exeter railway station looking for something good to read on his journey back to London: His choice was limited to popular magazines and poor-quality paperbacks – the same choice faced every day by the vast majority of readers, few of whom could afford hardbacks. Lane's disappointment and subsequent anger at the range of books generally available led him to found a company – and change the world.

'We believed in the existence in this country of a vast reading public for intelligent books at a low price, and staked everything on it'
Sir Allen Lane, 1902–1970, founder of Penguin Books

The quality paperback had arrived – and not just in bookshops. Lane was adamant that his Penguins should appear in chain stores and tobacconists, and should cost no more than a packet of cigarettes.

Reading habits (and cigarette prices) have changed since 1935, but Penguin still believes in publishing the best books for everybody to enjoy. We still believe that good design costs no more than bad design, and we still believe that quality books published passionately and responsibly make the world a better place.

So wherever you see the little bird – whether it's on a piece of prize-winning literary fiction or a celebrity autobiography, political tour de force or historical masterpiece, a serial-killer thriller, reference book, world classic or a piece of pure escapism – you can bet that it represents the very best that the genre has to offer.

Whatever you like to read – trust Penguin.